PALESTINE, ISRAEL, AND THE US EMPIRE

RICHARD BECKER

Published in December 2023 by
1804 Books, New York, NY

1804Books.com

This selection © 1804 Books, New York, NY
ISBN: 979-8-9882602-6-4
Library of Congress Control Number: 2023949974

Second edition, 2023 by 1804 Books
First edition, 2009 by PSL Publications

Cover by Vivek Venkatraman

TABLE OF CONTENTS

THE MIDDLE EAST

TURKEY
CYPRUS
SYRIA
LEBANON
PALESTINE
JORDAN
IRAQ
IRAN
KUWAIT
BAHRAIN
QATAR
U.E.A.
OMAN
SAUDI ARABIA
YEMEN
EGYPT
LIBYA

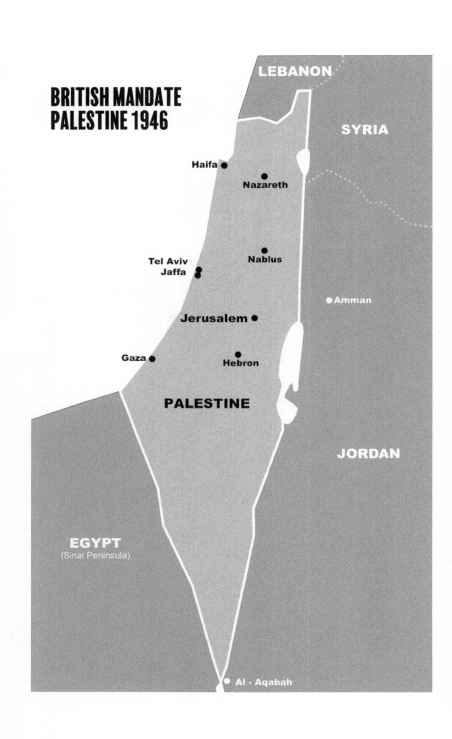

BRITISH MANDATE PALESTINE 1946

LEBANON

SYRIA

Haifa

Nazareth

Tel Aviv
Jaffa

Nablus

Amman

Jerusalem

Gaza

Hebron

PALESTINE

JORDAN

EGYPT
(Sinai Peninsula)

Al - Aqabah

PREFACE TO SECOND EDITION

On October 7, 2023, the Palestinian people broke out of the concentration camps and bulldozed through the apartheid wall surrounding Gaza—and in the first days after, the US and Israeli propaganda machines immediately launched a well-orchestrated campaign to suppress the movement for Palestine. Condemnation and criminalization echoed from the halls of the White House to university classrooms and television sets, denouncing both the resistance and all those who dared express solidarity with Palestine.

But despite the billions of dollars circulating between lobby groups, corporate media, and politicians ready to serve the interests of profit, the Israeli propaganda campaign was quickly forced into a defensive position. An enormous shift in public consciousness swept the United States, and mobilizations in solidarity with Palestine grew exponentially across the country. Tens of thousands of people took to the streets in genuine outrage and anger, defying massive police deployments and intimidation campaigns. There was no masking the genocidal nature of the Israeli state, and decades of a staunchly pro-Israel narrative fell apart in only a few days in the face of genuine humanity.

The world witnessed the largest demonstration in support of the Palestinian struggle in US history on November 4, 2023. Half a million people made their way to Washington, DC in planes and hundreds of buses and cars driving overnight from across the country, loaded with their families and neighbors. All joined in strong and unified demands to the White House: an immediate ceasefire, an immediate end to the siege on Gaza, an immediate end to US aid to Israel, and a free Palestine.

The national march on Washington, DC represented the culmination of these unprecedented mobilizations for Palestine, with thousands of actions occurring globally and millions pouring into the streets worldwide. The gathering of hundreds of thousands of people in the capital of the US empire represented not only opposition to US economic and political policy in support of Israel but a growing understanding of the true culpability of US imperialism in the genocide of the Palestinian people, as well as the anti-imperialist character of the Palestinian struggle.

As is discussed in the new edition of *Palestine, Israel, and the US Empire*, many theories attempt to explain the nature of the US empire's relationship to Zionism and the Palestinian struggle. Academics, politicians, and the media more broadly peddle a discourse that roots the basis of such relationship in a notion of shared Judeo-Christian or democratic values, the historical trauma of the Jewish people, a clash of civilizations, or one that overly centers the influence of the pro-Israel lobby. Ultimately, these explanations act to distort the true basis and character of the relationship between the US and the Zionist project.

Now more than ever, supporters of Palestine and anti-imperialism must understand that Israel is not an entity distinct or independent from the US empire but rather an extension of its agenda for global hegemony. The Zionist project, though not always fully dependent on US support, is now completely reliant on US collaboration for its very existence, just as the US presence in the region is equally reliant on the utilization of Israel as an extension of US military power in this resource-rich part of the world. The rapidly expanding global movement in solidarity with Palestinian people is recognized in Washington, DC and by the Israeli government as its potentially most formidable adversary. Ultimately, the Israeli regime exists as a proxy regime. It is a colonial project inside the borders of historic Palestine, but its stability is sustained only to the extent that it is valued by US imperialism as an extension of its larger neocolonial aims in the Middle East.

Armed with this precise analysis, it becomes clear that to support the Palestinian struggle is to support one of the most active fronts in the battle against US imperialism. This understanding transforms activists into revolutionaries, activism into movement, and drives people of conscience to move from outrage to a commitment to the anti-imperialist struggle. And there is no better school than the struggle itself. *Palestine, Israel, and the US Empire* is republished in a moment of high and active mobilization—read the following pages and return to the streets, sharpen your slogans and your demands, and prepare for the road to come. History is with us.

—Mohammed Nabulsi, Palestinian Youth Movement,
and Layan Sima Fuleihan, The People's Forum
December 2023

INTRODUCTION TO SECOND EDITION

As this updated edition of *Palestine, Israel, and the US Empire* goes to print, historic events are unfolding in Palestine, the Middle East, and beyond. The relentless oppression, murder, torture, and occupation carried out by the Israeli apartheid regime has precipitated an unprecedented counteroffensive by Palestinian resistance forces. In response, the Israeli leaders are attempting, by means of a genocidal air assault and total blockade on Gaza, to continue the ethnic cleansing that has been the hallmark of the Israeli state since its foundation in 1948.

Israel's war machine and its attendant systems of oppression are bought and paid for by US imperialism. US tax dollars fund the grinding oppression of the Palestinian people to the tune of $4 billion each year. In addition to calling for billions more to fund Israel's latest offensive, the warmongering Biden regime has provided billions for war in Ukraine and in preparation for a future war in the Pacific with China.

Biden and other US leaders' claims that their lavish support for Israel is based on sympathy with Jewish people remains nothing but a pretense. The saying, "the great powers have no permanent friends, only permanent interests," is as true today as ever. Imperialist politics have nothing to do with human needs or sentiments, and everything to do with profit and power. The top priority of the Biden administration, as has been true of every US administration since World War II, whether Republican or Democrat, has been to assure that the United States is the dominant world power.

As documented in this book, the immense funding of Israel is seen by Washington as an investment integral to its strategic objective of global domination. A highly militarized state, provided with many of the most technologically sophisticated weapons systems including nuclear bombs, Israel is effectively a projection of US military power in a key strategic region of the world.

Biden's repeated proclamations of "I am a Zionist" plays into the Israeli leadership's campaign to conflate Judaism, a religion, with Zionism, a reactionary colonialist ideology. A key element in the strategy of present Israeli prime minister Benjamin Netanyahu, as was true of all his predecessors, is the claim that Israel is the homeland and representative of all Jewish people no matter where they live in the world. But growing numbers of Jewish people in the US and elsewhere, particularly young Jewish people, are rejecting the attempts to identify them with a state based on racism and ethnic cleansing. In growing numbers, they are joining the multinational, multiracial movement in solidarity with Palestine.

The conflict in Palestine today can only be correctly understood as a struggle for national liberation like the struggles in Vietnam, Algeria, Korea, Angola, Cuba, China, and other formerly colonized countries. The colonization of Palestine by the Zionist movement was only made possible by the sponsorship of the British empire. The Zionist project that produced the state of Israel, like all European colonial projects, has no regard for the rights of Indigenous people whose territory it aimed to conquer. This racist view is expressed in the favored Zionist slogan calling Palestine a "land without people for a people without a land." The land of the Palestinian people was stolen from them, not centuries ago but over the past eight decades. As Israeli and Palestinian historians alike have irrefutably documented, the expulsion of the Palestinians in 1948–49 was accomplished by means of massacres and terror. It could not have been accomplished otherwise.

Since the publication of *Palestine, Israel, and the US Empire* in 2009, Israel, with the full backing of Washington, has intensified its relentless campaign designed to destroy Palestinian society and drive out as much of the population as possible. It is, in fact, a continuation of al-Nakba, the catastrophe of 1948–49, when 750,000 Palestinians were expelled from their homeland by means of terror to make way for the colonial-settler state of Israel. In the wars that followed, Israel conquered the remainder of what had been the British colony of Palestine, the West Bank and Gaza, as well as parts of Syria and Lebanon.

Despite paying lip service to a mythical "two-state solution," Israel has flooded the West Bank and East Jerusalem with hundreds of thousands of settlers, bands of whom rampage with impunity across the West Bank protected by the Israeli army. These racist gangs beat people, burn, and destroy Palestinian homes, farms, and shops on a daily basis, while the occupation army and police attack anyone who resists, often with lethal results.

The 2.3 million residents of Gaza have been trapped inside the world's largest open-air prison for more than seventeen years. Much of Gaza has been destroyed several times over—in 2009, 2011, 2014, 2021, and, most devastatingly, now in 2023—by Israeli war planes. Gaza has no air defenses that can confront one of the world's most advanced air forces, as Israeli pilots kill with impunity. That the Palestinians face a triple enemy of US imperialism, the Israeli Zionist state, and the reactionary Arab regimes has been dramatically reaffirmed by events of recent years, most dramatically by the so-called Abraham Accords. An initiative of the Trump administration in 2018, the accords opened diplomatic and other relations between Israel and some Arab monarchies with the aim of isolating the Palestinians.

For the Western mainstream media there is a set of carefully observed rules when it comes to reporting on the struggle in occupied Palestine. "Gunman" always refers to a Palestinian fighter with a gun but never to an Israeli soldier or settler toting one. Only Palestinians can be called "terrorists"; never the pilot who drops a five-hundred-pound bomb on defenseless people nor the commander who gave the order. And the right to "retaliate" is reserved to the Israeli side alone, thus constantly conveying the false idea that the Palestinians are the aggressors and the Israelis the victims. Reality is turned upside down.

In this process, the day in and day out oppression suffered by the Palestinians at the hands of the Israeli soldiers, settlers, and police is disappeared. The daily rampages of the fascist settler mobs in the West Bank—invariably protected by the Israeli occupation army—are only covered in the Western media when the Palestinians resist. The fact that Gaza residents under the age of eighteen have spent their entire lives trapped in a giant open-air prison simply because they are Palestinian is of no interest to the *New York Times* or *Washington Post*, leading mouthpieces of the imperialist establishment. Nor are the violations of international law committed against the Palestinians on a daily basis of any interest to the imperialist media.

More than five thousand Palestinian political prisoners are held illegally in Israeli prisons, 20 percent of whom are detained without charge and indefinitely as "administrative detainees." Transporting persons from an occupied territory into the territory of the occupiers is a clear violation of international law, as is settling people from the occupying power into occupied lands.

In 2022, an extreme right-wing government led by Benjamin Netanyahu took over in Israel. It included two openly fascist settler leaders who in the past had been excluded from running due to their openly racist stands. Itamar Ben-Gvir, leader of the "Jewish Power" party and a follower of the late Meir Kahane, was made minister of national security, a new position that gave him control of police forces and prisons and the power to create and arm a new settler vigilante militia. Belazel Smotrich was awarded the ministry of finance, but also a unique position inside the "defense" ministry that gave him control over much of the West Bank. Smotrich has openly proclaimed, "I am a fascist homophobe." Ben-Gvir kept a photo in his living room of Baruch Goldstein, another Kahane follower who murdered 29 Palestinians and wounded 125 inside the Ibrahim Mosque in Hebron in 1994. He begrudgingly took the photo down when told it was necessary in order for him to be made eligible to run for office.

Global Consensus that Israel is an Apartheid State

Palestine, Israel, and the US Empire originally included a chapter on the apartheid character of the Israeli state; it has since been documented in far greater detail by a wide and growing range of Palestinian, Israeli, and international human rights and other organizations. This includes eight Palestinian organizations, twelve Israeli groups, the International Commission of Jurists, Amnesty International, Human Rights Watch, the International Federation for Human Rights, numerous United Nations special rapporteurs on Palestine, the United Church of Christ of the US, and many others.

But the final confirmation that it is indeed an apartheid state came from none other than Israel's government itself!

In July 2018, the Israeli parliament ratified into law an apartheid system that has long been a reality. "Israel as the Nation-State of the Jewish People," was approved as a Basic Law in a country where such laws take the place of a constitution Israel has never had. The "nation-state law" had been under consideration for many years, but even many ardent Zionists had been opposed to it, not because they disagreed with its provisions but because it would remove all doubt worldwide about the apartheid character of the regime. For the same reason, many pro-Israel organizations and leaders in the United States spoke out against the law. Apartheid is a crime against humanity under the International Convention on the Suppression and Punishment of the Crime of Apartheid.

Fulsome support from the Trump administration, including moving the US embassy to Jerusalem, was the green light for many members of the parliament (Knesset) to vote for the bill in 2018. At the same time, the massive military and economic support, and diplomatic protection extended by Washington have made Israeli leaders increasingly dismissive of criticism from other governments. The vote for the law was 62–55, with most of the opposition—with the exception of thirteen Palestinian Arab members—still motivated by fears of international reaction to openly proclaiming Israel to be a racist state. Ahmed Tibi, one of the dissenting Palestinian legislators, called it, "the official beginning of fascism and apartheid." It is an openly racist law.

Point 1 of the "nation-state law," "Basic Principles," states:

A) The land of Israel is the historical homeland of the Jewish people, in which the State of Israel was established.

B) The State of Israel is the national home of the Jewish people, in which it fulfills its natural, cultural, religious, and historical right to self-determination.

C) The right to exercise national self-determination in the State of Israel is unique to the Jewish people.

It should be pointed out that the borders of the "land of Israel" were not defined, as they never have been since the formation of the state in 1948. This is not accidental. From the very beginning, the Israeli colonizers considered their original territory to be insufficient and temporary, and have waged several expansionist wars. Today, crossing into the West Bank one encounters no sign of a border. Not mentioned here, nor anywhere in the law, are the Palestinian people, who comprised 92 percent of the population a century ago.

The law's claim that the "right to exercise national self-determination . . . is unique to the Jewish people," explicitly denies any national rights to the Palestinians who make up 21 percent of the population inside the 1948 borders, and at least 50 percent of those living today in what was the British colony of Palestine—West Bank, Gaza and the present state of Israel. One of the aims of making the right of self-determination "unique" to Jewish people was to foreclose such a right for the Palestinians in the case of Israeli annexation of the West Bank. Not only were national rights denied to Palestinians in the law, but nowhere in the text are to be found the words "equality" or "equal rights" in regards to the population as a whole.

In the run-up to the final vote on the "nation-state bill" in June 2018, the leadership of the Knesset voted not to allow even the discussion of an opposing bill that called for equal rights and status for the "Arab and Jewish nationalities" inside the 1948 borders of the Israeli state. The bill, titled "State of All Its Citizens," was introduced by three members of the Balad party, Jamal Zahalka, Haneen Zoabi, and Jouma Azbarga. Balad was one of the parties representing the approximately 1.8 million Palestinians living inside Israel.

The speaker of the parliament, Yuli-Yoel Edelstein, an immigrant to Israel from Ukraine, called the bill "absurd" and explained why the indigenous Palestinian population must not, from his point of view, be accorded equal rights: "We cannot allow a proposal whose goal is to gnaw away at the foundations the State of Israel is built upon to be on the Knesset's agenda." Most of Edelstein's colleagues were in full agreement. Knesset Legal Adviser Eyad Yinon stated: "As a matter of principle and in its details, it's hard not to see this proposal as seeking to negate the State of Israel's existence as a state of the Jewish people." The admission that a law calling for equal rights for all would "negate" or "gnaw away at the foundations" of Israel demolished the oft-repeated mantra that Israel is the "only democracy in the Middle East." In fact, racism and exclusivism have always characterized Zionism.

While the Balad party's bill would have been overwhelmingly defeated had it come to the Knesset floor, that was an eventuality that Israeli political leaders sought to head off at all costs, given the embarrassing public relations consequences. Point 3 of the "nation-state law," "The Capital of the State," asserts that Jerusalem, complete and united, is the capital of Israel." This is in direct violation of the international understanding that East Jerusalem is a part of Palestine and that Israeli settlements in the city are illegal. Point 4 stated that Hebrew is the only state language and downgrades Arabic from an official state language to one with "special status," meaning that it will not have to be available in state institutions.

Point 5 on the "In-gathering of the exiles" states, "The state will be open for Jewish immigration." This is another blatant apartheid provision as the Israeli state continues to illegally deny the right of return to all Palestinian refugees. Point 7 stipulates that "The state views the development of Jewish settlement as a national value and will act to encourage and promote its establishment and consolidation." The settlements are to be Jewish-only. They constitute an obvious violation of international law in addition to the fundamental right of Palestinians to their land.

By passing the "nation-state law" the rulers of Israel themselves exposed the profoundly racist apartheid character of their state and society. There can be no more credible denials.

Despite all that they have suffered—and continue to suffer—the Palestinians have neither given up nor been defeated. Their steadfast refusal to surrender and leave, in the face of a brutal occupation designed to make life unbearable, is a special form of heroism. Now is the time for all people who believe in justice to join in solidarity with the heroic and long-suffering Palestinian people in their struggle for self-determination and liberation.

EDITOR'S NOTE

The first edition of this book was published in 2009. In this most recent edition, we have updated pertinent information to correspond to its current publication in the year 2023. We have changed original references to the "present" to reflect that they are now in the past, except where otherwise indicated.

A CHRONOLOGY OF THE STRUGGLE FOR PALESTINE

1882   Small numbers of Zionist settlers fleeing European anti-Semitism begin arriving in Palestine.

1894   November — Jewish artillery officer Alfred Dreyfus is falsely convicted of treason in France. The anti-Semitism surrounding the case convinces Hungarian Jewish journalist Theodore Herzl of the need for a Jewish state.

1896   Herzl publishes "The Jewish State," the founding manifesto of the Zionist movement.

1897   First Zionist Congress is held in Basel, Switzerland. It articulates the goal of creating "for the Jewish people a home in Palestine secured by public law."

1902   Herzl asks Cecil Rhodes for support.

1903   Russian Minister of the Interior Vyacheslav von Plehve orchestrates the Kishinev Pogrom on Easter. One year later, Herzl would obtain a promise from von Plehve for a charter for Jews in Palestine.

1904   July 3 — Herzl dies.

1905   Seventh Zionist Congress votes against a national home for Jews anywhere but in Palestine. Other sites, including Uganda, had been previously considered.

1913   Arab Congress in Paris demands self-government from the
         Ottoman Empire. Palestinians begin to organize anti-Zionist
         groups.

1914   June 28 — World War I begins.

1916   The Arab Revolt against the Ottoman Empire begins. Britain
         promises independence to the Arab people, but secretly
         negotiates the Sykes-Picot Agreement with France.

1917   November 2 — British Foreign Secretary Arthur Balfour issues
         the Balfour Declaration, promising the Zionists a "national
         home" in Palestine.

         November, the Bolshevik party leads the victorious Russian
         Revolution. The new socialist government publishes the secret
         treaties signed by the ousted czarist government, including
         Sykes-Picot.

1918   August — President Woodrow Wilson writes to US Zionist
         leader Rabbi Stephen S. Wise expressing support for the
         Zionist movement.

1919   The General Syrian Congress, with delegates from present-day
         Palestine, Lebanon and Syria, unanimously repudiates the
         Sykes-Picot Agreement.

         August — the US-based King–Crane Commission reports on
         its trip to Syria and Palestine, stating that the Zionist claim to
         Palestine "can hardly be seriously considered."

1920   Britain secures a mandate over Palestine in the aftermath of
         World War I. Riots erupt in Jerusalem.

1921   July 22 — British Foreign Secretary Arthur Balfour, Zionist
         leader Chaim Weizmann, British Prime Minister Lloyd George
         and Colonial Secretary Winston Churchill meet to discuss the
         situation in Palestine.

1923   Vladimir Jabotinsky publishes "The Iron Wall," arguing that the Zionist project could only succeed through the use of overwhelming force.

1933   Adolph Hitler comes to power in Germany. A new wave of Jewish settlers arrives in Palestine.

1936   Starting with a six-month general strike, Palestinians launch an armed rebellion against the British Mandate government in a struggle for independence.

1937   The British Peel Commission recommends the partition of Palestine and the creation of a small Jewish state.

1938   November — The "Kristallnacht" Nazi pogrom in Germany leaves more than 1,300 Jewish people dead and 7,000 businesses destroyed in one night.

1939   September 1 — World War II begins in Europe as Germany invades Poland.

        September, the British crush the Palestinian uprising that began three and a half years earlier. The British employ extreme violence with the assistance of the Jewish Agency and the main Zionist army, the Haganah.

1942   The Zionists shift their organizing focus to the United States and issue the Biltmore Program in New York City calling for the formation of a Jewish state in Palestine.

1944   January 13 — US Secretary of the Treasury Henry Morgenthau Jr. issues an unusual report, protesting the US government's failure to respond to the Nazi genocide. The government takes no remedial steps.

1947   November — without consulting the Palestinians, the United Nations votes to partition Palestine. War starts in Palestine between Zionists and Palestinian Arabs.

1948   March 10 — Plan Dalet begins. Palestinian villages not involved in the fighting are attacked by the Haganah and the Irgun.

April 9 — Nearly all residents of the village of Deir Yassin are wiped out by the Irgun.

May 15 — British troops withdraw from Palestine. The state of Israel is proclaimed, known as al-Nakba by the Palestinians. Arab League troops intervene on behalf of the Palestinians. By this date, three hundred thousand Palestinians are already in exile.

December 11 — UN Resolution 194 passes. It states that all refugees must be allowed to return and compensated for damages suffered. Israel continues to defy the resolution to this day.

1949   January — A ceasefire is reached. Israel occupies 80 percent of Palestine. Seven hundred-fifty thousand Palestinians are made refugees.

1953   August — Iran's nationalist leader, Mohammed Mossadegh, is overthrown in a CIA-engineered coup. The brutal shah is returned to power.

October 14 — The Israeli army attacks the West Bank village of Qibya and wipes out its population.

1956   July 26 — Egyptian President Gamal Abdel Nasser nationalizes the Suez Canal.

October 24 — Britain, France and Israel sign the Protocol of Sevres, sealing their agreement to wage war against Egypt. France agrees to help Israel start a nuclear program.

Five days later, Israel attacks Egypt. The United States and Soviet Union, for different reasons, intervene. Britain and France suffer an embarrassing defeat while Nasser's prestige soars.

1958   Fatah, the Palestine National Liberation Movement, is founded.

July 14 — the Iraq Revolution overthrows the pro-British monarchy. US and British troops immediately deploy to prevent the fall of the governments in Lebanon and Jordan.

1964   The Palestine Liberation Organization (PLO) is founded in Cairo.

1967   June 5 — The Six-Day War begins. Israel attacks Egypt, Syria, and Jordan, quickly tripling in size. The rest of Palestine, as well as the Egyptian Sinai and the Syrian Golan, are occupied. US imperialists are convinced that Israel will be an indispensable ally against Arab nationalism.

December — The Palestinian wing of the Arab National Movement, together with a number of smaller organizations, form the Popular Front for the Liberation of Palestine (PFLP) and declares its adherence to Marxism-Leninism.

1968   March — About two hundred Palestinian guerrillas, backed by elements of the Jordanian army, hold off a major Israeli attack in Karameh, Jordan.

1969   February — The Palestinian resistance assumes control of the Palestine Liberation Organization. The PLO adopts as its objective a "democratic secular state" in all of Palestine.

1970   Jordan's King Hussein oversees the massacre of more than fifteen thousand PLO fighters and civilians. The incident is known as "Black September." PFLP fighters seize three international airliners, take them to Jordan and blow them up without passengers on the airport's runway.

September 28 — Nasser dies. Anwar Sadat succeeds him as Egyptian president and begins moving away from the Soviet Union and toward the United States.

1973   The Palestine National Front forms in the West Bank and Gaza Strip.

October 6 — The 1973 Arab-Israeli War begins. Egypt and Syria launch a war to regain territories lost to Israel in 1967. No territory changes hands, but Israel is shown not to be invincible.

The International Convention on the Suppression and Punishment of the Crime of Apartheid becomes international law.

1974   Fatah, with the support of the Democratic Front for the Liberation of Palestine (DFLP) and others, begins advocating a "two-state solution" that would create a Palestinian state in the West Bank and Gaza. The PFLP opposes the two-state proposal.

October — The Arab Summit Conference votes to recognize the PLO as the sole legitimate representative of the Palestinian people.

November — PLO Chairman Yasser Arafat addresses the United Nations, where the PLO is granted observer status.

1975   April — The fascist Phalangist Party ignites civil war in Lebanon with the massacre of 30 people, mostly Palestinians.

November — The United Nations condemns Zionism as a form of racism and recognizes the "national rights" of the Palestinians.

1976   May — With the PLO and the Lebanese National Movement on the brink of victory, the Syrian army intervenes in Lebanon.

August 12 — The refugee camp of Tal al-Zaatar falls to rightists after six weeks of siege. The Syrian army blocks Palestinian reinforcements from lifting the siege.

October — The Riyadh Summit Conference establishes an uneasy peace in Lebanon.

1978   The Camp David Accords are signed, putting Egypt squarely into the US camp.

1979   February — The US-backed shah of Iran is swept out of power by the Iranian Revolution.

1980   September — The Iran-Iraq war begins.

1981   Israel bombs the Osirak nuclear power plant, derailing Iraq's nuclear program, with Washington's approval.

        October 6 — Egyptian President Anwar Sadat is assassinated by military officers in response to Camp David.

1982   June — Israel invades Lebanon with US backing. Three months of relentless bombing leave more than twenty thousand Lebanese and Palestinian civilians dead.

        September — PLO forces evacuate to Tunisia under a negotiated agreement. US, French and other military forces arrive in Lebanon.

        September 16 — Despite security guarantees, the Israeli military allows Phalangist forces to massacre Palestinians in the Sabra and Shatila refugee camps. More than two thousand people are slaughtered in forty-eight hours.

1983   October 23, a truck bombing kills 241 US troops in Beirut. US Marines evacuate soon afterward.

1987   Hamas is formed. It is an offshoot of the Egyptian Muslim Brotherhood.

        December — The 1987 Palestinian Intifada erupts. The emergence of a Unified National Leadership, bringing together the Palestinian resistance organizations, creates a situation of dual power for nearly four years.

1991   The defeat of Iraq in the Gulf War and the overthrow of the
         Soviet Union mark a shift in the world balance of forces with
         deep repercussions for the Arab liberation movements.

1993   September — The Oslo Accords are signed by Israeli leadership
         and PLO Chairman Yasser Arafat. They form the centerpiece
         of the so-called peace process. Under Oslo, the PLO is allowed
         to take control of small portions of the West Bank. Israel
         immediately breaks the accords by accelerating settlement
         construction. Nearly all of the Palestinian left organizations
         oppose the Oslo Accords.

2000   Lebanese resistance organizations, with Hezbollah emerging as
         the central force, push Israeli troops out of Lebanon.

         September 28 — The Al-Aqsa Intifada begins after Israeli
         Prime Minister Ariel Sharon's provocative visit to the Al-Aqsa
         Mosque.

         November — George W. Bush is elected US president.

2002   April — Israel bombs the West Bank refugee camp of Jenin,
         massacring dozens of Palestinians and demolishing homes
         with bulldozers supplied by US-based Caterpillar.

         Israel begins construction of the apartheid wall in the West
         Bank, effectively annexing large areas of Palestinian land.

2003   March 20 — The US military bombs and invades Iraq. Three
         weeks later, Baghdad falls.

2004   November 11 — Yasser Arafat dies.

2005   September — Israel withdraws troops and settlements from
         Gaza. Israel continues to surround Gaza and wages a campaign
         of bombings and targeted assassinations.

2006   Hamas wins the Palestinian parliamentary election. Israel
         imposes a blockade on Gaza.

July — Israel attacks Lebanon with US backing. Israel suffers relatively high casualties and is driven out by mid-August without achieving its goals. Hezbollah leads the resistance in Lebanon.

2008   June 19 — Hamas and Israel negotiate a cease-fire. Israel continues its blockade of Gaza.

November 4 — Israel kills six people inside Gaza in violation of the cease-fire. It seals off Gaza completely. Palestinian resistance forces resume rocket fire.

Barack Obama is elected US president.

December 27 — Israel launches massive air strikes on Gaza. The three-week offensive leaves 1,417 Palestinians dead, more than 5,500 wounded and causes over $2 billion in damage.

2009   A new Israeli government forms in the spring, led by the extreme right-wing prime minister, Benjamin Netanyahu, and his fascist foreign minister, Avigdor Lieberman. Labor Party leader Ehud Barak rounds out the alliance as defense minister.

US envoy George Mitchell meets with Netanyahu and Lieberman in April. The two Israeli leaders refuse to make any references to a Palestinian state.

May — The Israeli Knesset and cabinet approve a law that criminalizes any Israeli citizen who denies Israel is a "democratic and Jewish state." The law targets Palestinians with Israeli citizenship.

2010–11 Starting in Tunisia, hundreds of thousands take to the streets of Arab countries in spontaneous rebellion, beginning the "Arab Spring" across the Middle East and North Africa. In Egypt, the US-client military regime of Hosni Mubarak is overthrown when low-ranking officers refuse to fire on protestors. Two years later, a coup led by then-Defense Minister Abdel Fattah el-Sisi restored the generals to power

in a massacre of more than nine hundred people, with the
support of the US. Most of the murdered were members of
Muslim Brotherhood.

2011   March–October — Under the pretext of removing Libyan
head of State Muammar Gadaffi, eight NATO nations—
Belgium, Canada, Denmark, France, Italy, Norway, the United
Kingdom, and the United States—bomb this country of
six million people for seven months. Libya's head of state is
assassinated, its civilian infrastructure reduced to rubble and
its ability to operate as a sovereign nation destroyed.

March — An armed right-wing insurgency begins in Syria
aiming to replace the government of Bashir al-Assad.
Hezbollah and Iran back Syria while Washington and its
Saudi Arabian clients arm arch-reactionary jihadists such as
ISIS, which destroy Syria's economic base in Aleppo and cut a
murderous swath through the country, executing thousands.
Israel bombs Syria and provides medical attention for wounded
jihadists in the Golan Heights, a part of Syria that it occupies.
In 2014, the Pentagon sends in troops who continue to occupy
a third of Syria to this day, including its most fertile and oil-
rich lands.

2012   October — African National Congress National Chairperson
Baleka Mbete calls Israeli apartheid against Palestinians "far
worse than Apartheid South Africa."

November — Israel assassinates Hamas's military chief of staff,
Ahmad Jabari, followed by eight days of Israeli air raids on
Palestine killing more than one hundred.

2014   July 8 — Israel launches a massive aerial assault on Gaza, which
it calls "Operation Protective Edge." Israel also attempts a
ground invasion in order to militarily defeat Hamas. Defeated
in ground warfare, Israeli forces are forced to withdraw from
Gaza. Nevertheless, the invasion kills over two thousand
Palestinians.

2015   Saudi Arabia, with the military and diplomatic aid of the
        US, begins a war on Yemen, one of the poorest countries in
        the world, to oust the Ansar Allah (or Houthi) movement
        which had popularly taken power in the capital of Sana'a. By
        2022, the Saudi bombings and blockade are responsible for
        destruction of the civilian infrastructure, a cholera epidemic,
        indiscriminate civilian deaths, and starvation, in what the
        United Nations then called the world's worst humanitarian
        crisis. The US conducts its own operations in Yemen as part
        of the so-called war on terror. These operations include drone
        warfare, raids, and assassinations.

        April 2 — the Joint Comprehensive Plan of Action, also
        called the Iran nuclear agreement, is negotiated. It limits the
        Islamic Republic's nuclear energy capacity in exchange for
        the lifting of nuclear-related sanctions. Signing the agreement
        with Iran are the five permanent members of the UN Security
        Council: China, France, Russia, United Kingdom, and the
        United States—plus Germany. The agreement calls for the
        International Atomic Energy Agency to have regular access to
        Iranian nuclear facilities for inspections.

        September — Israeli forces storm Al-Aqsa Mosque in
        Jerusalem, firing at worshippers. Fears over the further
        restriction of religious rights for Muslims lead to
        demonstrations throughout the West Bank. More than two
        hundred Palestinians civilians are killed by Israeli forces there
        in the next six months.

2017   July — After ten years of Israeli siege, UNESCO declares Gaza
        to be "unlivable." Citing limited electricity, lack of water, food,
        health care and sanitation, and other factors, the UN bodies
        say that life there is "in perpetual crisis."

        December — In defiance of international law and the United
        Nations Security Council, the Trump Administration
        recognizes Jerusalem as the capital of Israel. The US moves its
        embassy there.

2018   May — President Trump unilaterally pulls the US out of the
            Iran nuclear deal, even though regular monitoring of Iran's
            nuclear facilities by the International Atomic Energy Agency
            found no violations. Trump announces that the US will
            reimpose "the highest level of sanctions" on Iran.

            July — The Israeli Parliament passes the "nation-state law,"
            declaring that national rights in Israel belong only to Jewish
            people. This formally enshrines Israel as an apartheid, Jewish-
            supremacist state. The law also establishes "Jewish settlement
            as a national value" and mandates that the state "will labor to
            encourage and promote its establishment and development."
            This gives a green light to the de facto annexation of the West
            Bank through further settlement.

            March 2018–December 2019 — The Great March of Return.
            Every Friday, Gazans organize peaceful marches to the Israeli
            border demanding the right to return to their homelands, and
            the lifting of the siege of Gaza. Israeli snipers regularly fire
            live ammunition on unarmed demonstrators. Two hundred
            twenty-three Palestinians are killed, forty-six of them children.
            Neary 10,000 are wounded and 155, mostly young men,
            require limb amputations.

2020   January — High-ranking Iranian General Qasem Soleimani
            and top Iraqi paramilitary commander Abu Mahdi
            al-Muhandis are assassinated by a US drone strike. Soleimani
            was known for assisting both the Syrian and Iraqi governments
            in fighting ISIS. The assassinations sparked large and angry
            anti-US demonstrations in Iran and Iraq, and a call by the
            Iraqi Parliament for the US to leave that country.

            September 15–December 22 — The United Arab Emirates,
            Bahrain, Morocco, and Sudan sign the Abraham Accords, a
            peace and normalization treaty with Israel.

2021   The Jenin Brigades, organized armed resistance groups, emerge
            specifically in response to the plight of Palestinian political
            prisoners in the West Bank.

In May, mass uprisings take place in both the West Bank and Gaza in response to a storming of Al-Aqsa Mosque during Ramadan and Israeli settler attempts to evict families by force from their homes in Sheikh Jarrah neighborhood of East Jerusalem. Hamas demands Israel withdraw security forces from the Al-Aqsa Mosque compound. Israel responds with air raids on Gaza, killing 256 Palestinians, wounding 2,000 and displacing more than 70,000.

2022　　Deadliest year for Palestinians in the West Bank since the end of the Intifada in 2005. A year after the attack on Palestinian families in Sheikh Jarrah, Israeli military and armed settler raids on Palestinian mosques and refugee camps intensify. More organized armed resistance movements begin to emerge in the West Bank, particularly the cities of Nablus and Jenin.

May 11 — While covering the aftermath of an Israeli raid on the Jenin refugee camp, well-known Palestinian American journalist Shireen Abu Akleh is assassinated by an Israeli sniper shot to her head. This sparks global protest and resistance throughout Palestine. Her funeral in Jerusalem is attacked by Israeli police.

December 29 — A newly formed Israeli government includes open fascists. The government establishes a paramilitary National Guard independent of the police and under the direct control of Minister of National Security Itamar Ben-Gvir, a settler on the West Bank, who openly applauds those who kill Palestinians. Another West Bank settler, Finance Minister Bezalel Smotrich, is given the additional role of overseeing the West Bank. Smotrich has called for the destruction of Palestinian villages, opposes Palestinian statehood, and denies the existence of the Palestinian people. In its first six months, the new government authorizes thousands of new settlements, bringing the number of Israeli settlers there to seven hundred thousand, in a move to permanently annex the West Bank.

2023　　January — Hundreds of thousands of Jewish Israelis demonstrate against legislation proposed by the right-wing government to weaken the judicial system, and grant itself unlimited power to enact its reactionary agenda. While protesters see this as limiting their rights, they find the issues of Palestinians "not relevant." Palestinians bringing Palestinian flags to the protest are forced to leave, and even beaten up.

July — Israel launches its deadliest and most intense military occupation in the West Bank since the Second Intifada, with the aim of destroying renewed armed resistance forces in the West Bank.

October 7 — Palestinian resistance forces launch the unprecedented Al-Aqsa Flood counteroffensive, sending hundreds of armed militants over the illegal border wall via motorized hang glider. Israel responds with their greatest acts of violence and repression since the start of the Nakba, enacting a complete blockade of Gaza and indiscriminately bombing hospitals, refugee camps, and residential complexes. As of December 2023, 20,000 Palestinians had been killed, 70 percent of whom are women and children.

SECTION I: FRAMING THE STRUGGLE

OVERVIEW

On January 22, 2009, George Mitchell was introduced as President Barack Obama's chief Middle East negotiator. At the press conference announcing his appointment, Mitchell spoke about his previous role as US representative in the Northern Ireland negotiations during the 1990s. He mentioned that the conflict in Ireland had been ongoing for eight hundred years. Then the former senator told the assembled media and US State Department staff a "joke:"

> Just recently, I spoke in Jerusalem, and I mentioned the 800 years. And afterward, an elderly gentleman came up to me, and he said, "did you say 800 years?" I said, "Yes, 800." He repeated the number again. I repeated it again. He said, "Ah, such a recent argument. No wonder you settled it."[1]

The reporters and officials laughed knowingly. They all "knew" that the Arab-Israeli (cast as a Muslim-Jewish) conflict—the supposed core of the problem in the region—has been going on for not hundreds, but thousands of years. The only problem with this well-accepted "fact" is that it is not true. It is a myth, a malicious misrepresentation of the real nature and causes of the struggle in the Middle East.

Government and corporate media spokespeople have so endlessly regurgitated this fundamental distortion of the source of conflict in the Middle East that it has become conventional wisdom. It is accepted by a large part of the US population. The conflict is presented as an ancient and bitter fight between two peoples or two religions, based on irreconcilable and mutual hatred. It is a convenient lie that lets the real sources of the conflict—imperialism and colonialism—off the hook. There is, in fact, an irreconcilable conflict in the Middle East, but it is not one between different peoples or faiths. It is instead the struggle between imperialism: Israel and the dependent Arab regimes on the one hand, and the oppressed peoples of this oil-rich and strategic region fighting for liberation and progress on the other.

At the very heart of this conflict is Palestine. The Palestinian struggle is a struggle against Western colonialism. It has been this way from the beginning, more than a century ago. As is the case with all conflicts and world events, what is going on today in Palestine and the Middle East can only be understood in its historical context.

The key event in reshaping the region was World War I, a war fought by empires for the purposes of redividing the world to suit their interests. It was the British and French takeover and division of the area as the spoils of World War I that created the artificial boundaries of the modern Middle East. Syria and Lebanon became part of the French Empire; Iraq, Egypt, Jordan, and Palestine were incorporated into the British Empire. The British and French imperialists viewed the desire of the Arab people for the creation of one Arab state as a threat to their domination. A widespread revolt in 1920 against the new colonizers was crushed. Without the sponsorship of the British Empire, the Zionist colonial project could not have succeeded. Three decades later, this project officially gave birth to the state of Israel.

After World War II, the United States emerged as the dominant power in the region. Contrary to its false image as a "beacon of democracy," Washington has sought to destroy every progressive government and popular democratic movement in the region for over sixty years. Washington has supported, and sometimes installed, the most reactionary monarchies and police states. The aim has been to clear all obstacles to the unrestricted exploitation of the region's vast oil resources, labor, and markets, while ensuring US military hegemony over the area.

Today, the United States occupies Iraq and Syria, while its bases and naval power dominate the Persian/Arabian Gulf and the entire region. Israel plays a key role in the US government's strategy of regional domination. Over the past forty years, the United States has sent billions of dollars in economic and military assistance to the small state of Israel annually—far more aid than it has sent to any other country or even to any continent. In 2023, Israel received $3.3 billion in military aid from Washington without strings attached, as it does every year, and the Biden administration has requested an additional $14 billion following the Palestinian counteroffensive on October 7, 2023 to assist in Israel's unparalleled destruction of Gaza.[2] Although Israel has a population of less than seven million people, it has been built up into a nuclear-armed power. It has repaid these incomparable "gifts" by playing a vital role in the US strategy of regional and global domination.

The appended pamphlet, *Israel: Base of Western Imperialism*, by the Egyptian historian Abdel Wahab el-Messiri, illustrates that in the 1960s the national liberation movements in the Middle East and the rest of the world saw Israel as a colonial-settler state, a garrison that served the interests of imperialism.[3] That description remains accurate today.

What is not accurate is the idea that Israel or a pro-Israel lobby controls US policy in the Middle East. Special attention will be paid to this question in the first section of this book, so that readers have a clear understanding of Israel's role in relation to US imperialism. Without such understanding, it is easy to adopt a skewed and misguided view of the entire struggle to liberate Palestine.

DOES THE ISRAEL LOBBY CONTROL US POLICY?

Growing numbers of people around the world oppose the US government's political support for Israel and the massive military and economic aid that is used to brutally suppress the Palestinian people. Many attribute this unparalleled and one-sided support to the power of the pro-Israel lobby inside the United States. Some believe that US Middle East policy is controlled by Israel through the medium of the pro-Israel organizations in the United States. Also, there are those on the far right, including fascist elements, who oppose US aid to Israel not based on solidarity with the Palestinians nor out of any concern for justice, but because of their own anti-Semitic prejudices. These racists often subscribe to conspiracy theories that portray Jewish people as "evil" and "power-hungry." The Nazis in Germany and their followers, like automobile mogul Henry Ford, propagated outlandish theories about a "Jewish Bolshevik/banker conspiracy" to take over the world.

These contemporary "theories" are latter-day incarnations of the anti-Semitism that was so pervasive in the Christian churches of the Middle Ages. Contrary to current mythology, it was the Christian churches and countries of Europe that were the main sources of anti-Semitic violence through history. Life in predominantly Muslim societies was typically much better for Jewish people than in predominantly Christian ones. When the Christian crusaders conquered Palestine in the early Crusades, they slaughtered Muslims and Jews alike. When the Christian kingdoms conquered Spain in 1492, their rulers expelled both Muslims and Jews.

Perhaps the most ambitious and certainly the most documented attempt to prove that pro-Israel forces in the United States dominate US Middle East policy is the 2007 book, *The Israel Lobby and US Foreign Policy,* by John J. Mearsheimer and Stephen M. Walt.[4] Although both authors are thoroughly mainstream liberal professors at elite academic institutions, the University of Chicago and Harvard University, respectively, Mearsheimer and Walt have predictably been accused of "anti-Semitism" by Israel's defenders in the United States. Smearing critics of Israel with the brush of "anti-Semitism" is the tried-and-tested method used to "change the subject" whenever irrefutable criticisms are raised about Israel. Mearsheimer and Walt certainly knew what was coming before they published their book, which is presumably why they dedicated 106 of 466 pages to footnotes.

The Israeli government and pro-Israel organizations in the United States and abroad seek to equate Zionism with Judaism—to draw an equal sign between a brutal colonial political ideology and a religion. This dishonest and dangerous equation becomes the basis for falsely accusing any and all critics of Israel of "anti-Semitism." To the extent that the practitioners of this tactic are successful, they actually encourage the growth of anti-Semitism. If critics of Israel are Jewish—and there are growing numbers of Jewish people who oppose Israeli apartheid and militarism—and reject the equating of Zionism with Judaism, they are invariably vilified as "self-hating Jews." Jewish critics are considered especially dangerous by the defenders of Israel. While Arab American professors, especially Palestinians, are targeted on a regular basis, special efforts are made to drive Jewish critics out of academia or positions of public influence.

The Mearsheimer–Walt book describes several of these cases. Particularly instructive is the case of Dr. Norman Finkelstein, a renowned author and the son of Holocaust survivors. Finkelstein was outrageously denied tenure at DePaul University in Chicago in 2007 due to an intense campaign by pro-Israel groups. Alan Dershowitz, a Harvard law professor and virulent Israel supporter, spearheaded the campaign. Four years earlier, Dershowitz had unsuccessfully attempted to prevent the publication of one of Finkelstein's books by the University of California Press. Of the campaigns of vilification and slander regularly directed against Palestinian and other Arab American professors who speak out, some have been successful and some have been defeated. A campaign in 2005 purged Dr. Rashid Khalidi, a member of one of the most prominent Palestinian intellectual families and a Columbia University professor, from a lecture program for New York City high school teachers. The following year, the New York City Council approved a study program on Israel "initiated by the public relations department of the Israeli Consulate in New York."[5]

The Israel Lobby and US Foreign Policy contains a great deal of interesting and useful information about US and Israeli policy in the Middle East as a whole. It details the workings of numerous pro-Israel organizations to influence US legislation and actions in support of Israel, and to stifle all real debate about Israel in the political process, media, universities, labor organizations, and society in general. It is not a question that pro-Israel organizations are well organized, well-funded, and influential. Nor is it in dispute that they can stampede nearly the entire Congress into voting for the most one-sided and outlandish positions of support for Israel. Some examples are measures passed during Israel's massive bombardment of Lebanon in 2006 and Gaza in 2008–2009. Neither lengthy resolution contained a single word of criticism of Israel, notwithstanding its indiscriminate use of some of the most diabolical weapons ever created against defenseless civilian populations.

But does the pro-Israel lobby—or Israel itself through the lobby—control and direct US policy in the Middle East? To put it another way, does the tail wag the dog? Is it really conceivable that a small, dependent country could call the shots for the most powerful empire in the history of the world? The answer to all of these questions is no. Israel is part of the US global empire, not the other way around.

The pro-Israel lobby has been empowered by the US ruling class and political establishment, which see Israel as an important instrument against the liberation movements of the Arab and other peoples of the Middle East. The pro-Israel lobby has been allowed to grow strong in the same way as the now-declining Cuban counterrevolutionary lobby. Advocates for progressive movements or governments have never been permitted to establish anything like what the pro-Israel and anti-Cuba forces have been allowed and encouraged to develop. The key factor is that the latter are moving in the same general direction as imperialism.[6] The US imperialists hate and fear the Arab and other liberation movements, which they see as a threat to their strategic position in the Middle East and their domination of the region's resources and markets. They have spent more than a half-century seeking to destroy these movements, especially the Palestinian movement. Likewise, the imperialists hate and fear the Cuban Revolution, and have a similar fifty-year history of trying to overthrow it. These actions are neither the product of irrationality nor powerful lobbies.

All useful aspects aside, there is a fatal flaw in the Mearsheimer–Walt analysis. It flows from a liberal capitalist world view, which—reflecting a somewhat surprising degree of naivete for distinguished professors—implicitly accepts the US government's own description of its role in the world. In describing what they believe would justify massive US aid and support to Israel, Mearsheimer and Walt write:

> America's willingness to give Israel extensive economic, military and diplomatic support would be easy to understand if it advanced America's overall strategic interests. Generous aid to Israel might be justified, for example, if it were a cost-effective way for the United States to deal with countries that Washington had previously identified as hostile. Steadfast US support might also make sense if the United States received substantial benefits in return, and if the value of these benefits exceeded the economic and political costs of US support. . . . In short, aid to Israel would be easy to explain if it helped make Americans more secure and more prosperous.[7]

The underlying Mearsheimer–Walt assumption is that there is one, classless "America," and that the aim of US foreign policy is to "make Americans more secure or more prosperous." This assumption has nothing in common with reality. The complementary and interlinked priorities of US foreign policy are global domination and the protection of capitalist interests. The over 750 US military bases in more than 40 countries around the world are not there to make the people of the United States "more secure and more prosperous." Nor is the often-uttered goal of "protecting democracy" in countries around the world, some of which have never had an election.

Understanding Israel's Role

Mearsheimer and Walt's statement that the aid would be justified if Israel undertook to "deal with countries that Washington had previously identified as hostile" is bizarre. In fact, Israel has nearly always done just that on behalf of US imperialism. In the 1950s and 1960s, while Israel did not send troops—at least openly—to join in the genocidal US wars against Korea and Vietnam, it found other ways to support the Pentagon and its puppet governments in both conflicts.[8]

Israel also gave key support to the apartheid government in South Africa in the 1970s and 1980s, particularly when it was "inconvenient" for Washington to be seen openly supporting the racist regime. In the mid-1970s, Israel built an electrified fence along the Namibian-Angolan border. Namibia was then a colony of South Africa, and the liberation movement, the South West Africa People's Organization (SWAPO), was waging an armed struggle to free the country. The SWAPO guerrillas had bases in Angola, a country that had just achieved its independence from Portugal. Israeli-South African collaboration led to South Africa testing a nuclear bomb in the South Atlantic in 1979. From Washington's point of view, this was a very positive development, one that the US leaders fully supported. The South African apartheid regime not only ruthlessly oppressed the African people inside its own borders and in Namibia, it also served as the enforcer of US and other imperialist interests in all of Africa below the equator. Apartheid South Africa's counterrevolutionary role in Africa was much like that of Israel's in the Middle East.

During the 1980s, Israel trained and armed the Guatemalan army when it was carrying out genocide against the Indigenous peoples of that country. The US Congress had cut off direct aid to Guatemala's extreme right-wing government, but the White House and Pentagon were dedicated to destroying the revolutionary movement. This was at the height of the US proxy wars in El Salvador and Nicaragua. The Israeli secret police joined with the CIA to train torturers in Chile and other countries of Latin America after CIA-coordinated military coups in the 1970s. Israel also gave military aid to Taiwan, and supported right-wing dictatorships in Africa.

Nowhere has Israel's role as a watchdog for imperialist interests more benefited its sponsor than in the Middle East. Israel has been an ever-menacing hammer against the Arab countries—especially more progressive governments—that won real independence in the two decades after World War II. Israel joined with the British and French imperialists in attacking Egypt and the new Nasser government in 1956. The thwarted aims of the war were to (1) overthrow Nasser and return Egypt to the status of a British neo-colony, (2) expand the Israeli state to the Suez Canal at the expense of Egypt, and (3) undermine the Algerian Revolution. The 1956 War occurred before the US-Israeli relationship was fully cemented. At this time, Israel relied primarily on France and Britain for arms and funding, although the US government supported it as well. In this rare case, Tel Aviv and Washington were not on the same side, but things soon changed.

Israel became a satellite for US imperialist interests in the region. Israel's victory in the 1967 Six-Day War was a major blow to the more progressive nationalist forces, especially in Syria and Egypt. It was after this war that the US-Israel alliance became what it is today. In the mid-1970s, Israel intervened to support the fascist elements in Lebanon's civil war. In 1978 and 1982, Israel invaded Lebanon. In 1982, Israel occupied Beirut and carpet-bombed the capital throughout the summer. In 2006, Israel's five-week assault on Lebanon deliberately destroyed much of the infrastructure, which had just been rebuilt after years of civil war that Israel helped fuel. Israeli bombers destroyed an Iraqi nuclear power plant that was under construction at Osirak in 1981. This was at a time when the Iran-Iraq War was raging. The US government was publicly "supporting" Iraq in its war against Iran—where the US-installed Shah had been overthrown in 1979—and did not want to take responsibility for such an extremely hostile act. As the Iran-Contra affair later revealed, the United States was supporting Iran as well as Iraq in the hopes that they would destroy each other.[9] In a thousand different ways, the existence of the state of Israel as an artificial and colonial state in the heart of the Arab world has profoundly distorted regional development for the benefit of imperialism, and to the detriment of the Arab and other peoples of the region.

The leaders in Washington are above all businesspeople or their representatives. They are investors, who do not hand out money based on sentimentality or generosity. Sentimentality and imperialist diplomacy are mutually exclusive categories. As it has often been said: "The great powers have no permanent friends, only permanent interests." US leaders have sent hundreds of billions of dollars to Israel. Most of them view the money as being well spent. Because they are hard-headed investors, that assessment is subject to revision at any time. The possibility of a shift in the US-Israeli relationship cannot be dismissed. US and Israeli interests in the region are complimentary but not identical.

Events that have occurred since 2006 have complicated the US-Israeli alliance. The US-backed Israeli wars on Lebanon in 2006 and on the Palestinians in Gaza in 2008–2009 failed to achieve their essential objectives. They did, however, cause immense death, destruction, and suffering for the Arab people. Israel's continued inability to destroy the Lebanese and Palestinian resistance movements, combined with the failure of US interventions in Iraq, Iran, Syria, and elsewhere to achieve their goals, could lead to a tactical shift in US policy under the Obama administration. Given Israel's essential role in the Middle East vis-à-vis US imperialism, the White House will not put a long-term strategic shift on the table. But even a tactical shift has the potential to cause serious conflict between Washington and Tel Aviv. Nevertheless, the two-term presidency of Barack Obama saw an increase in the Washington-led partnership between Israel and the US. This alliance has since been doubled down on by both the Trump and Biden administrations, most heinously by the latter in the ongoing slaughter of Gaza.

Having an understanding of Israel's basic relationship with US imperialism is key for partisans in the struggle against Zionism and imperialism today. It is also important to know the conflict's colonial roots, the origin and development of Zionist thought, and the dynamics of the ongoing Palestinian struggle for liberation. These are some of the points this book will attempt to address and explain.

SECTION II: RECOLONIZING PALESTINE

DIVIDING THE MIDDLE EAST

At the start of the twentieth century, much of what is known today as the Middle East was still part of the Ottoman Empire based in Turkey. What later became Syria, Lebanon, Jordan, and Palestine were until 1918 part of the vilayets (provinces) of Syria and Beirut and the independent sanjak (sub-province) of Jerusalem. The vilayets of Mosul, Baghdad, and Basra, which together form modern Iraq, were also under Ottoman rule. Egypt and the Arabian Peninsula were still formally under Ottoman administration, but Ottoman influence was declining and rival British power was growing in both areas. The Suez Canal, which runs through Egypt, was Britain's vital lifeline to its richest colonies in Asia. British troops occupied key parts of Egypt in 1882.

During World War I, which began in 1914, the British sent a military emissary, T. E. Lawrence, to enlist the support of Arab leaders, particularly the Hashemite King Hussein bin Ali, who ruled the Hejaz region of the western Arabian Peninsula.[10] The British promised support for an independent Arab state in return for Arab military participation in the war against Turkey. At the same time as these promises were being made, the foreign ministers of the British, French, and Russian empires, along with their allies in Italy and Greece, were secretly drawing up a plan to divide the Ottoman Empire in the aftermath of the war. The 1916 Sykes-Picot Agreement became public only after the Russian Revolution of November 1917.[11] The new Soviet Commissariat of Foreign Affairs published the secret treaties signed by the ousted Czarist government, includ-

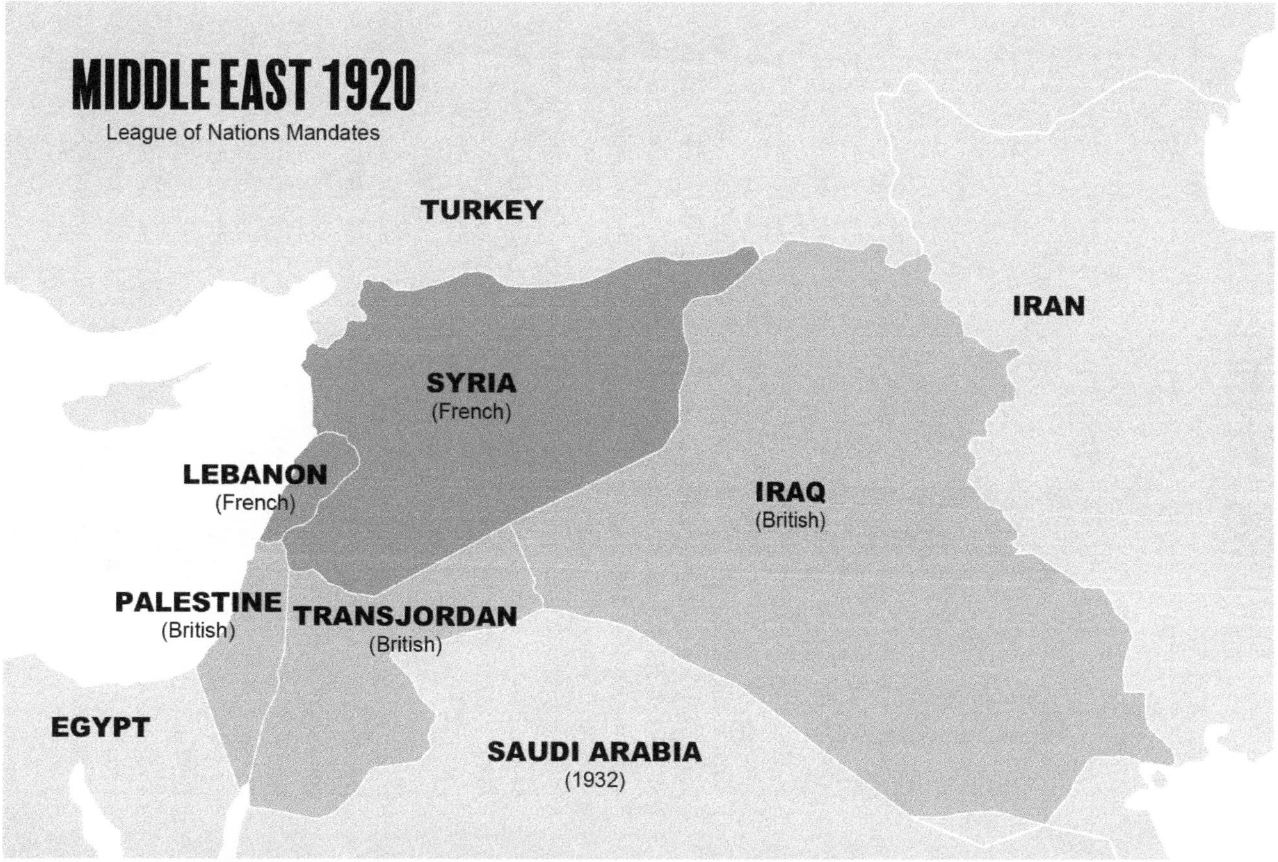

MIDDLE EAST 1920

League of Nations Mandates

TURKEY

IRAN

SYRIA
(French)

IRAQ
(British)

LEBANON
(French)

PALESTINE
(British)

TRANSJORDAN
(British)

SAUDI ARABIA
(1932)

EGYPT

ing Sykes-Picot. The new Soviet state, led by Vladimir Ilyich Lenin's Bolshevik party, also renounced all territorial ambitions against other nation-states.

That same month, more than a year before the war's end, and while Palestine was still nominally under Ottoman rule, Britain's foreign secretary, Arthur Balfour, sent a letter to Lord Rothschild, a member of the British House of Lords and one of the world's richest men. The infamous Balfour Declaration of November 2, 1917, read:

> Dear Lord Rothschild:
>
> I have much pleasure in conveying to you, on behalf of His Majesty's Government, the following declaration of sympathy with Jewish Zionist aspirations which has been submitted to, and approved by, the Cabinet:
>
> "His Majesty's Government view with favour the establishment in Palestine of a national home for the Jewish people, and will use their best endeavours to facilitate the achievement of this object, it being clearly understood that nothing shall be done which may prejudice the civil and religious rights of existing non-Jewish communities in Palestine, or the rights and political status enjoyed by Jews in any other country."
>
> I should be grateful if you would bring this declaration to the knowledge of the Zionist Federation.
>
> Yours sincerely,
> Arthur James Balfour[12]

Underlining the colonialist character of the note is the phrase: "nothing shall be done which may prejudice the civil and religious rights of existing non-Jewish communities in Palestine." The "existing non-Jewish communities"—the Palestinian Arabs—went unnamed, despite comprising 92 percent of the population at the time. While national rights were emphasized for the tiny settler minority, no mention was made of the same rights for the indigenous majority.

As Palestinian scholar Dr. Ismail Zayid wrote about the Balfour Declaration:

> It is interesting to note that the four-letter word "Arab" occurs not once in this document. . . . To refer to the Arabs who constituted 92 percent of the population of Palestine and owned 89 percent of its land, as the non-Jewish communities, is not merely preposterous but deliberately fraudulent. . . . Palestine did not belong to Balfour to assume such acts of generosity.[13]

The Balfour Declaration sparked great outrage, particularly among the rapidly growing urban populations, which were the centers of political activity in the region. The Balfour Declaration and the Sykes-Picot Agreement were widely viewed by the Arab masses as a double betrayal by Britain. Instead of liberation, Arabs from Jerusalem to Damascus to Baghdad found themselves as colonial subjects under the domination of the world's two largest empires. What made the new colonialism even worse was that the imperial rulers had designated their land as a "national home" for another people. The resistance against these new colonial realities would decisively shape the struggle in the Middle East for decades to come.

New Colonial Masters

At the end of World War I, the British army occupied Jerusalem in Palestine, Damascus in Syria, Iraq, and Transjordan (now Jordan). French troops occupied Beirut in Lebanon. Expecting the British to keep their wartime commitments, Hussein sent one of his sons, Faisal, to Damascus. On July 2, 1919, the General Syrian Congress, with delegates elected from areas throughout present-day Palestine, Lebanon, and Syria, met in Damascus. The delegates unanimously repudiated the Sykes-Picot Agreement, the Balfour Declaration, and the Zionist project. They asked:

> How can the Zionists go back in history two thousand years to prove that by their short sojourn in Palestine they have now a right to claim it and return to it as a Jewish home, thus crushing the nationalism of a million Arabs?[14]

Within the emerging Arab nationalist movement, the creation of a Greater Syria was a very popular idea. The people were organizing in preparation for independence. The leaders of this movement were also encouraged by the rhetoric of US President Woodrow Wilson. Point twelve of Wilson's famous "Fourteen Points," enunciated in a speech to the US Congress on January 8, 1918, while war was still raging, read in part:

> The Turkish portions of the present Ottoman Empire should be assured a secure sovereignty, but the other nationalities which are now under Turkish rule should be assured an undoubted security of life and an absolutely unmolested opportunity of autonomous development.[15]

In a follow-up speech on July 4, 1918, Wilson called for:

> [T]he settlement of every question, whether of territory or sovereignty, of economic arrangement, or of political relationship, [should be determined] upon the basis of the free acceptance of that settlement by the people immediately concerned, and not upon the basis of material interest or advantage of any other nation or people which may desire a different settlement for the sake of its own exterior influence or mastery.[16]

The following month, however, Wilson completely contradicted his public statements. He wrote to Rabbi Stephen S. Wise, an American Zionist leader, in a message titled, "Rebuilding Palestine:"

> I welcome an opportunity to express the satisfaction I have felt in the progress of the Zionist movement in the United States and in the Allied countries since the declaration by Mr. Balfour.[17]

The aspiring state of Greater Syria had a very short life. In 1920, the British made good on their Sykes-Picot commitments and allowed the French army to enter Damascus, overthrow the new government headed by Faisal, and occupy present-day Syria and Lebanon.

The oppressed peoples of the region responded with a widespread revolt in 1920. This engulfed the region in response to the imperialist takeover. Eventually, the revolt was suppressed. In the aftermath, Greater Syria was dismembered. One part, Palestine—it was known as Southern Syria at the time—was designated for Zionist settlers from Europe. The French imperialists developed Lebanon into the Western banking center and entertainment capital of the region. Puppet monarchs were placed on the thrones of Transjordan, Iraq, and Syria. The petroleum resources of Iraq and the entire region were reserved exclusively for the benefit of the US, British, French, and Dutch oil monopolies.

The chopping up of Greater Syria, the creation of new statelets like Kuwait and other tiny Gulf kingdoms, and the drawing of new borders across the region were intended to thwart Arab nationalism and to benefit the dominant imperialist powers. As a consolation for being ousted in Syria, the British crowned Faisal in 1922 as king of their new colony, Iraq. His brother, Abdullah, was made emir (monarch) of another new British colony, Jordan. For the masses of people there was no consolation, only new colonial masters. Faisal and Abdullah would soon show themselves to be compliant collaborators with both British colonialism and its newly-anointed project, Zionism.

ZIONISM: A COLONIAL PROJECT

Modern political Zionism—the idea of creating an exclusively Jewish state—began to gather momentum in the late nineteenth century as a response to the anti-Semitic bigotry that prevailed in so much of Europe and the United States. In Eastern Europe, particularly the Russian Empire, horrific anti-Jewish pogroms, or massacres, were commonplace. Small numbers of Zionist settlers began arriving in Palestine in 1882. Like the first European settlers in North America nearly three centuries earlier, the early Zionist settlers survived only thanks to the assistance of the indigenous Palestinian Arab population. These settlers in Palestine comprised a tiny part of the Jewish population that emigrated from Europe due to oppression and poverty during the late nineteenth and early twentieth centuries. More than a million Jewish immigrants arrived in the United States during the same period.

In the 1890s, the Zionist movement began to take on a more organized form. Theodore Herzl, an Austrian Jewish journalist, emerged as the movement's preeminent leader. Herzl reportedly became a Zionist after covering the 1894 trial of a Jewish junior military officer, Alfred Dreyfus, in France. Using anti-Semitism, Dreyfus' superiors framed him, which resulted in his conviction for treason and being sent off to the notorious Devil's Island prison. In 1896, Herzl published *The Jewish State,* generally regarded as the founding manifesto of the Zionist movement. The First Zionist Congress was held the next year. While the Zionist project, headed by Herzl, was a response to European anti-Semitism, it was at the same time thoroughly European. Its leaders fully subscribed to the colonialist and racist outlook pervasive among the European ruling classes.

The early Zionists considered a number of possible sites for their projected homeland including Uganda and Argentina, as well as Palestine. They soon settled on Palestine, the site of the biblical kingdoms of Israel and Judah, small states that existed in ancient times. The first Jewish kingdom came into being around 1000 BCE when an Israelite army led by David conquered the Canaanites. The Canaanites had built Jerusalem as a fortified city with a sophisticated water system more than eight centuries earlier.[18] The last of the ancient Jewish kingdoms, Judah, fell in 586 BCE—nearly twenty-five centuries before the modern Zionist project was launched.[19] Since the seventh century CE, Palestine has been predominantly Arab and Muslim. Over time, many of the Canaanites, Israelites, and other peoples who lived in the region in earlier generations intermarried with the Arabs, who came originally from the Arabian Peninsula, as well as others who arrived later from Europe, Africa, and East Asia.

Using the Bible as a real estate deed, or going back thousands of years in history to determine who has the right to what territory is unworkable to say the least. As Jewish writer Erich Fromm said many years ago, "If all nations would suddenly claim territory in which their forefathers had lived two thousand years ago, this world would be a madhouse."[20] From the beginning of the Zionist movement, the leaders—most of whom were secular rather than religious—had a common goal: the establishment of an exclusively Jewish state. In the early twentieth century, the state they envisioned, Eretz Israel (Greater Israel), included parts of what is today Jordan, Lebanon, Syria, Iraq, Egypt, the West Bank, and Gaza, as well as the present state of Israel.

In the late nineteenth and early twentieth centuries, Zionism represented a small minority among Jewish people. It was mainly a movement of the middle class, with support from a few wealthy sponsors, particularly the Rothschild oil and banking interests.[21] Jewish workers and intellectuals of that time played a vital role in the socialist, communist, and other progressive movements in Europe and the United States. They fought for equality rather than separation. Prior to World War II, political Zionism was widely regarded as a reactionary nationalist and dangerous ideology in progressive circles, Jewish and non-Jewish alike.

'Married to Another Man'

The goal articulated by the First World Zionist Congress, held in Basel, Switzerland, in 1897 and presided over by Herzl was, "to create for the Jewish people a home in Palestine secured by public law." The use of the word "home" instead of "state" was both deliberate and deliberately misleading. In his diary, Herzl wrote: "At Basel I founded the Jewish State. If I said this out loud today, I would be answered by universal laughter. Perhaps in five years, and certainly in fifty, everyone will know it."[22] Following its meeting, the World Zionist Congress sent an investigatory delegation of two Austrian rabbis to Palestine. The delegation's telegrammed report to the Congress was brief and telling: "The bride is beautiful, but she is married to another man."[23] In other words, another people already inhabited Palestine. As a British report two decades later emphasized, there was virtually no arable land in Palestine that was not already under cultivation.[24]

This undeniable reality did not deter the Zionist leaders. They were imbued with the predominant colonialist attitudes of the day toward the peoples of the Middle East and all of Asia, Africa, and Latin America. Nor did it prevent the Zionists from relentlessly propagating the racist slogan that Palestine was "A land without people for a people without a land." For the Zionists and most other European leaders, "a land without people" meant a land without Europeans.

In the early 1900s, British Colonial Secretary Joseph Chamberlain proposed to Herzl that the Zionists should colonize Uganda, another already inhabited land. The British, French, and other colonizing powers favored the establishment of European settlement in their far-flung colonies as a means of fortifying control. Herzl argued in favor of Uganda as the site of the projected Zionist state at the Sixth World Zionist Congress in 1903. The proposal was defeated at the Seventh Zionist Congress in 1905, one year after Herzl's death.

From its very beginnings, political Zionism was a colonial-settler project. When European settlers began arriving in Palestine in the early 1880s, Jews comprised about 5 percent of the Palestinian population. About 20 percent of the population was Christian, and

75 percent were Muslim. Regardless of whether their religion was
Muslim, Christian, or Jewish, nearly the entire population was Arab.
A large majority of the indigenous Jewish population opposed Zionist
settlement, as did most Arab Jews in other countries of the Middle
East, fearing that it would lead to conflict.

The settler movement raised funds in Europe and the United
States to purchase land. The land was acquired mostly from absentee
feudal landlords, evicting Palestinian peasants in the process. Much
of the countryside was still feudal or semi-feudal, and many of the
peasants were tenant farmers. The owners of large landed estates
often lived in Beirut, Damascus, or Jerusalem. While the Ottoman
Empire had divided the region into different provinces, much of the
population did not recognize these distinctions.

Land evictions led, as the indigenous Palestinian Jewish population had feared it would, to friction between religious groups,
which previously had been minimal. Middle East scholar Don Perez
described the percolating hostility:

> Tensions began after the first Zionist settlers arrived in the
> 1880s . . . when [they] purchased land from absentee Arab
> owners, leading to dispossession of the peasants who had
> cultivated it.[25]

In a 1921 *Atlantic Monthly* article, renowned archeologist Albert T.
Clay, who had just returned from visiting Palestine, wrote:

> Political Zionism is strongly opposed by many ortho-
> dox Jews in Palestine; especially because they recognize
> that, through the fanaticism of the Zionist leaders, it has
> become most difficult for them to maintain their former
> amicable relations with the other natives.[26]

Contrary to Zionist propaganda claims, Palestinian Arab resistance
to Zionist settlement was not motivated by anti-Semitism any more
than Native people's resistance in the Americas or African people's
resistance to apartheid South Africa were anti-white. In all three situations, the indigenous peoples were fighting against dispossession—
the theft of their homelands.

'Because it is Something Colonial'

Herzl and the other early Zionist leaders were well aware that settlement alone could not bring their colonial project to fruition. In 1902, Herzl solicited Cecil Rhodes, the arch-racist symbol of British colonialism. Herzl wrote to Rhodes:

> You are being invited to help make history. That cannot frighten you nor will you laugh at it. . . . It doesn't involve Africa but a piece of Asia Minor, not Englishmen but Jews. But had this been on your path, you would have done it by now. . . . How then do I happen to turn to you? Because it is something colonial.[27]

Essential to the success of the Zionist project was obtaining the sponsorship and protection of one of the great powers of the day. To several of the European empires, Herzl offered a variety of propositions, all of which boiled down to this: "Support our project and the resulting state will serve your interests." This quid pro quo was necessary. After all, the European empires had colonized much of the world and were not in the habit of doing favors for any oppressed people. Herzl and his associates shopped their project around to the German, French, Italian, British, Russian, and Ottoman empires.

In 1904, shortly before his death, Herzl met with the Russian Minister of the Interior, Vyacheslav von Plehve. The discussion between Herzl and von Plehve reveals much about the counterrevolutionary nature of political Zionism. The viciously anti-worker, anti-Semitic von Plehve was notorious for orchestrating pogroms. These violent, Ku Klux Klan-like terrorist attacks against Jews often involved rape, torture, burning, and lynching. Pogroms were a favored instrument of the Russian imperial government as a means of social control, a way to deflect the anger of the oppressed peasants away from their real oppressors—the Russian ruling class. Major pogroms were not spontaneous affairs. On Easter 1903, the year before his meeting with Herzl, von Plehve organized a particularly infamous pogrom in Kishinev, Bessarabia, which left at least forty-five Jews dead and more than five hundred injured.

Von Plehve agreed to meet with Herzl in the hope that the Zionists could help pull Jewish youth away from the rapidly growing socialist

movement in Russia. "The Jews have been joining the revolutionary parties," von Plehve told Herzl. "We were sympathetic to your Zionist movement as long as it worked toward emigration. You don't have to justify the movement to me. You are preaching to a convert."[28] Afterwards, Herzl explained the "deal" he had struck with von Plehve to Chaim Zhitlovsky, a leader of the mainly peasant Russian Social-Revolutionary Party. Herzl wrote:

> I have just come from Plehve. I have his positive, binding promise that in 15 years, at the maximum, he will effectuate for us a charter for Palestine. But this is tied to one condition: the Jewish revolutionaries shall cease their struggle against the Russian government. If in 15 years from the time of the agreement Plehve does not effectuate the charter, they become free again to do what they consider necessary.[29]

Zhitlovsky responded by informing Herzl that the Social-Revolutionary military organization was already planning to assassinate the murderous von Plehve. Zhitlovsky went on to tell him:

> We Jewish revolutionaries, even the most national among us, are not Zionists and do not believe that Zionism is able to resolve our problem. To transfer the Jewish people from Russia to Eretz-Israel is, in our eyes, a utopia, and because of a utopia we will not renounce the paths upon which we have embarked—the path of the revolutionary struggle against the Russian government, which should also lead to the freedom of the Jewish people.[30]

Lenin, leader of the Bolshevik Party, wrote in 1903: "[T]his Zionist idea is absolutely false and essentially reactionary."[31]

Herzl's meeting with von Plehve appalled the Russian-born Chaim Weizmann, who was soon to succeed Herzl as the preeminent Zionist leader. Weizmann recognized that if the meeting became known, it could fatally discredit Zionism in the eyes of the masses of the oppressed Jews in the Russian Empire. But Weizmann, who had immigrated to England, was as eager to seek the support of the imperialists as was Herzl. Weizmann focused on gaining the support of the British Empire, then the most powerful in the world. Weizmann emphasized both the value that a future Israeli state could have for British imperialism and his movement's Euro-supremacist outlook in a 1914 letter:

> Should Palestine fall within the British sphere of influence and should Britain encourage Jewish settlement . . . [we could] develop the country, bring back civilization to it, and form a very effective guard for the Suez Canal.[32]

The British conquest of most of the Middle East in 1918, combined with the Balfour Declaration issued the previous year, set the stage for the Zionist project to take off.

BUILDING A SETTLER STATE AMERICAN-STYLE

With British sponsorship and new sources of funding from the United States, the Zionist project gained momentum after World War I. Jewish settlements and land acquisition in Palestine rapidly grew. Though Palestine was now a British colony, the Jewish Agency was set up as a de facto government in the Zionist-controlled areas. The Agency began building its own militia and, later, a regular army.

In the post–World War II period, the Zionist leaders would seek to legitimize their cause in the eyes of the world by painting it as "anti-colonial"—in opposition to the British Mandate. But, in truth, it was always purely colonial. The Zionist project could not have succeeded without British imperial patronage. While there were inevitable and sometimes serious clashes between the British sponsors and the Zionist leadership, the nature of the relationship was unlike any other in the far-flung British Empire. It was not one between the colonizer and the colonized, but instead between two colonizers, one much stronger than the other, but both colonizers nonetheless.

The nature of the relationship was highlighted by a meeting that took place July 22, 1921, at the home of British Foreign Secretary Arthur Balfour to discuss the situation in Palestine. In addition to Balfour, the attendees were Zionist leader Chaim Weizmann, British Prime Minister Lloyd George, and Colonial Secretary—and future prime minister—Winston Churchill. Describing the meeting, Israeli historian Tom Segev wrote, with considerable understatement:

> It is doubtful that there were many other national leaders [leaders in other British colonies] able to arrange such a

high-level meeting. Weizmann led the discussion; Lloyd
George and Balfour went out of their way to please
him. . . . The encounter was extraordinary from every
point of view.[33]

It would have been inconceivable for any leader of a genuine national
liberation movement to be treated with such deference and respect by
the top officials of the British Empire. Certainly no Palestinian Arab
leaders were invited to London to meet with the prime minister at the
foreign secretary's home.

The British government was at the time the chief organizer of the
international imperialist campaign to overthrow the Russian Revolution. How this related to their heightened interest in Zionism was
explained in a virulently anti-Semitic, anti-revolutionary, and pro-
Zionist feature article written by Churchill for London's *Illustrated
Sunday Herald* in 1920. Following a section simply headlined "Good
Jews and Bad Jews," Churchill offered his true point of view:

> From the days of Spartacus-Weishaupt to those of Karl
> Marx, and down to Trotsky (Russia), Bela Kun (Hungary),
> Rosa Luxembourg (Germany), and Emma Goldman
> (United States), this world-wide conspiracy for the over-
> throw of civilization . . . has been steadily growing. It
> played, as a modern writer, Mrs. Webster, has so ably
> shown, a definitely recognizable part in the tragedy of the
> French Revolution. It has been the mainspring of every
> subversive movement during the Nineteenth Century;
> and now at last this band of extraordinary personalities
> from the underworld of the great cities of Europe and
> America have gripped the Russian people by the hair of
> their heads and have become practically the undisputed
> masters of that enormous empire.

He continued in the section titled, "Terrorist Jews:"

> There is no need to exaggerate the part played in the cre-
> ation of Bolshevism and in the actual bringing about of
> the Russian Revolution, by these international and for the

most part atheistical Jews. It is certainly a very great one; it probably outweighs all others. With the notable exception of Lenin, the majority of the leading figures are Jews. Moreover, the principal inspiration and driving power comes from the Jewish leaders.

But then the future prime minister of the British Empire offered what he saw as a saving grace:

> Zionism offers the third sphere to the political conceptions of the Jewish race. In violent contrast to international communism, it presents to the Jew a national idea of a commanding character. It has fallen to the British government, as the result of the conquest of Palestine, to have the opportunity and the responsibility of securing for the Jewish race all over the world a home and a center of national life. The statesmanship and historic sense of Mr. Balfour were prompt to seize this opportunity. Declarations have been made which have irrevocably decided the policy of Great Britain.

> Zionism has already become a factor in the political convulsions of Russia, as a powerful competing influence in Bolshevik circles with the international communistic system. Nothing could be more significant than the fury with which Trotsky has attacked the Zionists generally, and Dr. Weizmann in particular. The cruel penetration of his mind leaves him in no doubt that his schemes of a world-wide communistic state under Jewish domination are directly thwarted and hindered by this new ideal, which directs the energies and the hopes of Jews in every land towards a simpler, a truer, and a far more attainable goal. The struggle which is now beginning between the Zionist and Bolshevik Jews is little less than a struggle for the soul of the Jewish people.[34]

Whether meeting with high-ranking imperial officials or expanding their colonial foothold on the ground, the Zionist leaders made their

aims crystal clear. They took lessons from their colonial predecessors, in Britain and elsewhere. Similar to the colonial-settler pattern
in North America against the Native peoples, when the Zionists
acquired an area, their goal was to make it exclusively Jewish. They
wanted to rid the land of the Indigenous population altogether.
Zionist settlements and businesses were urged or required to hire only
Jewish labor. Jewish-owned businesses that disobeyed—often in the
interest of garnering greater profits by hiring Palestinians at lower
wages—were subjected to boycott or violence by other Zionists.

As the settler population increased from about 10 percent in
the early 1920s to nearly 30 percent by the end of the 1930s, the
discussion about "transfer" intensified among Zionist politicians.
"Transfer," in the Zionist discourse, was a code word for expelling
the indigenous Arab population from Palestine to make way for the
envisioned state. It is beyond question that this was the intention of
the main Zionist leaders from the beginning. In 1919, the US-based
King–Crane Commission traveled to Syria and Palestine to investi-
gate the situation. Their report stated, in part:

> The commissioners began their study of Zionism with
> minds predisposed in its favor. . . . The fact came out
> repeatedly in the Commission's conferences with Jewish
> representatives that the Zionists looked forward to a prac-
> tically complete dispossession of the present non-Jewish
> inhabitants of Palestine, by various forms of purchase. . . .

> If that principle [of self-determination] is to rule, and so
> the wishes of Palestine's population are to be decisive as to
> what is to be done with Palestine, then it is to be remem-
> bered that the non-Jewish population of Palestine—nearly
> nine-tenths of the whole—are emphatically against the
> entire Zionist program. . . . To subject a people so minded
> to unlimited Jewish immigration, and to steady financial
> and social pressure to surrender the land, would be a gross
> violation of the principle just quoted. . . .

> The initial claim, often submitted by Zionist representa-
> tives, that they have a "right" to Palestine based on occu-

pation of two thousand years ago, can barely be seriously considered.[35]

It became clear to the Zionist leaders that the only way to achieve their objective of "transfer" was through military superiority. As they were well aware, the Palestinians were not about to give up their land voluntarily.

'Labor Zionists' and Revisionists

The building up of Zionist armed forces was not a controversial subject, but how to talk about it publicly was. This led to a split in the Zionist movement. In the early 1920s, David Ben-Gurion, who had emigrated from Poland in 1906, emerged as the central Zionist leader inside Palestine. Another key leader was Vladimir Jabotinsky, who wrote two articles titled "The Iron Wall," published in *Ha'aretz* in 1923. Jabotinsky argued that the Zionists should be honest with themselves and the world by saying outright that theirs was a settler project that could only be achieved by overwhelming force—what he called the "Iron Wall":

Settlement can thus develop under the protection of a force that is not dependent on the local population, behind an IRON WALL which they will be powerless to break down. . . . A voluntary agreement is just not possible. As long as the Arabs preserve a gleam of hope that they will succeed in getting rid of us, nothing in the world can cause them to relinquish this hope, precisely because they are not a rubble, but a living people. And a living people will be ready to yield on such fateful issues only when they give up all hope of getting rid of the Alien Settlers.

The Arabs loved their country as much as the Jews did. Instinctively, they understood Zionist aspirations very well, and their decision to resist them was only natural. . . . There was no misunderstanding between Jew and Arab, but a natural conflict. . . . No agreement was possible with the Palestinian Arab; they would accept Zionism only when they found themselves up against an "iron wall," when they realize they had no alternative but to accept Jewish settlement.[36]

Jabotinsky continued his "honesty" in a letter to Jewish lawyer and friend Oscar Grusenberg: "We Jews are Europeans. . . . What do we have in common with the 'Orient?' And everything that is 'oriental' is doomed."[37]

Ben-Gurion and mainstream leaders, such as Weizmann, Golda Meir and other "Labor Zionists" wanted to pursue a more diplomatic course. They publicly disavowed Jabotinsky's open advocacy of racism and terrorism. The fact that this disagreement was more rhetorical than substantive was clarified by subsequent developments. But it led to a major split in the Zionist movement at the time. Ben-Gurion and his Labor and other "socialist" Zionists would go on to form the pseudo-left Labor Party (Mapai) that dominated the Israeli government for the first three decades of its existence as a nation-state.

While Ben-Gurion and many of the founders of Israel spoke in the name of "socialism," this had more to do with the popularity of socialism among the working class and petit-bourgeoisie of the time than with any Zionist principles. The irreconcilable nature of Zionism—really a form of reactionary nationalism—and socialism is best explained in the analysis of a real revolutionary, V.I. Lenin:

> Marxism cannot be reconciled with nationalism, be it even of the "most just," "purest," most refined and civilized brand. In place of all forms of nationalism, Marxism advances internationalism, the amalgamation of all nations in the higher unity, a unity that is growing before our eyes with every mile of railway line that is built, with every international trust, and every workers' association that is formed (an association that is international in its economic activities as well as in its ideas and aims).

> The principle of nationality is historically inevitable in bourgeois society and, taking this society into due account, the Marxist fully recognizes the historical legitimacy of national movements. But to prevent this recogni-

tion from becoming an apologia of nationalism, it must be strictly limited to what is progressive in such movements, in order that this recognition may not lead to bourgeois ideology obscuring proletarian consciousness.[38]

While making clear his view on the relationship between nationalism and Marxism, Lenin advocated an alliance between the working class in the imperialist countries and the genuine national liberation movements struggling against colonialism. Both face the same main enemy: the imperialist ruling classes.

At the same time, Lenin and the Bolsheviks fought against narrow nationalism—advocating internationalism instead. The British especially relied upon pitting one oppressed nationality—whose leaders would receive favors and benefits—against other oppressed nationalities in their far-flung empire. The practice has been perpetuated by the United States in Vietnam, Iraq and other countries, ever since it became the dominant global power. The Bolsheviks, whose top leadership apart from Lenin was largely of Jewish descent, were adamantly opposed to Zionism as a reactionary ideology. They believed that anti-Semitism could only be ended through socialist revolution.[39] One of the first decrees of the Bolshevik government after the October 1917 revolution banned discrimination against Jews and other oppressed peoples in the former czarist empire.

The Jews of the Russian, German, and Austro-Hungarian empires—all three of which included parts of Poland with its large Jewish population—and other European countries were a persecuted and subjugated people. But, the Bolsheviks maintained, although European Jews shared a common religion and in some areas a common language and culture, they lacked a contiguous territory and did not constitute a nation. The Zionists, while aiming to create a Jewish nation-state, did not seek to acquire territory in Eastern Europe where most of the European Jewish population was concentrated and most violently repressed. Instead, the Zionists offered to make themselves available to be transported as settlers to any number of places in the colonized continents of Asia, Africa, and Latin America, before settling on Palestine. Political Zionism was thus a unique form of narrow nationalism. Lacking its own indigenous land base, it could only hope to succeed as an extension of European colonialism. Unlike any genuine national liberation movement, Zionism was always completely dependent on imperialist sponsorship.

This reality shaped the Zionist movement and its political alliances. The priority of Ben-Gurion and the Labor Zionists was never really socialism nor the well-being of the workers. In his 1954 book, *Rebirth and Destiny of Israel*, Ben-Gurion tellingly looked back on the earlier days of settlement: "We were not just working—we were conquering, conquering, conquering a land. We were a company of conquistadors."[40] Their modus operandi was clear. Ben-Gurion and the Labor Party were simply reactionary bourgeois nationalists posing as socialists. Their support for trade unionism—specifically as leaders of the Histadrut (the Zionist labor federation)—both before and after the founding of Israel was aimed at only winning the support of Jewish workers. This kept the Palestinian workers both separate and unequal. And it succeeded in imbuing Jewish workers with chauvinism and racism toward the colonized Palestinians. The Labor Party's collaboration—in fact, complete integration—with Zionism had the effect of channeling the radical leanings of Jewish workers into a narrow and backward ideological framework. It was a necessary ingredient to the Zionist project.

Ben-Gurion candidly addressed the need for a Zionist "workers' movement" in December 1922:

> How can we run our Zionist movement in such a way that [we] will be able to carry out the conquest of the land by the Jewish worker, and which will find the resources to organize the massive immigration and settlement of workers through their own capabilities? The creation of a new Zionist movement, a Zionist movement of workers, is the first prerequisite for the fulfillment of Zionism. . . . Without a new Zionist movement that is entirely at our disposal, there is no future or hope for our activities.[41]

Zionism gained strength in the aftermath of World War I, a period that was fertile ground for the growth of reactionary nationalist and fascist movements in Europe, such as those in Germany, Italy, Hungary, Poland and a number of other countries. It was also a time of emerging progressive national movements against imperialism in the colonized world of Asia, Africa, and Latin America. Though it had its own distinct roots, Zionism shared some of the characteristics of the reactionary European movements. It fiercely opposed the anti-colonial and genuine national liberation movements. Zionism's opposition to true liberation movements is well documented in *Israel: Base of Western Imperialism.*[42] It could not have been otherwise, due to both the Zionists' dependence on the world's largest empire, Britain, and its character as a European colonial phenomenon.

Vladimir Jabotinsky did not conceal his connections to the most reactionary nationalism of his time. His political faction was known as the Revisionists, because they wanted to "revise" the Balfour Declaration to include both banks of the Jordan River in their projected state—in other words, they wanted at least all of present-day Palestine and Jordan. The Revisionists formed the Betar Party, which included avowed supporters of the Italian fascist dictator, Mussolini. Jabotinsky was himself photographed proudly wearing an Italian fascist officer's uniform.

Betar gave birth to the self-identified terrorist paramilitary organizations Irgun and Lehi (Stern Gang) in the 1930s and 1940s. Among their leaders were two future Israeli prime ministers, Menachem Begin and Yitzhak Shamir. After 1948, Betar became the Herut party, and two decades later Herut, in turn, served as the core of the Likud bloc, which became the dominant force in Israeli politics in the late 1970s. When Menachem Begin visited America soon after the creation of the Israeli state in 1948, a letter to the *New York Times* signed by twenty-eight Jewish liberals and progressives, including Albert Einstein and Hannah Arendt, denounced him as a "terrorist, right-wing chauvinist." His movement, the letter stated, was "closely akin in its organization, methods, political philosophy, and social appeal to Nazi and Fascist parties. . . . Within the Jewish community they have preached an admixture of ultranationalism, religious mysticism, and racial superiority. Like other Fascist parties they have been used to break strikes, and have themselves pressed for the destruction of free trade unions. In their stead, they have proposed corporate unions on the Italian Fascist model."[43]

Because Israel was a colonial implantation that could only succeed by crushing the Indigenous population, the "Iron Wall" doctrine eventually triumphed and, along with it, the politics of Revisionist Zionism. It is today an integral part of Israeli state ideology and strategy. Overwhelming military force has long been accepted as essential across the entire Zionist political spectrum. The dispossession of an entire people has never been possible anywhere except by extreme, often genocidal, violence. Palestine is no exception. While Jabotinsky is less well-known in the United States than his Labor Zionist counterparts, and although his followers were treated as marginal figures in the early decades of Israel's existence, his brutal doctrine has dominated Israeli politics since the state was formed.[44]

THE REVOLUTION OF 1936–1939 IN PALESTINE

The aim of the Zionists to dispossess Palestinians of their land and rights was no mystery to the Palestinian population. Throughout the 1920s and 1930s there were numerous uprisings against British colonialism and Zionist settlements, the most famous and protracted of which was the 1936–1939 revolution. In 1936, Palestinians launched a general strike that lasted six months—the longest general strike in history. The strike was followed by a guerrilla war that lasted nearly three and a half years. It was mainly based in the countryside among poor peasants. The war tied down a large part of the British army. It was not until September 1939—the same month that World War II began in Europe—that the British finally succeeded in crushing the rebellion by brute force. The Palestinian fighters were hampered by the lack of a revolutionary party to lead the struggle. Despite this critical problem and a lack of sufficient arms and equipment, they carried on an intense and protracted struggle against the world's most powerful empire.

During the revolt, the British occupiers imposed repressive laws, called Emergency Regulations, on the Arab population. Many of the regulations are still used today by the Israelis against Palestinians in the West Bank. These "emergency" measures legalized a number of the colonial government's arbitrary actions, including detention and imprisonment without charge and house demolitions.

The revolutionary writer and leader Ghassan Kanafani, who was assassinated by the Israeli secret service in 1972, elaborated on this point in his pamphlet, *The Revolution of 1936–1939 in Palestine*:

With regards the first of these means (violent repression), the British Emergency Regulations performed their purpose with great effectiveness. Al-Sifri gives a list of sentences issued at the time to exemplify the repressiveness of the regulations: "Six-year prison sentence for possession of a firearm; twelve years for possession of a bomb; five years hard labor for possession of twelve rounds of ammunition; eight months for giving a group of British soldiers wrong directions; nine years for the possession of small explosives; five years for attempting to buy ammunition from soldiers; two weeks for possession of a stick; etc."

According to a British estimate reported to the League of Nations, the number of Arab casualties over the course of the 1936 Revolution was around one thousand killed, not counting those injured, missing, or imprisoned. The British also adopted a policy of widescale home demolition. On June 18, 1936, British authorities blew up and destroyed a large part of the city of Yafa, with an estimated 220 homes demolished and around 6,000 people rendered homeless. In addition to this, in the suburbs surrounding Yafa they destroyed 100 huts in al-Jabaliyah, 300 in Abu Kabir, 250 in al-Shaikh Murad, and 75 in 'Arab al-Dawudi.

It is evident that the inhabitants of the Yafa neighborhoods and outskirts whose homes were destroyed were poor peasants who had moved to the towns from the countryside. As for the villages, al-Sifri counted 143 homes razed under pretexts directly related to the revolution. These homes belonged to poorer peasants, some medium peasants, and a very small number of feudal landowning families.[45]

In the course of the struggle, the British had aided—and were aided by—the armed police of the Jewish Agency, which became a training ground for thousands of troops in the Zionists' main army, the Haganah. Also weighing in on the side of the British Empire was its puppet monarch in Jordan, King Abdullah. One of the tactics of the Palestinian resistance was to blow up the oil pipeline the British built from Kirkuk, Iraq to Haifa, Palestine. After a number of these attacks, the British assigned the Zionist police to guard the pipeline inside Palestine. Abdullah's forces were assigned a similar role in Jordan. The reactionary triple alliance of imperialism, Zionism, and Arab reaction first clearly appeared in opposition to the revolutionary movement in Palestine in this period. That counterrevolutionary alliance—with the United States taking Britain's place as the lead imperialist power in the 1950s—has confronted all revolutionary movements in the region ever since.

The Palestinian defeat in the 1936–1939 Intifada (uprising) had a profound effect on the future shape of the conflict. When World War II broke out in Europe in 1939, the Zionist forces were greatly strengthened, while the Palestinians were decimated. As Kanafani concluded his pamphlet:

> By 1947, conditions were ripe for the Zionists to harvest the fruit of the 1936 Revolution's defeat, a harvest delayed by the Second World War. As such, the second chapter of the revolution's defeat—from late 1947 to mid-1948—was remarkable for its brevity: it was only the epilogue to a long and bloody chapter endured from April 1936 to September 1939.[46]

Both the justice of the Palestinian resistance and colonial nature of Zionism had been admitted in the midst of the revolt by none other than the central Zionist leader, Ben-Gurion:

> In our political argument abroad we minimize Arab opposition to us. But let us not ignore the truth among ourselves. . . . A people which fights against the usurpation of its land will not tire so easily.[47]

Ben-Gurion also said:

> When we say that the Arabs are the aggressors and we defend ourselves—that is only half the truth. As regards

our security and life we defend ourselves. . . . But the fighting is only one aspect of the conflict, which is in its essence
a political one. And politically we are the aggressors and
they defend themselves.[48]

Such candid admissions—which were quite common from Zionist
leaders before the state of Israel was established—in no way deterred
the Jewish Agency leadership from its colonizing course. What the
Zionists were planning was captured in the words of Joseph Weitz,
director of the Jewish National Land Fund, in 1940:

Among ourselves it must be clear that there is no room for
both people in this country . . . and there is no way besides
transferring the Arabs from here to neighboring countries, to transfer them all; except maybe for Bethlehem,
Nazareth, and Old Jerusalem, we must not leave a single
village, a single tribe.[49]

This extreme racism was deeply embedded in the Zionists' logic. In the
midst of the Palestinian revolt in 1937, the British Peel Commission
recommended the partition of Palestine and the creation of a small
Jewish state. Many Zionist leaders opposed the proposal because it did
not meet their goals. Ben-Gurion argued for accepting it, though only
as a short-term solution. He viewed the proposal as merely a first step
toward taking over all of Palestine in the name of Zionism:

Just as I do not see the proposed Jewish state as a final
solution to the problems of the Jewish people, so I do not
see partition as the final solution of the Palestine question.
Those who reject partition are right in their claim that
this country cannot be partitioned because it constitutes
one unit, not only from a historical point of view but also
from that of nature and economy.[50]

Just years later, the Zionists would implement the most bloody means
in an attempt to realize their goal.

WORLD WAR II: ANTI-SEMITISM AND GENOCIDE

In 1939, the Nazi armies invaded Poland, signaling the start of World War II in Europe. By mid-1941, Germany, Italy, and their fascist allies occupied nearly all of continental Europe west of the Soviet Union; on June 22 of that year they launched an all-out attack on the Union of Soviet Socialist Republics (USSR). David Ben-Gurion, who was to become Israel's first prime minister, wrote in 1939 that while World War I had brought the Balfour Declaration, the Second World War would result in the creation of a Zionist state.[51]

The capitalist governments of Western Europe and the United States paid scant attention to the mass murder of Jews and other peoples at the hands of the Nazis as they were taking place. Suffused with anti-Semitism themselves, many in the US ruling class in the 1930s viewed Nazi Germany as a weapon against their main enemy of the time—the Soviet Union. A number of US capitalists regarded Nazi Germany as having an ideal business climate. The Nazis had smashed the powerful German labor unions and had fused German corporations closely with the state. Among those who shared Nazi sympathies and business connections were Henry Ford, Joseph Kennedy Sr. (father of John, Robert, and Ted Kennedy), and Prescott Bush (father and grandfather of US presidents).

In November 1938, the "Kristillnacht" Nazi pogrom killed more than 1,300 Jewish people in Germany and destroyed seven thousand businesses in one night. It was followed by the start of the large-scale deportation of Jews to concentration camps. The following year, the Wagner-Rogers bill was submitted to the US Congress. It called for twenty thousand German Jewish children to be admitted to the United States, outside of the existing quota. The bill died after then-President Franklin D. Roosevelt refused to support it. Typifying the anti-Semitism so prevalent in US ruling circles at that time, Roosevelt's cousin, Laura Delano Houghteling, the wife of the US commissioner of immigration, explained her opposition to the bill. Houghteling said: "twenty thousand charming children would all too soon grow into twenty thousand ugly adults."[52]

One month after the Kristillnacht pogrom, Ben-Gurion expressed his calculated perspective on the relationship between what was happening in Germany and the Zionist project in Palestine:

> If I knew it was possible to save all [Jewish] children of Germany by their transfer to England and only half of them by transferring them to Eretz-Israel, I would choose the latter—because we are faced not only with the accounting of these [Jewish] children but also with the historical accounting of the Jewish People.[53]

His words expose the cold pragmatism of Zionism. To the Zionist leaders, it was preferable to have an exclusivist state controlled by them than to benefit Jewish people.

The imperialists' compassion was no greater. Even after entering the war and being informed of the mass murder underway in the fascist concentration camps, there was little sign of concern from ruling circles in Washington and London. The US high command was so indifferent to people suffering in the Nazi death camps that they refused to bomb the rail lines, which brought the boxcars crammed with victims into the camps and the gas chambers that were used for mass murder.[54]

US Secretary of the Treasury Henry Morgenthau Jr. was the only Jewish member of President Roosevelt's cabinet. Like most Treasury secretaries, Morgenthau was a representative of Wall Street and a conservative. On January 13, 1944, he issued a report that was highly unusual for someone in his position. In it, Morgenthau protested how his own government was failing to respond to the Nazi genocide, which was then in full swing:

One of the greatest crimes in history, the slaughter of the Jewish people in Europe, is continuing unabated. This Government has for a long time maintained that its policy is to work out programs to serve those Jews of Europe who could be saved.

I am convinced on the basis of the information which is available to me that certain officials in our State Department, which is charged with carrying out this policy, have been guilty not only of gross procrastination and willful failure to act, but even of willful attempts to prevent action from being taken to rescue Jews from Hitler.

I fully recognize the graveness of this statement and I make it only after having most carefully weighed the shocking facts which have come to my attention during the last several months. Unless remedial steps of a drastic nature are taken, and taken immediately, I am certain that no effective action will be taken by this government to prevent the complete extermination of the Jews in German controlled Europe, and that this Government will have to share for all time responsibility for this extermination.[55]

The US imperialists took no remedial steps. During the Nazi genocide, six million Jews were murdered. Millions of Roma and Slavic people, lesbians and gays, disabled people, communists, and anyone who resisted fascism also were killed. Among the Jewish survivors who wanted to leave Europe, as many as 80 percent hoped to go to the United States.[56] It would not have been difficult for the United States to absorb four hundred thousand Jewish refugees, particularly since the US mainland had suffered no damage during the war and its economy was booming. But US corporate and government leaders opposed opening the doors to the survivors of Nazi persecution, fearing that many were influenced by communist and socialist ideas.

The Zionist leaders were also well aware of the desire of the European Jewish survivors to come to the United States. They were equally opposed to the notion because it threatened the realization of their core goal. As Chaplain Klausner, a Zionist organizer put it: "I am convinced that the [Jewish refugees] must be forced to go to Palestine."[57] To build a Jewish state, the Zionists needed to get as many refugees as possible to Palestine.

Although the US government had done little before or during World War II to aid the Jewish victims of fascism, it quickly used the very real horrors of Hitler's death camps to rally public opinion in favor of establishing the state of Israel. The Zionists succeeded in this regard as well, building support for their colonial project among otherwise progressive Jewish organizations, church groups, and labor unions throughout the United States and Europe. Once the war was over, the gathering momentum behind the plans to create Israel became seemingly unstoppable.

ILLEGAL UN PARTITION

The conflict in Palestine intensified following World War II. The British government, bankrupt and seeking to hold on to their most profitable colonies, announced in the spring of 1947 it was turning over its Palestine "mandate" to the recently formed United Nations. Britain set May 15, 1948, as the date on which it would withdraw its troops. After months of debate, the UN General Assembly set November 29, 1947, as the date for a vote on partitioning Palestine.

The Palestinians—who had had nothing to do with European anti-Semitism or genocide—were not consulted before the UN vote. There was no plebiscite or vote of the people to determine how the Indigenous people felt. If there had been, the outcome would not have been in doubt: one unitary state in Palestine would have been the overwhelming choice. The UN partition vote was an illegitimate act, a violation of the Palestinians' right to self-determination.

The two-thirds majority required to pass Resolution 181 was only achieved through intense US pressure. The vote ended up 33–13 with 10 abstentions. The administration of President Harry S. Truman leaned heavily on its neocolonies and client states, particularly the Philippines, Liberia, Haiti, and Thailand, all of which initially opposed the resolution and subsequently switched their votes. Without those four votes, the resolution would have failed.

The Soviet Union and its allies, who later became key supporters of the Arab liberation struggles, also provided crucial votes without which the partition resolution would have failed. What was behind this decision? The Soviet leadership mistakenly believed that Israel would be a friendly state. The Soviet Red Army, after all, had been the main force that defeated Nazism and liberated the concentration camps in Poland and eastern Germany. The Soviet Union had borne the full fury of the Nazi war machine beginning in June 1941. In the four years that followed, more than twenty-seven million Soviet soldiers and civilians died at the hands of the fascists. Much of the country's infrastructure was destroyed. The heroic Soviet Red Army fighters broke the back of the Nazi war machine, leading directly to its historic defeat. In contrast, the United States suffered around four hundred thousand killed in the war in both the European and Pacific theaters, and no internal destruction. There was great goodwill among the Jewish survivors of the Nazi Holocaust toward the USSR.

Soviet support for Resolution 181 was an unmitigated disaster for the Palestinians and the Arab anti-colonial struggle, as well as for the communist parties in the Arab world. All of the communist parties in the Arab world, with the exception of the Iraqi party, unfortunately supported the Soviet position, which compromised them—and communism—in the eyes of the Arab masses. In the United States, the Communist Party, then the largest left organization, also supported the creation of Israel.

Israel received crucial political and military support from the Soviet Union and its allies in 1947 and 1948. At that time, much of the Israeli population was pro-socialist and pro-Soviet. But neither of those facts mattered. Israel's fundamental relationship to the imperialist West could not be altered. After all, without imperialist patronage, the Zionist project never would have gotten off the ground. The early support of the Soviet leadership and many communist parties for Israel contributed greatly to disorienting the progressive movement, especially in the United States, with long-lasting effect. Zionism was not understood for what it really is—an ideology rooted in colonialism and racism.[58]

The UN partition vote led to celebration among the Zionists. Despite owning just 6 percent of the land and constituting 35 percent of the population, Resolution 181 granted the soon-to-be state of Israel 55 percent of Palestine. The Palestinian Arabs were to receive 44 percent of the territory, with the remaining one percent to be an "international zone." The zone included Jerusalem. On the Palestinian side, there was justified anger and rebellion. All parties knew ahead of time that partition meant war.

The 1948 War

Fighting broke out immediately. Contrary to one of Israel's creation myths, the Zionist military forces possessed superior equipment, training, and numbers from the start of the war. This advantage only increased over the following year. Since the defeat of the 1936–1939 Revolution, Palestinians had been forbidden—often under penalty of death—to possess weapons. Many of the leaders, organizers and fighters of the 1936–1939 Intifada had been killed or exiled.

On the other side, the Haganah had grown much stronger, as had the Irgun and Lehi (Stern Gang). Most Haganah soldiers had military training, having joined the British army during World War II. Funds from the United States, England, and other countries were pouring in to support what became the state of Israel. The British still held state power in Palestine when the fighting started. They declared an arms embargo. The poorly equipped Palestinian paramilitary forces were largely prevented from being rearmed. Nevertheless, the Haganah received a major weapons shipment from Czechoslovakia.

Ben-Gurion and his military commanders were determined not to accept "merely" 55 percent of Palestine and immediately began to carry out military operations to seize as much territory as possible, including Jerusalem. But as a number of Israeli and Palestinian historians have documented, their aim was not just to take control of land. The other equally essential goal of the Zionist leaders was to uproot and expel as much of the Arab population as possible from all of Palestine. Addressing the Central Committee of the Histadrut on December 30, 1947, Ben-Gurion made it clear that he had no intention of accepting a significant Arab presence—even with a subjugated status—in his projected state:

> In the area allocated to the Jewish state there are not more than 520,000 Jews and about 350,000 non-Jews, mostly Arabs. Together with the Jews of Jerusalem, the total population of the Jewish State at the time of its establishment will be about one million, including almost 40 percent non-Jews. Such a [population] composition does

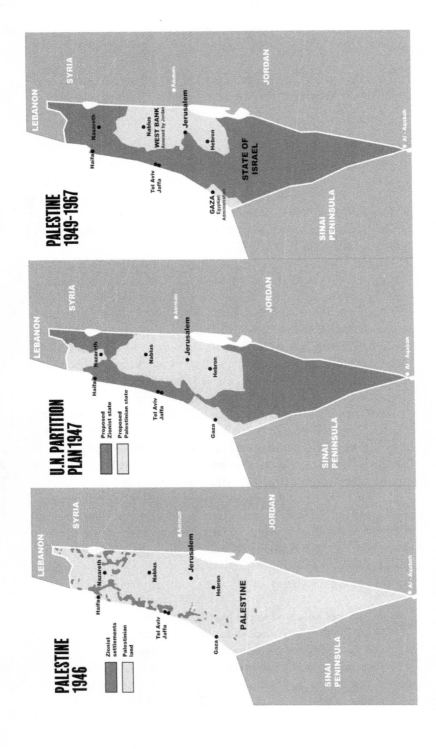

not provide a stable basis for a Jewish state. This [demo-graphic] fact must be viewed in all its clarity and acute-ness. With such a [population] composition, there cannot even be absolute certainty that control will remain in the hands of the Jewish majority. . . . There can be no stable and strong Jewish state so long as it has a Jewish majority of only 60 percent.[59]

The "ethnic cleansing" of Palestinians that began almost immediately after partition delighted Ben-Gurion. Speaking to the council of his Labor Party on February 8, 1948, he said:

> From your entry into Jerusalem, through Lifta, Romema [East Jerusalem Palestinian neighborhood] . . . there are no [Palestinian] Arabs. One hundred percent Jews. Since Jerusalem was destroyed by the Romans, it has not been Jewish as it is now. In many [Palestinian] Arab neigh-borhoods in the west one sees not a single [Palestinian] Arab. I do not assume that this will change. . . . What had happened in Jerusalem . . . is likely to happen in many parts of the country . . . in the six, eight, or 10 months of the campaign there will certainly be great changes in the composition of the population in the country.[60]

But what so delighted Ben-Gurion in early 1948 was not yet reflected in most of the country. In the first months of fighting, while the Zionists generally prevailed in battle, the objective of driving out the Palestinian population was not being achieved. Palestinian villagers would retreat, but only to nearby villages, waiting for the fighting to stop. Until March 1, 1948, the population had been driven out from less than 5 percent of Palestinian villages. This constituted a serious problem from the point of view of the Zionist leaders, one that threat-ened their entire plan.

Two additional factors made the problem a potential crisis for the Zionists. One was a shift in Washington. While the Truman admin-istration had played a key role in pushing the partition plan through the UN General Assembly, it was now evidencing second thoughts. The partition plan had not brought a settlement or peace, and the war raging in Palestine had angered the entire Arab world. Much of that anger was directed at Washington. The US government began floating other alternatives in hopes of pacifying the situation. One idea floated by the State Department called for scrapping the partition plan and replacing it with a five-year UN trusteeship over the area. The Zionist leaders rejected it outright, but were acutely conscious of the fact that they were losing critically needed support. The approach of May 15, 1948—the date for British withdrawal—was the other factor creating a crisis atmosphere for the Zionist commanders.

On March 10, 1948, Ben-Gurion and his inner circle began to implement a new doctrine, "Plan Dalet." Under the plan, the Haganah, along with its supposed rival, the Irgun, began staging attacks on "quiet" Palestinian villages—those not involved in fighting.[61] Israeli historian Ilan Pappe asserts that Ben-Gurion and his cohorts actually saw "quiet" villages as a bigger problem than those that resisted. Resistance provided the Zionists with a pretext for carrying out harsh repression and removal.[62]

Plan Dalet escalated the level of violence directed against the Palestinian civilian population to the extreme. A typical operation carried out by Haganah and Irgun units would plant explosives around Palestinian houses in the middle of the night, drench them with gasoline, and then open fire. The point was to terrorize and drive out the Palestinian population. Arbitrary executions became routine, particularly directed against men and boys who were designated as being of fighting age—whether they were involved in resistance or not. But the Zionist leaders decided that more was needed.

BORN OF MASSACRES AND ETHNIC CLEANSING

Deir Yassin, on the outskirts of Jerusalem, was a "quiet" village, in which there was no apparent resistance activity. There was even reported cooperation with the Jewish Agency. The Jewish Agency had transformed itself in May 1948 into the new Israeli government.

On April 9, 1948, the Irgun nearly wiped out the entire population of Deir Yassin. The Irgun soldiers arrived in the village and announced that the residents had fifteen minutes to leave. Then the attack began. The Zionist soldiers blew up homes with their inhabitants still inside, fired at will and at close range, and committed other atrocities. When it was over, more than two hundred lay dead. Many of the women in the village were raped before being killed.[63] An eleven-year-old Deir Yassin survivor described the horrors committed by the Zionists:

> As soon as the sun rose, there was knocking at the door, but we did not answer. They blew the door down, entered and started searching the place; they got to the store room, and took us out one-by-one. They shot the son-in-law, and when one of his daughters screamed, they shot her too. They then called my brother Mahmoud and shot him in our presence, and when my mother screamed and bent over my brother, carrying my little sister Khadra, who was still being breastfed, they shot my mother too. We all started screaming and crying, but were told that if we did not stop, they would shoot us all. They then lined us up, shot at us and left.[64]

Despite attempts by the Jewish Agency to stop him, Jacques de Reynier of the International Red Cross visited Deir Yassin a few days later. He found Irgun soldiers in the midst of "cleaning up." De Reyier wrote:

> I found some bodies cold. Here the "cleaning up" had been done with machine guns, then hand grenades. It had been finished off with knives, anyone could see that. . . . As the [Irgun] gang had not dared to attack me directly, I could continue. I gave orders for the goodies in this house to be loaded on the truck, and went to the next house, and so on. Everywhere it was the same horrible sight. I found only two more people alive.[65]

The Irgun paraded the few Palestinian survivors through the streets of Jerusalem where they were jeered and spit on. With Deir Yassin, Plan Dalet had been raised to a new level of brutality. The massacres in Deir Yassin, Tantura, and other villages were meant as warnings to all Palestinians. While the Jewish Agency officially condemned the Deir Yassin massacre in words, on the same day it brought the Irgun into the Joint Command of the military with the Haganah.

Twelve days after the Deir Yassin massacre, on April 21, 1948, the British commander in Haifa—a city in the north with a mixed population—advised the Zionist forces that he would immediately begin withdrawing his forces. He did not inform the Palestinians. The same day, joint Irgun-Haganah forces launched a lethal attack on the Palestinian areas of Haifa. They rolled barrel bombs filled with gasoline and dynamite down narrow alleys in the heavily populated city while mortar shells pounded the Arab neighborhoods from overhead. Haganah army loudspeakers and sound cars broadcast "horror recordings" of shrieks and screams of Arab women, mixed with calls of: "Flee for your lives. The Jews are using poison gas and nuclear weapons." The Irgun commander reported that many Palestinians cried "Deir Yassin, Deir Yassin," as they fled.[66]

Within a week, similar terror tactics led 77,000 of 80,000 Palestinians to flee the port city of Jaffa. Comparable operations were repeated many times. By May 15, 1948, when Israel's independence was proclaimed, 300,000 Palestinians were living and dying in abominable conditions of exile in Lebanon, Gaza, Syria, and the Jordan Valley. By the end of that year, the number of dispossessed Palestinians had grown to over 750,000. Without the tactic of massacre, the ethnic cleansing of Palestine would not have been possible. Without massacres, the Israel that its creators envisioned could not have come into being.

None of the Palestinians who were driven out were allowed to return to their homes, despite UN Resolution 194, passed in December 1948. The resolution states unequivocally that all refugees must be allowed back and compensated for any damages suffered.[67] To justify this illegal refusal, the Israeli authorities claimed that the refugees had left "voluntarily." This was another of Israel's contradictory creation myths—contradictory because it collides with another historical fabrication. After all, if Palestine was truly a "land without people," why would anyone have had to leave? The myth that the Palestinians "left voluntarily" has been demolished. It is today undeniable that Palestinians who fled did so because of a deliberate campaign of terror. But whether refugees leave due to violence, the threat of violence or for any other reason, their right to return to their homeland remains inalienable according to international law and any sense of justice.

Al-Nakba's Wake

The people of Palestine and the entire Arab world remember the year 1948 as al-Nakba—the Catastrophe. The Palestinian historian Walid Khalidi wrote about al-Nakba and its physical remnants today:

> By the end of the 1948 war, hundreds of entire villages had not only been depopulated but [also] obliterated, their houses blown up or bulldozed. While many of the sites are difficult to access, to this day the observant traveler of Israeli roads and highways can see traces of their presence that would escape the notice of the casual passerby: a fenced-in area, often surmounting a gentle hill, of olive and other fruit trees left untended, of cactus hedges and domesticated plants run wild. Now and then a few crumbled houses are left standing, a neglected mosque or church, collapsing walls along the ghost of a village lane, but in the vast majority of cases, all that remains is a scattering of stones and rubble across a forgotten landscape.[68]

After the 1948 war, the remaining 22 percent of Palestine was divided. Jordan annexed the West Bank—named after the west bank of the Jordan River; Gaza came under Egyptian administration. More than 750,000 Palestinians were dispossessed of their farms, shops, and homes and forced into wretched concentration camps. The expropriated Palestinian land, workplaces, houses, and public buildings constituted an essential material basis for the new Israeli state and its economy. The Palestinians had seemingly disappeared, at least for much of the world. In the United States press they lost all nationality, becoming only "refugees."

The process of "disappearing" the Palestinians was very important to Israel. The post-war period was the epoch not of rising colonialism, but of its opposite—decolonization. The imperialist powers were all being confronted by national liberation struggles in Asia, Africa, Latin America, and the Middle East. Under these circumstances, the Israeli leaders and their US patrons did not want Israel to be perceived as a colonial-settler state. Their way out was simply to proclaim that Palestine had been an empty, barren land. The fact that tens of thousands of Israelis were now living in the homes of Palestinians, working their fields, and harvesting the fruit of century-old trees was conveniently forgotten in the glowing accounts of how Israel had "made the desert bloom." This fiction appeared as the dominant narrative in most US media outlets.

Israel Seeks a 'Second Round'

Despite having taken control of most of Mandate Palestine, Israeli leaders, including Ben-Gurion, were far from satisfied with their new state. Moshe Dayan, a young military officer and Ben-Gurion protégé, was quoted by a Tel Aviv-based US diplomat in 1949 as saying: "Boundaries-Frontier of Israel should be on Jordan [River]. . . . Present boundaries ridiculous from all points of view."[69] As events would soon show, it was not just the West Bank to which Dayan was referring. Parts of neighboring Lebanon, Egypt, and Syria were also in the Zionist leaders' expansionist dreams.

The leaders of the new Israeli state did not rely on dreams to fulfill their aspirations. No sooner did Israel come into being than Ben-Gurion and his ruling cabal began looking for a new war. They were ready for a second round of battle to realize their goals. A key figure in Israel's aggressive policy was the war criminal and future prime minister, Ariel Sharon. Sharon's half-century-long bloody trail of massacres—from Qibya to Gaza, from Sabra and Shatila to Jenin— parallels the history of Israel itself. Sharon and his cohorts always hid their mass murders behind the pretext of "retaliation." This soon became Israel's unnamed policy when it would employ mass violence or provoke a war with its hostile neighbors.

In the first years after their expulsion, Palestinians frequently crossed the illegal and artificial border established by the Zionist state, usually to return to their stolen lands and homes. Most often this happened during the planting and harvest season. Smaller numbers returned as groups of fighters, or fedayeen, seeking to continue the struggle.[70] Israeli army—Israeli Defense Forces (IDF)—orders were to kill any "infiltrators," including those who were unarmed. In response to any fedayeen attack, the Israeli army would often carry out large-scale attacks and massacres. The aim was not only to punish. "Retaliation" really meant provocation; the intent was to get Jordan or Egypt to react militarily to the massacres, which could then be used by Israel as a pretext for a new war of conquest. Israeli writer, Benny Morris explained in his book, *Righteous Victims*:

> Major Ariel ("Arik") Sharon, the Israeli officer who came to embody the "retaliatory policy," was placed in charge of the new Unit 101, designed especially for such actions. On October 14, 1953, Unit 101 attacked Qibya, a small border village, and wiped out its population of more than 60 people. Many of the villagers were burned alive inside their homes. There were no IDF casualties.[71]

Sharon was then the favorite officer of Israeli Gen. Moshe Dayan. The general, who later became defense minister, was a major proponent of the "retaliation" policy. The Qibya massacre elicited world condemnation, but not the new war with Jordan that Israeli leaders were seeking as a pretext to seize the West Bank. Israel and its backers in the United States have continued to make use of the "retaliation" doctrine up to the present. The word "retaliation" implies an act of self-defense.

When Israel launches devastating assaults on the Palestinians or any other country or people, the corporate media and politicians universally describe them as "retaliation."

There is nothing new about this kind of propaganda. In similar ways, newspapers justified the response to the 1831 Nat Turner slave revolt in Virginia, the extermination campaigns against the Native nations of this continent and the US war on Korea in the early 1950s. The oppressors are always magically transformed into victims, the oppressed into the aggressors. Such descriptions are patently false. They turn the true narrative of history upside down. The Israeli government continued its policy of provocation, cloaked as "retaliation," leading up to the 1956 Suez war against Egypt. In that war, Israel made a temporary alliance with the British and French imperialists. They temporarily conquered the Gaza Strip and Sinai Peninsula.

SECTION III: ISRAELI EXPANSION, PALESTINIAN RESISTANCE

WATCHDOG FOR THE WEST

From its beginnings, Israel has required vast amounts of outside aid—economic and military—to survive. In 1950, its imports exceeded its exports by a ratio of ten-to-one. No economy can endure under those circumstances without massive assistance. Because its population was overwhelmingly made up of European immigrants, many of whom would have gone to the United States if given the choice, the Israeli leaders were very aware that European-like living standards had to be maintained. Otherwise, much of the population would have soon departed. Their problem was that Palestine was not in Europe and did not have a developed industrial economy.

Israel survived these first years thanks to a nonstop infusion of aid on an extraordinary scale, combined with the takeover of Palestinian private and personal property. As an artificial state, this was the only way to ensure Israel's existence. In 1952, Ben-Gurion's government consummated an agreement to receive "reparations" from West Germany for the following fifteen years. The "reparations" agreement caused a huge controversy among Jews, but was deemed essential by Ben-Gurion and associates.[72] In 1951, an editorial appeared in *Ha'aretz,* a leading Israeli newspaper, outlining how the new state could repay the aid:

> Therefore, strengthening Israel helps the Western powers to maintain equilibrium and stability in the Middle East. Israel is to be a watchdog. . . . If for any reason the Western powers should sometimes prefer to close their eyes, Israel

could be relied on to punish one or several neighboring
states whose discourtesy toward the West went beyond the
bounds of the permissible.[73]

An early opportunity for Israel to demonstrate its watchdog role came
in 1956. On July 26 of that year, the nationalist Egyptian government
led by Gamal Abdel Nasser nationalized the Suez Canal, the strategic
waterway connecting the Mediterranean Sea to the Indian Ocean.
Under Nasser, Egypt was a leading force in the decolonization struggle in the Middle East. In October 1956, Britain, France, and Israel
launched a surprise attack on Egypt.

The 1956 Suez War was the product of a secret plot hatched by top
officials of the three aggressor states. The French and British imperialists were frantically seeking to retain their colonies and neocolonies
in the Middle East. Their posture brought them into conflict not only
with the peoples of the region, but also their senior ally, the United
States. Like most real conspiracies, details of this one did not stay
secret for long. As is almost always the case when more than a handful
of people are involved, participants in the planning for the 1956 Suez
War soon leaked information to the media. *Time* magazine printed
the plot's details and how it had come about a week after it ended.

France, Britain, and Israel—the invading powers—had separate,
but complementary reasons for launching the war, and they shared a
common enmity toward Egypt. Egypt's old colonial order was overthrown along with King Farouk in 1952. The Free Officers Movement
sought to free the country from British domination and embark on a
course of modernization. By 1954, Nasser had emerged as the leading
figure of both the new government and the Pan-Arab national movement that was sweeping the region. By 1955, his government was
providing assistance to Algeria's National Liberation Front (Fronte de
Libération Nationale, FLN) in its struggle against French colonialism.

With the Suez War, the British wanted to reassert their control over
the recently nationalized Suez Canal and restore their domination
over their former colony, Egypt. France's priority was crushing the
Algerian Revolution, which had begun two years earlier. The French
imperialist government, then headed by the Socialist Party, believed
that the Algerian FLN would collapse without Egyptian support.[74]
Success against Egypt also would have meant the restoration of the

French share in the Suez Canal and adjoining Canal Zone, which it had previously co-owned with the British. Israel's main objective was to vastly expand its territory by conquering the entire Sinai Peninsula.

The leaders of all three aggressor countries agreed that Nasser's nationalist government should be overthrown and replaced by a puppet regime. They essentially sought a repeat of what the US Central Intelligence Agency had done three years earlier in Iran. In 1953, the CIA engineered the overthrow of Iran's first elected government led by Mohammed Mossadegh and put the shah (king) back in power. By 1955, France had become Israel's main state ally and arms supplier. France agreed in October of that year to provide warplanes, artillery and other weapons to the Israeli army. At the time, much of the Middle East was still governed by pro-Western regimes, and neither the US nor the British government wished to appear too closely tied to Israel. Israel had turned to France for arms in the early 1950s after the Eisenhower administration declined to provide them.

In 1956, France greatly increased its military aid to Israel. It sent seventy-two high-tech Mystère fighter-bombers as well as other advanced weapons. By early summer, joint planning for an attack was moving forward, involving at first France and Israel. Both governments sought to bring Britain into the plan, in order to provide additional cover for them and to strengthen their alliance. When Nasser announced the nationalization of the Suez Canal in July, the British ruling class' reaction was rabid fury. The canal was a central symbol of British imperial power. It was also the key economic route to the British colonies and neocolonies in Asia and East Africa. Nasser's takeover of the Suez Canal Company was done within the bounds of bourgeois legality. The share owners were compensated. But this did nothing to calm the hysteria in the British, French, and other capitalist media. A typical reaction was exemplified by the *New York Daily News'* full-page headline that branded Nasser as "Hitler of the Nile." Inside Egypt, meanwhile, huge crowds celebrated the country's break with imperialism and restoration of sovereignty.

Ben-Gurion's 'Fantastic Proposal'

From October 22 to 24, 1956, a secret conference was held in Sèvres, near Paris, to put the final touches on the war plans. Ben-Gurion surprised the other leaders in attendance by presenting what he called a "fantastic proposal" for the complete reorganization of the Middle East. Jordan, he suggested, was not a viable state and should become part of Iraq—which was still under British domination—with one condition: the new Iraq would have to agree to resettle all the Palestinian refugees from 1948 on the East Bank of the Jordan River. The West Bank, minus the Palestinians living there, would become part of Israel. Next, Ben-Gurion proposed, Israel would take over southern Lebanon up to the Litani River. The rest of Lebanon would become a "Christian state" with the restoration of French domination. Lebanon had been a French colony until 1943.

The Nasser government would be overthrown, the Suez Canal would be "internationalized," and British influence would be restored in Egypt. This would mean, in effect, British control of the canal. Israel would take over the Sinai Peninsula, the Straits of Tiran, and the Gulf of Aqaba leading to the Red Sea. The downfall of Nasser, according to the Israeli plan, would undermine both the Pan-Arab movement and the Algerian Revolution, to the benefit of all three conspiring states. Israel's territory would be tripled in size by this plan. And while Ben-Gurion himself called the plan "fantastic," he was dead serious about it.[75]

Ben-Gurion's proposal was too overreaching for the imperialist leaders of Britain and France. The plan they agreed on, however, was only slightly less ambitious. On October 24, they signed a seven-point document known as the Protocol of Sèvres. According to this plan, on October 29, 1956, Israel would launch a full-scale invasion of Egypt, seeking to reach the Suez Canal as quickly as possible. The pretext for the invasion was to be the familiar excuse of "retaliation"—Israel was striking back against a fabricated Egyptian attack. Then, as the Israelis neared the canal, the British and French would issue an "appeal" to Israel and Egypt to both withdraw their forces to ten miles from the canal, so as to "protect" the waterway. To make sure that Egypt could not accept this, an additional and insulting demand was made that British and French troops be allowed to occupy the Canal Zone, again in the interests of "protection." Finally, if Egypt failed to accept this ultimatum within twelve hours, there would be a joint Anglo-French attack on Egypt on October 31, including the bombing of Egyptian cities and a ground invasion. Outside the formal negotiations, the Israelis offered the French a joint oil venture in the to-be-conquered

Sinai. France agreed to provide Israel with the technology to launch a nuclear power and weapons program.

The plan of attack was implemented beginning October 29, but the collusion between the three attackers was immediately transparent. For one thing, the so-called appeal to protect the Suez Canal was issued before the Israeli troops even got close to the canal. Facing off against overwhelming military superiority, the Egyptian army and civilians inside the Canal Zone fought fiercely against the British and French invaders. An estimated 2,700 Egyptians were killed and wounded in the battle for Port Said. Numerous Egyptian military and civilian facilities were destroyed, especially in the cities near the Suez Canal. Euphoric in what at first seemed a victory, Ben-Gurion wrote that the newly conquered lands would become "part of the third kingdom of Israel." But it was not to be.

Soviet Union, US Intervene—for Different Reasons

The ostensible British-French-Israeli victory did not stand. There was worldwide outrage at the invasion. The 1956 Suez War was seen widely as a blatant attempt to resurrect colonialism—especially in the Middle East, but also across the world. Israel was widely condemned as a pawn of imperialism.

Both the United States and Soviet Union responded swiftly and strongly to the Tripartite Invasion—but for very different reasons. The Eisenhower administration reacted furiously for not having been informed in advance by either its imperialist allies or Israel. On October 30, 1956, the United States introduced a UN Security Council resolution condemning the invasion. Britain and France both used their veto power to defeat it. More fundamental than any emotion was the US ruling class's opposition to the restoration of British and French imperial power in the strategically key and oil-rich Middle East. From World War II to the present day, every administration—including Eisenhower's—has held US domination of the region as a central objective. Nor would Washington tolerate Israel serving as proxy for other imperialist powers. The message was sent to the Israeli government that if it did not withdraw from Egypt, all aid from official sources as well as private fundraising efforts in the United States would be cut off. Further, the United States would allow Israel to be expelled from the United Nations.[76]

Soviet premier Nikolai Bulganin warned the British, French, and Israeli governments that his country would unleash rocket attacks on their cities if they did not immediately withdraw. These warnings had to be taken very seriously, particularly because Eisenhower had ordered the withdrawal of the US protective nuclear shield over the three countries. The Soviet leadership also stated that if the war continued, Soviet volunteers would join the fight on the side of the Egyptians. Egypt and the Soviet Union had just entered into their first economic and military relations in the months before the invasion. Those relations were vastly expanded after the 1956 Suez War.

Facing such irresistible pressures, the invading powers were forced out. As they withdrew, the Israelis waged a scorched-earth campaign, destroying every road, railroad and structure of any value in Egypt. The outcome of the war was a humiliating defeat for the aggressors, especially the British and French. For the Israelis, while their "third kingdom" would have to be put on hold, significant gains were made from the episode. Israel acquired both vital military aid and the beginning of a nuclear weapons program. The 1956 Suez War led within a very short time to Israel being brought fully into the US camp. By its next war against the Arab world in 1967, Israel was closely aligned with and supplied by the US military.

The 1956 Suez War, rather than defeating the Arab national liberation movement, propelled it forward. The prestige of Nasser and Egypt was greatly enhanced. Less than two years later, on July 14, 1958, the Pan-Arab movement scored another victory when another movement of nationalist military officers overthrew the pro-British monarchy in Iraq. The Iraq Revolution was a huge blow to both the United States and Britain. Iraq was the center of the Baghdad Pact—a military alliance organized by Washington against both the Soviet Union and the rising tide of radical Arab nationalism. US leaders had been working to build up Iraq militarily as a counterweight to Syria and Egypt in the Arab world. The July 1958 Iraq Revolution shocked both Washington and London. President Eisenhower called it "the gravest crisis since the Korean War." It ended British-US domination of that country. Within months, the British air bases were forced to close, the Baghdad Pact collapsed and Iraq began the nationalization of its rich oil resources. Up until 1958, 100 percent of Iraq's petroleum was foreign-owned, 95 percent of it by US, British, French and Dutch oil companies.

The revolution energized revolutionary movements in other Arab countries. Without the intervention of 20,000 US Marines in Lebanon and 6,600 British paratroopers in Jordan in the days immediately following July 14, the pro-Western governments in those countries likely would have fallen as well. Military intervention to overturn the Iraq Revolution was contemplated by US and British leaders, but plans had to be abandoned—for the time being—because of its mass popular base and international support. It is hardly a coincidence that, forty-five years later, the same imperialist powers invaded Iraq and returned it to its former colonial status.

FORTIFYING THE US-ISRAELI ALLIANCE

In the late 1950s and early 1960s, significant US military aid began arriving in Israel. With the invaluable assistance of France and the United States, Israel developed nuclear weapons. Then, in a lightning strike in 1967, Israel achieved its goal of conquering the remainder of historic Palestine and more. The June 1967 War—the Six-Day War—was another watershed event in the history of the Middle East. It signaled the end of one phase of the post-World War II national liberation struggle in the region, and the start of a new phase, led by a resurgent and revolutionary Palestinian movement.

The 1967 Six-Day War convinced US leaders that Israel could be a highly effective weapon against the Arab liberation struggle, and should be supplied with nearly unlimited quantities of economic and military aid. After a period of rising tensions and deepening radicalization in the Arab world, the Israeli military, using US equipment and intelligence data, launched coordinated strikes against Egypt, Syria, and Jordan on June 5, 1967. The US Sixth Fleet in the Mediterranean Sea and the 82nd Airborne Division, among other military units, were on alert, ready to intervene in the name of "protecting American lives" if the surprise attack by the Israeli Defense Forces went awry.[77]

Most of the mainstream media, along with Israel's apologists in the United States, propagated the notion that the war was a rerun of the biblical David versus Goliath battle. Israel was pictured as the heroic underdog, with God once more on its side. The misnamed, US-based "Anti-Defamation League," which has long served as propagandist for the Israeli regime, said that "Israel launched a preemptive strike against Egypt," suggesting that it only did so to avert annihilation.[78] None other than the extreme right-wing Israeli Prime Minister Menachem Begin later exposed the utter falsity of the renewed "retaliation" claims. Fifteen years after the war, in an August 2, 1982 speech to the Israeli National Defense College, Begin said: "We must be honest with ourselves. We decided to attack him [Egyptian President Gamal Abdul Nasser]."[79] It was not just Begin who exposed the myth. Ten years earlier, Gen. Mattiyahu Peled, one of the Israeli commanders in the 1967 Six-Day War, told the Israeli newspaper *Ha'aretz*: "The thesis that the danger of genocide was hanging over us in June 1967 and that Israel was fighting for its physical existence is only a bluff, which was born and developed after the war."[80]

Three decades later, Israel's minister of defense at the time of the 1967 Six-Day War, Moshe Dayan, talked to the *New York Times* about the events leading up to the war on the Syrian-Israeli front. He stated that the Israeli kibbutz (cooperative farm) residents in the area wanted to take over the rich farmland of Syria's Golan Heights: "They didn't even try to hide their greed for that land."[81] Describing Israel's by now familiar use of provocation disguised as retaliation, Dayan recounted:

> We would send a tractor to plow some area where it wasn't possible to do anything, in the demilitarized area, and knew in advance that the Syrians would start to shoot. If they didn't shoot, we would tell the tractor to advance further, until in the end the Syrians would get annoyed and shoot. And then we would use artillery and later the air force also, and that's how it was. . . . The Syrians, on the fourth day of the war [June 9, 1967], were not a threat to us.

Israel succeeded in achieving its long-held objective of expanded territory through the war. The remaining 22 percent of historic Palestine—the West Bank and Gaza—was conquered by Israel's surprise attack, along with Syria's Golan Heights and Egypt's Sinai Peninsula. More than thirty-five thousand Arabs were killed, many of them burned to death by Pentagon-supplied napalm bombs. Thousands more were wounded. Most of the Egyptian, Syrian and Jordanian air

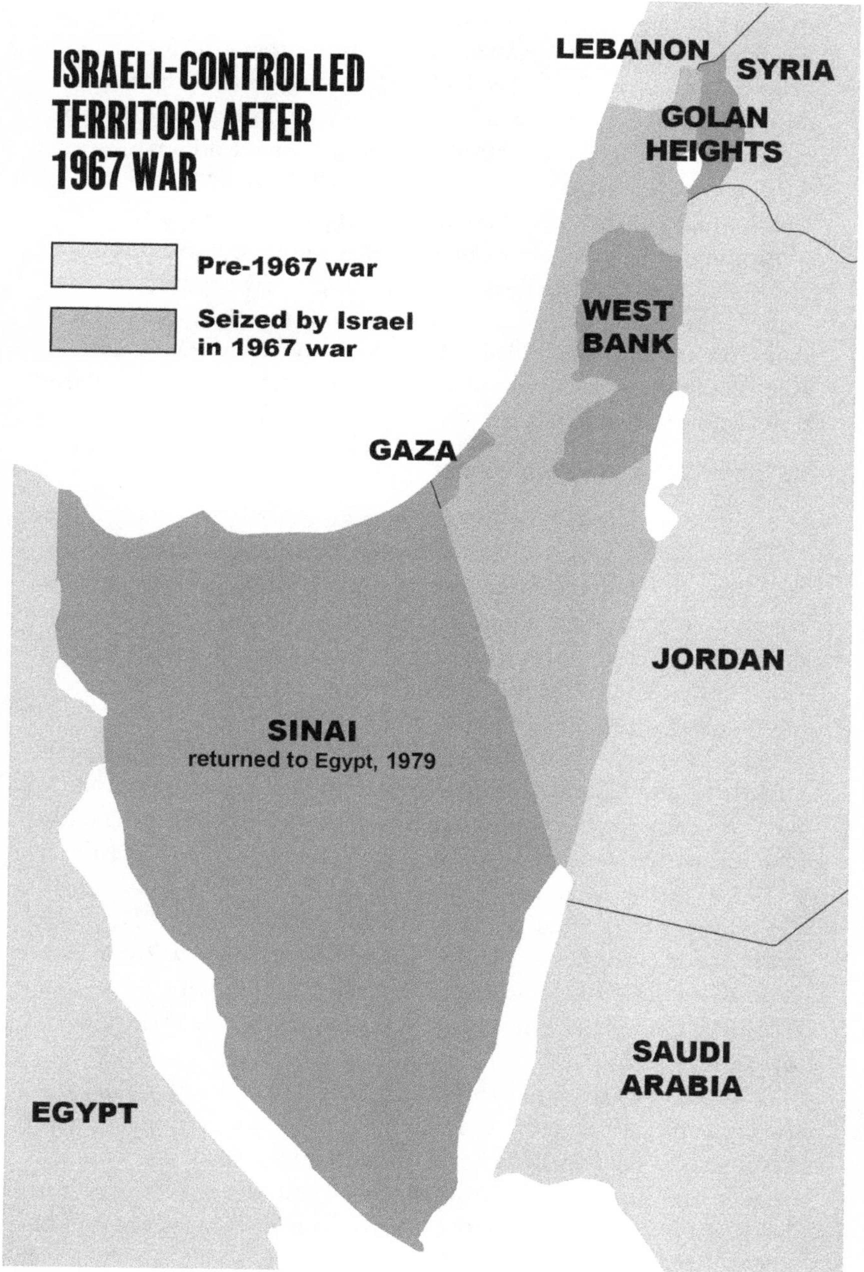

ISRAELI-CONTROLLED
TERRITORY AFTER
1967 WAR

Pre-1967 war

Seized by Israel
in 1967 war

LEBANON

SYRIA

GOLAN
HEIGHTS

WEST
BANK

GAZA

JORDAN

SINAI
returned to Egypt, 1979

EGYPT

SAUDI
ARABIA

and armored forces were destroyed in the opening days of the surprise attack. The Israeli army drove more than ninety thousand Syrians and Palestinians out of the Golan Heights, an agriculturally rich region north of the Sea of Galilee. Many of the Syrian villages and Golan's main city, Quneitra, were bulldozed by the Israeli military. Israeli settlers began arriving in Golan in July 1967. In 1981, the Israeli Knesset (parliament) passed a law annexing the Golan Heights. The continuing occupation of Golan, as well as the West Bank and Gaza, defies scores of UN resolutions. Possessing overwhelming technological superiority, Israeli casualties were low. Officially, around one thousand Israelis were killed. More than three hundred thousand Palestinians were made refugees in the war—many of them for the second time in two decades.

US Imperialism—The Big Winner

In addition to Israel, Washington was the other big winner of the 1967 Six-Day War. Gerald Ford, who was then-House of Representatives minority leader and later president, said while the war was still raging, "Israel has done a pretty good job of bailing out US interests in the area."[82] Ford meant that Israel had dealt a major blow to rising Arab nationalism in the oil-rich Middle East, at a time when the US military was preoccupied with its war on Vietnam.

The Egyptian Cairo Radio expressed the sentiments of anti-imperialist and nationalist forces throughout the region. "Our battle today is against the United States firstly, secondly and thirdly; lastly it is against the Zionist [Israeli military] bands, very much lastly."[83] A 1987 Library of Congress Country Study of Syria summed up the meaning of the war to the states attacked by Israel: "The traumatic defeat of the Syrians and Egyptians in the June 1967 war with Israel discredited the radical socialist regimes of Nasser's Egypt and Baathist Syria. . . . The defeat strengthened the hands of the moderates and the rightists."[84]

This was exactly the outcome sought by US political leaders and the oil, banking and military-industrial interests who employ them. According to Rita Freed in her 1972 pamphlet *War in the Mideast,* officials in Washington regarded Syria—where the left wing of the Baath Party had taken over the government six months earlier—as "the Cuba of the Middle East."[85]

The West Bank and Golan Heights remain under Israeli occupation today. So does Gaza. Although Israeli military forces withdrew in 2005, Gaza remains militarily surrounded and cut off from the world. A demilitarized Sinai went back to Egypt under the terms of a 1979 peace treaty with Israel, which was rooted in the 1978 Camp David Accords between Israel, Egypt, and the United States. The 1979 agreement removed Egypt from the Arab military alliance and brought it into the US government's orbit.

The Nixon Doctrine Means Massive Aid

The 1967 Six-Day War signaled a definitive shift in the US-Israeli relationship. It also marked the beginning of a truly massive flow of US military and economic assistance to the Zionist state. Since then, Israel has received aid unlike that granted to any other country in the world—and with far fewer strings attached. Most of the hundreds of billions of dollars sent to Israel have been in the form of non-repayable grants.[86] Many of what were originally called "loans" were later forgiven.

Shortly after the war, Israel and Iran—then ruled by the US-installed Shah Reza Pahlavi—became the linchpins and enforcers of the counterrevolutionary Nixon Doctrine. The Nixon Doctrine outlined a strategy for control and policing of the Middle East that was premised on a US-Israeli-Iranian axis. Of course, this was a partnership based on hegemonic control by one of the three "partners." Essentially, Washington relied on proxy Israeli and Iranian forces to control the oil-rich Middle East. The doctrine was necessitated by the fact that more than 550,000 US troops were tied down in a losing war in Vietnam. Washington and Wall Street were extremely worried about revolution in the Middle East, a region of the world looked upon by corporate interests as far more strategically important than Indochina.

US aid to Israel increased exponentially from about $151 million in 1967, to $3.3 billion in 1971, to $11.4 billion in 1974 and to $14.4 billion in 1979.[87] Two-thirds of this amount was officially military aid. The astronomical military assistance, which included high-tech weaponry not available to any other state, enabled Israel to become the world's fifth-ranked military power, despite its population of less than five million people. Israel has repaid this aid in many ways—doing Washington's dirty work in the Middle East and other parts of the world.

THE PALESTINIAN STRUGGLE TAKES CENTER STAGE

With the 1967 conquest of the remaining 22 percent of Palestine, it appeared that the fate of the Palestinians was sealed. This was certainly the dominant view in Israel. But in a seeming paradox, the 1967 Six-Day War led to a dramatic revival of the Palestinian movement and a new wave of popular radicalization across the region.

The defeat suffered by the Egyptian and Syrian armies was indeed a crushing one. But while it weakened the more radical bourgeois nationalist forces in favor of more conciliatory or comprador ones in both countries, it had a very different effect on the people of the Middle East. In describing the impact of the June 1967 Six-Day War on popular consciousness in the region, the September 1967 issue of *Fortune* magazine reported, "Not since the Boxer Rebellion [1899 in China] has there been as rapid a revulsion against a foreign power as against the United States in the Middle East."[88] Revolutionary fervor swept across much of the Middle East, spearheaded by remarkable developments in Palestine and among Palestinian refugees in Jordan, Lebanon and elsewhere.

Until 1967, radical Palestinian groups such as the Palestine National Liberation Movement (Fatah), founded under the leadership of Yasser Arafat and others, and the Arab National Movement (ANM), led by George Habash, had placed their main hopes for the restoration of lost lands and rights with Nasser and the other Arab leaders. Many believed the Arab armies would liberate Palestine. The outcome of the 1967 Six-Day War brought that period to a close. Out of the ashes of defeat arose an independent Palestinian revolutionary movement that transformed the region's politics. In both the West Bank and Gaza, the brutal Israeli occupation met with armed resistance, beginning with actions by Fatah in August 1967.

In December 1967, the Palestinian wing of the ANM together with a number of smaller organizations formed the Popular Front for the Liberation of Palestine and declared its adherence to Marxism-Leninism.[89] A number of other fedayeen organizations followed.

The Arab League established the Palestine Liberation Organization (PLO) in 1964 with an appointed leader named Ahmed Shukeiry. During the 1967 war, Shukeiry, who had no base in either the Palestinian population or militant organizations, gave bombastic radio broadcasts, vowing to "drive the Jews into the sea." Arafat's Fatah denounced Shukeiry's comments and anti-Semitism:

> [Palestinian military] operations . . . are in no way aimed at Jewish people. Nor do they intend to "drive them into the sea." . . . [O]n the day the flag of Palestine is hoisted over their freed, democratic peaceful land, a new era will begin in which the Palestinian Jews will again live in harmony, side by side, with the original owners of the land, the Palestinian Arabs.[90]

Shukeiry soon was ousted for making "misleading statements," condemned by Fatah, the Popular Front for the Liberation of Palestine (PFLP), the General Union of Palestinian Students and other organizations. The leadership of the PLO then passed into the hands of the Palestinian revolutionary organizations. The movement expanded rapidly.

In 1968, the PLO reemerged as an independent entity and began a multi-faceted struggle against Israel. Over the following years, the PLO and its constituent organizations like Fatah, the PFLP, the Democratic Front for the Liberation of Palestine (DFLP)—a 1969 split from the PFLP—and others organized trade unions, women's and youth organizations as well as armed resistance. The PLO issued a charter that proclaimed its aim to be the creation of a democratic, secular state in Palestine with equal rights for all in place of the state of Israel. The PFLP and the smaller DFLP called for the establishment of a "democratic, secular and socialist" state.

The Israelis used the most brutal forms of repression to try to crush the burgeoning struggle. Shootings, arbitrary arrests, wholesale and systematic torture of all arrested for political activity, expulsions, house demolitions, massive uprooting of fruit and olive trees, and extreme economic deprivation—these were the tools of the occupiers. The repression in the newly occupied West Bank and Gaza took a heavy toll on the early resistance movement, which was forced to concentrate its military forces in Jordan and Lebanon—the other two states with the largest refugee populations. The refugee camps, both inside and outside occupied Palestine, became the most indomitable centers of resistance, a reality that persists today.

Victory, Defeat in Jordan

The battle of Karameh, Jordan, on March 21, 1968, had a transformative impact on the resistance.[91] Approximately two hundred Palestinian fighters, backed by elements of the Jordanian army, fought off a far larger and more powerful Israeli force equipped with tanks and planes. "Many of our men who had run out of ammunition hurled themselves under the tanks, carrying explosives," said Taher Saadi, a Palestinian guerrilla who fought in the battle. "The first martyr to do that was Rarbi; he threw himself under a tank. I knew him well. We stuck it out that day, so as to wipe out the memory of June 1967."[92]

The effect of the Battle of Karameh was electrifying, especially in contrast to the devastating defeat suffered by the Arab states nine months earlier. Newspapers across the region featured photos of burned-out Israeli tanks. Thousands of young Palestinians, including women, lined up in the streets of cities and camps in Jordan and Lebanon to join the resistance organizations.

The Palestinian resistance presence in Jordan grew exponentially and threatened the regime of King Hussein, who had succeeded his collaborator grandfather Abdullah after his assassination in 1951 by a Palestinian refugee. Hussein was on the CIA payroll for at least two decades, starting in the 1950s. Palestinian refugees made up two-thirds of Jordan's population. Jordan's defeat in the 1967 Six-Day War meant that it lost control of East Jerusalem—the third-holiest site of Islam—and the entire West Bank, the richest part of the kingdom. The rapidly growing power of the Palestinian movement led Hussein to offer Yasser Arafat the position of prime minister in

1970, in an attempt to co-opt the resistance. Arafat declined. In the summer of the same year, heavy fighting broke out, with the wing of the resistance led by the PFLP attempting to seize power. The US- and British-supplied Jordanian army and air force answered by bombing and shelling the Palestinian refugee camps. The Israeli military was on standby to intervene if Hussein's forces faltered.

Syria, then governed by the left-wing of the Arab Baath Social-ist Party led by Salah Jadid, sent tank columns across the border to support the resistance fighters. The Syrian forces could have been a decisive factor, but were withdrawn under threat of destruction by Israeli bombers. The pullback weakened Jadid, who was overthrown the following year by the more centrist Baath party leader Hafez al-Assad. This episode was one more dramatic example of Israel's service to imperialism and its destructive impact on the Arab world.

In the end, the Jordanian military prevailed, massacring more than fifteen thousand PLO fighters and civilians in what came to be known as "Black September." As the wholesale killing, torture, and repression of the Palestinians raged on, the PFLP seized three international airliners and commanded the pilots to fly to Jordan. At the Amman airport, PFLP fighters emptied the airplanes of pas-sengers and blew them up on the runway. The PFLP's objective was to draw world attention to the slaughter taking place. Among those who carried out the operation was a young Palestinian revolutionary whose family was expelled from Haifa in 1948, Leila Khaled. After the defeat in Jordan, the center of the Palestinian resistance shifted to Lebanon, where hundreds of thousands of Palestinians live in desti-tute refugee camps.

The 1973 War—Israel Not Invincible

Out of all of Israel's many wars, the only one that it did not initiate took place in October 1973. This war also came close to becoming a nuclear conflict.

On October 6, 1973, Egypt and Syria launched simultaneous offensives, seeking to regain the territory they had lost in 1967. In the first days of the war, the Arab forces—which had been greatly strengthened since the 1967 defeat through aid from the Soviet Union and its allies—inflicted heavy casualties on Israel and made territorial gains. On October 8, Israeli Prime Minister Golda Meir ordered that thirteen atomic bombs be fitted on missiles aimed at targets in Egypt and Syria.[93] During the three weeks the war lasted, the US government sent more than fifty-five thousand tons of weapons and ammunition to Israel. Included were weapons systems so new that the United States dispatched military advisors to provide crash training for the Israeli soldiers. The United States also provided vital high-altitude intelligence information for the Israeli military's counterattack.

The Israeli military soon regained the offensive and recaptured all of the Sinai and Golan Heights, and then drove further into Syria. Iraqi and Jordanian forces entered the war, and a joint Iraqi-Syrian tank force turned back the Israelis who were driving toward Damascus. Algerian and Cuban units also entered the war on the side of Egypt and Syria. The Soviet Union sent more than sixty thousand tons of military supplies.

On October 22, the UN Security Council passed Resolution 338, calling for a ceasefire. The Israeli army violated the agreement the next day. It surrounded the Egyptian army instead, cutting it off from food, water and ammunition. The Soviet Union responded by demanding that the Israelis withdraw to their pre-ceasefire positions, and threatened to send their own forces in support of the trapped Egyptian military. Two days later, the United States put its nuclear forces on global alert, raising the threat of a nuclear world war. Even though no territory changed hands during the 1973 War, the outcome was very different from 1967. The early victories of the Arab armies showed that the Israeli military was not invincible.

The war raised the stature of the al-Assad government in Syria and the Anwar Sadat government in Egypt. Sadat was the new president of Egypt, following Nasser's death in September 1970. After the 1973 Arab-Israeli War, Sadat utilized his strengthened position to begin to move toward Washington and away from the Soviet Union. This shift culminated in the 1978 Camp David Accords and precipitated a serious split in the Arab world.

The 1973 Arab-Israeli War also brought a boycott by the Arab oil-producing states against the United States and other imperialist countries that supported Israel. The boycott, and the manipulation of it by the oil monopolies to increase their profits, caused the 1973–74 energy crisis. Gas and home heating prices doubled and tripled, and many gas stations in the United States and Europe went dry for a time.

'Sole Legitimate Representative'

Two developments in the wake of the 1973 Arab-Israeli War greatly advanced the Palestinian cause. In October 1974, the Arab Summit Conference meeting in Rabat, Morocco, voted to recognize the PLO as "the sole legitimate representative of the Palestinian people." The following month, PLO Chairman Yasser Arafat became the first representative of the organization to address the UN General Assembly. Arafat gave one of the most noted speeches in the history of the United Nations on November 13, 1974. His speech was greeted with great enthusiasm, especially by representatives of states that had won independence from colonialism in the years since World War II. Arafat's speech concluded:

> I know well that many of you present here today once stood in exactly the same resistance position I now occupy and from which I must fight. You once had to convert dreams into reality by your struggle. Therefore, you must now share my dream. . . . I have come bearing an olive branch and a freedom fighter's gun. Do not let the olive branch fall from my hand.[94]

By a vote of 105–4, the General Assembly voted to recognize the Palestinian people's right to self-determination and to grant the PLO observer status at the United Nations. Two of the dissenting votes were predictably cast by the United States and Israel, the other two by Dominican Republic and Bolivia, two countries that were the recent victims of US-backed coups.

Following this diplomatic recognition, the United Nations passed a series of resolutions reaffirming the right of Palestinians to return to their traditional homes (the right of return), to recover occupied East Jerusalem, to eliminate illegal Israeli settlements, to gain freedom from occupation, and to struggle by all means necessary, including "military resistance," to secure these rights. Gaining recognized legitimacy on the world stage was a major victory for the Palestinian resistance movement.

LEBANON: CIVIL WAR AND OCCUPATION

In the early 1970s, political polarization in Lebanon was accelerating rapidly. Lebanon is a small country with a very diverse population, including Arab Sunni and Shiite Muslims, Catholic and Orthodox Christians, and Druze. More than 10 percent of the population is made up of Palestinian refugees, and there is also a significant Armenian population. Many political parties and armed organizations had surfaced by the 1970s.

On one side were the pro-Western and fascist elements, grouped mainly around the Phalangist Party. The founders of the Phalangist Party were Maronite Catholics, but not all Lebanese Christians— or even all Maronites—followed them. The Phalangist Party based itself on a fascist ideology and their "special relationship" with the French former colonizers. They copied their party name from that of the Falangists in Spain, led by the dictator Gen. Francisco Franco. The Phalangists liked to portray themselves as "Phoenicians," not Arabs. Their fascist tendencies notwithstanding, the Phalangists were armed, supplied, and embraced by the Israeli government, who wished to make them the rulers over all of Lebanon.

On the other side were the progressive forces, comprised of the rapidly growing Lebanese National Movement (LNM), with representatives from all the numerous religious and ethnic communities in the country, and their allies in the Palestinian resistance movement. After the repression in Jordan, the Palestinian refugee camps in Lebanon had become the main base of the PLO. The LNM called for an end to the "confessional system" and its replacement with a democratic government. The French colonizers created the confessional system before Lebanon achieved formal independence in 1943. Under this system, which still exists, the president must always be a Maronite Catholic, the prime minister a Sunni Muslim, the speaker of the parliament a Shiite Muslim, and so on. Christians were guaranteed a majority in the parliament—since amended to 50–50—and the Maronites were given control of the army. Among other points, the LNM program called for universal conscription to build a strong army against Israel. It emphasized the right of the Palestinian resistance to carry out the liberation struggle from Lebanese territory. The Arab League also officially endorsed the right of the Palestinians to conduct armed resistance from inside Lebanon.

On April 13, 1975, a Phalangist massacre of thirty people, most of them Palestinians, was the spark that ignited full-scale civil war. In 1976, at the height of the Lebanese Civil War, the progressive alliance of the LNM and the PLO was on the brink of defeating the US/Israeli-backed Lebanese fascist/right-wing alliance. Then in May 1976, the Syrian army entered Lebanon with the blessing and backing of the United States, thereby blocking the victory of the progressive forces. While it was opposed to Israel and imperialist domination of the region, Syria's bourgeois nationalist government, led by the centrist al-Assad, was fearful that: (1) a revolutionary victory in Lebanon could promote a similar development inside Syria, and (2) such a victory would lead to a US-backed Israeli invasion of Lebanon and possibly a new attack on Syria.

A particularly horrendous episode in the war was the siege of the Tal al-Zaatar refugee camp, home to more than thirty thousand Palestinians and some Lebanese. In June 1976, the Syrian military gave the green light to the fascist militias to launch an all-out attack on the camp, which was a center of resistance. The fascists blockaded the camp. Syrian army forces proceeded to prevent Palestinian fighters from reinforcing the camp and lifting the siege. Despite deteriorating conditions and lack of food and medicine, camp defenders held out for six weeks, until trickery using the International Red Cross allowed the Phalangists to gain entry. The fascists executed every male they could find between the ages of fourteen and forty years old, and many other people. More than two thousand people were murdered; four thousand wounded and thousands more once again displaced.[95]

The Syrian intervention was disastrous for the working class and poor peasants of Lebanon, and for the country as a whole. Blocking the LNM-PLO alliance from achieving a decisive victory did not bring an end to the struggle. Instead, the conflict dragged on with shifting alliances until 1990, destroying much of the country and particularly its capital, Beirut. Syria's actions also did not prevent Israel—with full US backing—from invading and occupying Lebanon in 1982.

Camp David Brings New War

Following the death of Nasser in 1970, Anwar Sadat became Egypt's president. Sadat broke Egypt's alliance with the Soviet Union, and soon after the 1973 Arab-Israeli War entered into a negotiating process that led to the 1978 Camp David Accords. US President Jimmy Carter brokered the accords. Carter was awarded the Nobel Peace Prize along with President Sadat and Prime Minister Menachem Begin of Israel. Under the agreements and the "peace" treaty that followed, Egypt recognized Israel and the two states exchanged ambassadors. Sadat even traveled to Jerusalem and addressed the Israeli Knesset.

While hailed in the West, the Camp David Accords were widely viewed in the Arab world—including by most Egyptians—as a betrayal of the Palestinian and Arab cause. The accords detached the most populous and militarily powerful state from the Arab camp. Rather than bringing "peace," they paved the way for Israel's devastating 1982 invasion and eighteen-year occupation of Lebanon, which took tens of thousands of Lebanese and Palestinian lives. No other Arab country had the power to challenge Israel's US-funded and supplied military. The accords also had the effect of pulling Egypt firmly into Washington's orbit. Egypt soon became the second largest recipient of US aid—next to Israel. But unlike the military aid sent to Israel, which could be and was used for offensive purposes, "security assistance" to Egypt was intended for use primarily against the Egyptian population.

Military officers assassinated Sadat in 1981 in response to Camp David. His successor, Hosni Mubarak, followed Sadat's policies, despite mass opposition. Mubarak remained a dependent and dependable US ally until forced out during the Arab Spring in 2011. In 1981, when Carter was being hailed as a "Middle East peacemaker" his administration was doing everything in its power to help the murderous shah of Iran rollback the rising revolutionary tide in that country. Tens of thousands of Iranians were slaughtered in the streets with US-supplied weapons, but the revolution could not be stopped. In February 1979, the shah fled the country.

Israel's 1982 Invasion

In June 1982, using the pretext of the assassination of Israel's ambassador to Britain, Israel launched a long-planned invasion of Lebanon. Israel had occupied a large part of southern Lebanon since 1978, but the 1982 invasion was of a much greater scope and magnitude than any previous Israeli attack. The invasion had the full backing of the US administration headed by President Ronald Reagan. Within a few days, the Israeli army reached Beirut and occupied more than half the country. For the following three months, Israel—supplied by the Pentagon—rained bombs nonstop on West Beirut and the Palestinian refugee camps. The Israeli occupation had the dual objective of creating a new Lebanon under the leadership of the Phalangists and its leader Bashir Gemayel, and the complete destruction of the PLO in its main bases. Israeli leaders hoped to liquidate the Palestinian struggle once and for all.

After the bombing, Beirut was in ruins. More than twenty thousand Lebanese and Palestinian civilians were killed, and many more were wounded or made homeless. An agreement was signed. PLO and Fatah chairman Yasser Arafat agreed to evacuate the PLO military forces to Tunisia, far from Palestine in North Africa. In return, according to the accord brokered by a US diplomat, Philip Habib, the Palestinian refugee camps would be "guaranteed" protection by the military forces of several countries, including the United States. The PLO aimed to prevent the fascist militias from murdering Palestinian civilians. These were the same militias that had carried out the Tal al-Zaatar massacre just six years earlier. The Popular Front for the Liberation of Palestine (PFLP) opposed the evacuation of the PLO military forces, arguing that it posed a grave danger to the resistance and that there was no basis for putting any faith in the imperialists' "security guarantees." In early September 1982, PLO military forces left and US Marines and French army and other forces came ashore in Lebanon. On September 14, the leader of the Phalangist Party, also the newly anointed president of Lebanon, Bashir Gemayel, was killed in a bombing carried out by an opponent who was also a Lebanese Maronite. Gemayel was the presidential pick of Washington and Tel Aviv.

Despite the US "guarantee" of safety for the camps, on September 16, 1982, the Israeli military surrounding the Sabra and Shatila refugee camps allowed the Phalangist militia to enter the camps. Ariel Sharon, who was then Israeli minister of defense, was kept "fully informed" throughout the forty-eight-hour massacre that followed. More than two thousand Palestinians and Lebanese—nearly all children, women and elderly men—were slaughtered.

For the next year, US forces waged war against a rising Lebanese resistance movement. US warships off Lebanon's Mediterranean coast lobbed shells, which President Reagan bragged about being "the size of Volkswagens," into unsuspecting Lebanese mountain towns, sometimes entirely obliterating small villages.[96] The US occupation ended following an October 23, 1983, truck bombing of the Marines' Beirut barracks, killing 241 US troops. A similar attack killed 58 French occupation soldiers. The Marines evacuated soon afterwards.

Over the next seventeen years, the Lebanese resistance gained strength, finally forcing the Israeli occupiers to withdraw from nearly all of the country in 2000. The resistance encompassed several organizations, with Hezbollah (the Party of God), based mainly in Lebanon's large Shiite community, emerging as the central force.

Palestinian Resistance after Lebanon

The 1982 war exacerbated the already existing differences within the PLO over strategy, tactics and objectives. This was hardly surprising, since the major organizations represented different class forces within the national liberation movement. Fatah was the largest resistance organization and encompassed fighters and militants from all social classes. It represents the Palestinian bourgeoisie, or capitalist class. This class was and still is oppressed by imperialism and Israel, but it is also an exploiting class that wishes, like all such classes in the world, to gain control over a national territory where it can rule. The PFLP is a Marxist party. It too has attracted militants from different social classes. Its program represents the interests of the national liberation movement as a whole, with particular emphasis on the interests of the working class and other oppressed sectors, both inside Palestine and among the Palestinian diaspora. The Palestinians living in the fifty-nine refugee camps inside and outside Palestine suffer some of the greatest oppression and deprivation.

Beginning in 1974, Fatah—with the support of the DFLP and other groups—began openly advocating for a "two-state solution" to resolve the conflict with Israel. The two-state solution means the creation of a Palestinian state in the West Bank and Gaza. Given the extreme repression inflicted on the Palestinians by the Israeli occupation, any relief from Israeli rule would be welcomed by all Palestinians. All the major forces were in agreement that truly liberating any Palestinian territory would be a step forward. But a final agreement that accepted a Palestinian state on 22 percent or less of Palestine would: (1) create an entity that was dominated by its highly militarized "neighbor," Israel; and (2) ignore the right of return for the millions of Palestinians expelled in 1948 and their descendants. It would deny their right to come back to their homes and land inside what is Israel today. The most adversely affected would be the most impoverished, particularly those living in the camps in surrounding Arab countries. At the same time, gaining economic and political control over even a relatively small area was very appealing to many in the tiny Palestinian bourgeoisie.

The PFLP opposed the two-state proposal, viewing it as renunciation of the Palestine National Charter[97] and the historic aims of the PLO. Despite numerous political and strategic differences, there was a reunification of the PLO in early 1987. A few months later, Gaza and the West Bank erupted in a new Intifada, the most massive in Palestinian history.

INTIFADA, 'PEACE PROCESS,' INTIFADA

The 1987 Intifada began in the Gaza refugee camps in December after four Palestinians working inside Israel were killed when an Israeli tank transporter hit their vehicle. Within days, hundreds of thousands of Palestinians in the West Bank, inside the 1948 borders of Israel, and in Gaza took to the streets in the largest demonstrations in Palestinian history. Hundreds of thousands more marched and protested in the Palestinian camps in Lebanon, Jordan, and Syria. Solidarity demonstrations erupted in countries around the world. An underground "National Unified Leadership" (NUL) was formed, made up of representatives of Fatah, PFLP, DFLP, the Palestine Communist Party, other organizations within the PLO, and independents. The NUL issued flyers calling for various actions, including demonstrations, strikes, and boycotts. Out of the Intifada and the NUL came a new generation of Palestinian leaders, including Marwan Barghouti of Fatah and Ahmed Saadat of the PFLP, who today remain among the most popular Palestinian leaders. They were both elected members of the Palestinian Legislative Council, and both were illegally convicted and imprisoned inside Israeli jails.[98]

The Israeli military used the most vicious means to attempt to crush the Intifada. Early in the uprising, Israeli troops employed CS gas, a highly lethal brand of tear gas, firing multiple canisters into homes and other enclosed areas, causing many deaths. The CS gas, produced by Federal Labs in western Pennsylvania, had an especially deadly effect on the very young and very old.[99] Israeli army Chief of

Staff Yitzhak Rabin, who would later become prime minister, proclaimed a policy of "breaking bones" of demonstrators, which was taken up by the occupation forces. Video images of Israeli troops holding down and breaking the hands, arms, and legs of Palestinian children and youth inflamed world public opinion.

Despite the savage repression, which included the arrest, systematic torture, and imprisonment of tens of thousands of Palestinians, the Intifada could not be defeated. A situation of dual power existed for nearly four years, pitting the Israeli occupiers against the organized resistance under the leadership of the NUL. Palestinian American activist Muna Coobtee characterized the importance of the Intifada in the January 2005 issue of *Socialism and Liberation*:

> The Palestinian Intifada had few precedents in history. It was an ongoing general strike of an entire people. As a consequence of their heroism, many Palestinians were deprived of employment, education, and access to the essential necessities of life.
>
> The image of school children confronting Israeli tanks with nothing more than stones became emblematic of a people whose very survival and identity was dependent on their capacity to struggle.[100]

The 1987 Intifada transformed the situation in Palestine. It put to rest any and all versions of what was referred to as the "Jordanian option"—proposals for Palestinian "autonomy" of some parts of the West Bank linked to the regime of the US client, King Hussein. Seeing the writing on the wall, Hussein renounced Jordanian ambitions to rule over the West Bank in 1988.

The breadth, depth, and intensity of the uprising proved to the world that there could be no solution to the conflict without self-determination for the Palestinian people. The prolonged 1987–1991 Intifada forced the US leaders to rethink their position. It became clear that all the killing, bone-breaking, torture, house demolitions, and economic deprivation that the Israelis inflicted had not succeeded in crushing the Palestinians.

Relationship of Forces Changes

The year 1991 marked a qualitative shift in the world relationship of forces. Early that year, the US-led military coalition delivered a smashing blow to Iraq and the Arab world as a whole, in the first Gulf War. Iraq had been the strongest of the Arab countries militarily for years. Then, late in the year, the Soviet Union, which had been a strategic ally of the Palestinian and Arab liberation movements, was overthrown and dissolved. So, although the Palestinians had proven through determined struggle that they could not be disregarded or wished away, their position in 1991 was seriously weakened by developments over which they had no control. This combination of factors, and the understanding that the Arafat leadership was now willing to come into the US orbit, made the time ripe for "peace" negotiations in Washington's view.

The negotiating process began in Madrid, Spain, and culminated in the Oslo (Norway) Accords of 1993. On September 13, 1993, President Clinton forced Israeli Prime Minister Yitzhak Rabin to shake Yasser Arafat's hand at a much-celebrated White House signing ceremony. Rabin's reluctance was not just personal, but symbolic of the opposition of all Israeli leaders to giving up any Palestinian territory. The Oslo Accords called for an interim agreement. During the "interim," the PLO would take over the administration of Jericho and most of Gaza, to be followed by the eight largest cities in the West Bank and small surrounding areas. The areas in which the PLO had both civilian and security responsibility never increased to more than about 12 percent of the West Bank.

Under the terms of Oslo, within five years there were to be "final status" negotiations on the following issues: (1) The status of Jerusalem, (2) the status of Palestinian refugees, and (3) the status of Israeli settlements in the West Bank and Gaza. A phased turnover of land to full Palestinian control would supposedly take place during that time. But Israel immediately stonewalled, blocking implementation on all main points.

The Palestinian left organizations vehemently opposed Oslo—with good reason. So too did Hamas, the Islamic Resistance Movement, which formed in 1987. Hamas, an offshoot of the Egyptian Muslim Brotherhood, had in the beginning been allowed by the

Israeli authorities to operate its social services quite freely in the West Bank and Gaza. Hamas was not part of the PLO, and Israel originally saw it as a vehicle for drawing forces away from the resistance organizations. But as the 1987–1991 Intifada progressed, Hamas transformed into an active resistance organization. Hamas was not negatively impacted by the 1991 developments in the way that the secular leftist organizations were. After Oslo, disillusionment over the accords set in as it became clear that Israel was tightening its hold on the West Bank, not turning it over as promised. Hamas grew very rapidly in the immediate post-Oslo years. It became the largest organization opposing Oslo and carrying out armed resistance.

Rabin was assassinated by a more extreme Zionist in 1995. But by the time the Oslo "process" collapsed in 2000, Israel was far more entrenched in the West Bank than it had been in 1993. While most of the world—and certainly the Arafat leadership—expected that Oslo would lead to the emergence of a Palestinian state, however limited, successive Israeli leaders undermined any such possibility. As soon as Oslo was ratified, the Israeli leaders began breaking the agreement. Of particular significance were the Israeli violations of Article 31, Clause 8, which stated in part: "[T]he two parties view the West Bank and Gaza Strip as a single territorial unit, the integrity and status of which will be preserved during the interim report." Israel set out on an accelerated settlement and Jewish-only road-building campaign in the West Bank. Between 1993 and 2001, the number of Israeli settlers in the West Bank, including Jerusalem, increased from about 150,000 to 370,000. Today, the number stands at more than 500,000.[101]

In October 1998, Palestinian American writer Fawaz Turki described the magnitude of Oslo's failure:

> The five years have passed and the Palestinians are not a jot closer to independence, or even the trappings of independence. They have little control over their land, and none over their borders, water resources, trade, customs, population mobility and the rest of it. In fact, Israeli authorities have continued to treat the Palestinians like a conquered people rather than, as one would have assumed after the Oslo Accords were signed at the White House lawn, as peace partner.[102]

When Clinton's last-ditch attempt to reach a final agreement at Camp David in summer 2000 collapsed, US leaders blamed the Palestinians for having rejected Israel's "best and most generous offer." In reality, it was a joint US-Israeli proposal. During the course of the talks, US negotiators, led by Clinton's Middle East envoy Dennis Ross, often posed as "neutral" when in reality they were delivering Israeli proposals.

In the deal, all the details of which were not revealed until years later, the Palestinians would have received Gaza and about 75 percent of the West Bank, with Israel annexing the remainder. The Palestinian West Bank was to be broken up into four chunks of land completely surrounded by Israeli settlements and soldiers. The US-Israeli team demanded that the Palestinians renounce the right of return for refugees. The Palestinian "state" was to be demilitarized, with Israel in control of its borders, airspace and water resources. There was nothing generous about this offer.

Al-Aqsa Intifada Breaks Out

Seven years of declining living standards, relentless repression, and great frustration led to the 2000 Al-Aqsa Intifada, which began September 28, 2000. The event that triggered the new uprising was a "visit" by Ariel Sharon to the Al-Aqsa Mosque in Jerusalem. It was no ordinary visit. Sharon was surrounded by 1,500 armed police for his provocative intrusion into one of the world's most important Muslim religious sites. Another factor in the new Intifada was the withdrawal of Israeli troops from south Lebanon after twenty-two years of occupation. It was clear that what ended the occupation of Lebanon was not negotiating, but armed resistance led by Hezbollah and its allies.

The new Intifada began with massive street demonstrations and thousands of young people throwing stones at Israeli troops. The Israelis were positioned in their tanks and armored vehicles in the Palestinian cities, towns and refugee camps that were supposedly under Palestinian Authority (PA) control. As this writer witnessed firsthand, the Israeli soldiers fired tear gas, so-called rubber bullets—steel bullets with a hard plastic coating—live ammunition without plastic coating, and tank shells into the Palestinian crowds. Within a few weeks, the Israelis began using airpower—F-16s and attack helicopters. Israel's hugely superior firepower was deployed indiscriminately against Palestinian civilian areas in the West Bank and Gaza.

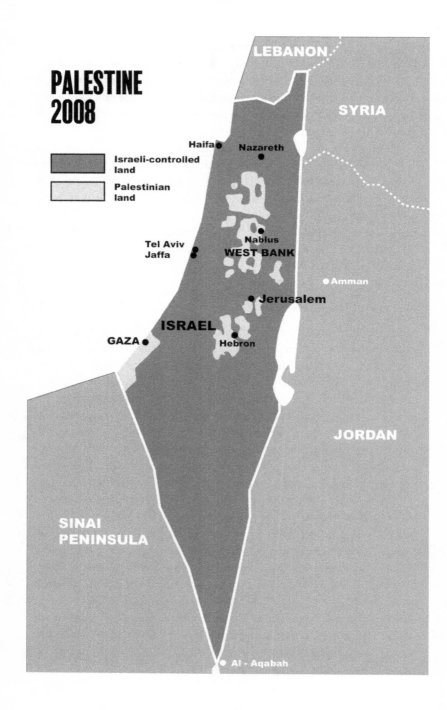

PALESTINE
2008

Israeli-controlled
land

Palestinian
land

LEBANON

SYRIA

Haifa   Nazareth

Tel Aviv   Nablus
Jaffa   WEST BANK

Amman

Jerusalem

ISRAEL

GAZA   Hebron

JORDAN

SINAI
PENINSULA

Al - Aqabah

Thousands of Palestinians were killed, thousands more wounded and imprisoned, and immense damage was deliberately inflicted on civilian buildings, businesses, hospitals, homes, schools, churches, and mosques. It was clear to this writer, who participated in a delegation to the West Bank and Gaza a month after the Al-Aqsa Intifada began, that Israeli troops sought to cause maximum damage to the civilian infrastructure. New housing developments that had been constructed recently in impoverished Gaza were damaged or destroyed by Israeli fire. These new buildings had been built with international funding and were meant to help relieve the acute housing problems in Gaza, where 70 percent of the population are refugees.[103]

Having no tanks, air force, or regular army, the Palestinian resistance forces responded with a variety of tactics, including a wave of suicide bombings inside Israel. Hamas carried out the great majority of these operations, but other organizations, including the PFLP, the Islamic Jihad, the Popular Resistance Committees, and the DFLP, also engaged in armed resistance. Only the Palestinian actions were labeled "terrorism" by the US corporate media. Between 2001 and 2004, the suicide bombings caused significantly more casualties on the Israeli side than were seen in the 1987–1991 Intifada. Still, the Palestinian death toll between 2000 and 2008 was far higher than that of the Israeli: 4,907 on the Palestinian side, 1,062 on the Israeli side.[104] The lightly armed PA security forces attempted to defend the cities against Israeli assault, but were soon overwhelmed by the massively superior firepower on the Israeli side. All PA security positions were destroyed. But the resistance did not stop.

In March 2002, a number of Arab governments proposed a settlement plan: Israel would withdraw from the West Bank and Gaza, which would then become a Palestinian "state." In exchange, all the Arab countries would recognize Israel. The Ariel Sharon-led Israeli government reacted in predictable fashion by launching a series of new assaults on the Palestinians, leading to the full reoccupation of all the West Bank and Gaza cities and towns. PA President Yasser Arafat's Mukataa compound in Ramallah was bombed and bulldozed; he was forced to live in what remained of the compound until his death in 2004.

Particularly devastated was the Jenin refugee camp in the northern West Bank. After several days of bombing and shelling, Israeli militarized bulldozers—supplied by the US-based Caterpillar Corporation—worked day and night for seventy-two hours to demolish the camp. Dozens of Palestinians died, many laid under piles of rubble for weeks, undiscovered. The extraordinary brutality of the Jenin Massacre was condemned worldwide. But once again, the United States, this time under the administration of President George W. Bush, protected Israel from suffering any type of international sanction despite its ongoing and obvious violations of international law. The Israeli military also launched a campaign of "targeted assassinations" against the leaders and cadres of resistance organizations. Those who were not killed were arrested. Today, more than nine thousand Palestinian activists remain locked away in Israeli prisons.

In 2002, the Sharon government began building an "Apartheid Wall" inside the West Bank. The wall separates the main Israeli settlement blocs from the Palestinians, while effectively annexing large chunks of the West Bank. The wall separated many Palestinian villages from their agricultural land. The International Court of Justice—the UN's highest judicial authority—declared the wall illegal in 2004, opining that it should be torn down. Israel and the United States ignored the ruling, decrying it as unfairly biased. In fact, the second Bush administration made no attempts to disguise its unequivocal support for Israel. The murderous Sharon—Israel's prime minister from 2001 to 2006—visited the White House more than any other foreign leader. Only in Bush's last year in office was the president of the Palestinian Authority, Mahmoud Abbas, invited to Washington, and then only for symbolic talks.

IMPERIALIST FAILURE: THE 'NEW MIDDLE EAST'

From the start in 2001, the Bush administration was determined to create a "New Middle East" through war and threats of war. Israel played a central role in its calculations. Bush and his top "national security" advisers, Vice President Dick Cheney, Defense Secretary Donald Rumsfeld, Deputy Defense Secretary Paul Wolfowitz, and others, saw Israel as an invaluable ally. This view of Israel was not dissimilar to that of prior administrations.

Also central to the Bush administration's goals was toppling independent regimes and defeating resistance movements in the region. This put Iraq in the crosshairs immediately. The unprovoked US invasion of Iraq in 2003 followed nearly thirteen years of Democratic and Republican Party support for genocidal sanctions and bombing campaigns. Attacking Iraq was on the agenda at the first meeting of the Bush cabinet, January 29, 2001—more than seven months prior to the September 11 attacks in New York and Washington, DC. The US government wanted to overthrow the Saddam Hussein-led government and replace it with a puppet regime. Washington wanted to dominate this strategically located country with its massive oil reserves. But the Hussein government refused the role of neocolonial subservience. Knowing full well that Iraq posed no threat to the United States, the Bush administration—with key support from leading Democrats in Congress—carried out its "Shock and Awe" invasion in March-April 2003. Much of Iraq's infrastructure was destroyed, along with its sovereignty. For the neoconservatives who dominated Bush's foreign policy, Iraq was meant to be a crucial first step in extending US hege-mony over the entire Middle East.

Baghdad fell to the invaders April 9, 2003. The same day, Rums-feld triumphantly warned Iran, Syria, and North Korea to draw the "appropriate lesson" from Iraq.[105] Based on what the United States had done in Iraq over the previous thirteen years—criminal sanctions and bombings that killed over 1.5 million Iraqis—Rumsfeld's words could only be understood as a terrorist threat, which translated: "Obey the dictates of Washington or we will bomb your cities, starve your people and reduce you to the status of colony, as we have done to Iraq."

Rumsfeld was not speaking off-handedly. Over the next four years, the US government carried out sustained efforts to bring about regime change in Iran, Syria, Sudan, and Lebanon. In Lebanon, they used the guise of the pro-imperialist "Cedar Revolution." At the same time, Washington sought to marginalize all Palestinian forces except its preferred leader, Mahmoud Abbas.

The brutal invasion and occupation of Iraq was meant not only to subjugate that country and seize its oil—previous to 1990, Iraq was the most developed of the Arab states—but also to have a "demon-stration effect." The invasion and occupation, the idea went, would "demonstrate" the supposed invincibility of US power and, conversely, the futility of any attempt to resist. So confident was the Bush admin-istration that on May 1, 2003, three weeks after the fall of Baghdad, they arranged to have the president land on an aircraft carrier off the coast of San Diego under a banner reading, "Mission Accomplished."

Their triumph was short-lived. Instead of bowing before the new empire, the fierce resistance that had characterized Iraq's fight against British colonialism from 1920 to 1958 reignited. What was demon-strated in Iraq was the exact opposite of what the Washington war planners anticipated. Despite its vast superiority in weaponry and ability to inflict massive casualties, the occupation army was shown to be vulnerable to a determined, popular resistance. Far from being a demonstration of invincibility, Iraq came very close to being a cata-strophic defeat for the United States. Although the armed resistance is not at the levels of 2005–2006 for a number of reasons, Iraq is very far from being "pacified."

The extreme aggressiveness of the Bush regime did not succeed in gaining its objectives in Iran, Syria, Sudan, or Lebanon. In Lebanon, despite the US-backed 2005 "Cedar Revolution," which forced Syrian troops to leave the country, the alliance of popular forces led by Hezbollah gained strength.

A Hole in the 'Iron Wall'

The failure of Washington's attempt to control Lebanon led directly to Israel's attack in summer 2006. This war should really be called a US-Israeli war. That's what it was. While the Israeli army, air force, and navy carried out the assault, the US government supplied arms, money, and political and diplomatic cover. Using the capture of two Israeli soldiers as the pretext, Israel launched six weeks of air attacks on Lebanese apartment buildings, hospitals, bridges, roads, power, water and sewage treatment plants, and more. It waged war on Gaza at the same time, using the same pretext of a "kidnapped" Israeli occupation soldier.

Over 1,200 Lebanese were killed and thousands more wounded. Much of what had been rebuilt after decades of a destructive civil war was destroyed again. In the midst of the war, it was revealed that US and Israeli leaders had met months earlier to discuss a new war, and that Israeli war plans had been in the works for over a year. In the early stages of the war, with its many Lebanese civilian casualties, US Secretary of State Condoleezza Rice rejected a ceasefire proposal by the UN Security Council. Rice arrogantly dismissed the Israeli assault and its casualties as "the birth pangs of a new Middle East." It seemed then that Israel was bound to prevail because of its overwhelming military advantage, as it had in earlier wars.

But that did not happen. The death and destruction inflicted on Lebanon was horrendous, but the war was not the one-sided affair anticipated by Israel, the United States, and much of the world. The Israeli military was never able to suppress rocket and missile fire into northern Israel that was a response to Israel's bombing campaign. When the Israeli infantry and armored forces invaded Lebanon, they were repelled, suffering relatively heavy casualties of 119 soldiers killed and 450 wounded.[106] Israeli civilian casualties were reported at 43 killed, around 100 seriously wounded, and 1,400 lightly wounded. On the Lebanese side, about 320 fighters and 900 civilians were killed, and more that 4,400 wounded.[107]

After a ceasefire agreement—vigorously sought by Israel and Washington—was reached on August 12, 2006, the Israeli military scattered more than a million cluster bomblets across southern Lebanon. This calculated act of terrorism continues to take the lives and limbs of Lebanese children and adults today. But even that could not alter the outcome: Hezbollah and its allied popular resistance forces had unmistakably punched a hole in Israel's much-vaunted "Iron Wall."

The 2008 Gaza Massacre

Two years later, in the Bush administration's closing days, Israel launched another US-backed assault, this time solely on besieged and densely populated Gaza. Israel pulled out its forces and settlements from inside Gaza in September 2005, but since that time it has maintained the occupation by surrounding and blockading the 1.5 million people inside. In time-honored fashion, US politicians and media assigned all blame for Israel's war on Gaza to the Palestinian side. Rep. Howard Berman (D-CA) authored House Resolution 34. Pushed through Congress by Speaker Nancy Pelosi (D-CA) on January 8, 2009, it read in part:

> (5) Calls on all nations—
>
> > (A) to condemn Hamas for deliberately embedding its fighters, leaders, and weapons in private homes, schools, mosques, hospitals, and otherwise using Palestinian civilians as human shields, while simultaneously targeting Israeli civilians; and
> >
> > (B) to lay blame both for the breaking of the "calm" and for subsequent civilian casualties in Gaza precisely where blame belongs, that is, on Hamas.

The resolution passed by a vote of 390–5, with 16 abstentions. It contained not one word of criticism of Israel, which by then had been heavily bombing and shelling civilian areas for more than ten days.

The congressional resolution was a complete falsification of history. After Hamas won the Palestinian parliamentary election in January 2006, Israel resolved to starve the people in Gaza as a form of collective punishment. Collective punishment—like West Bank and Golan Heights settlements, the imprisonment of Palestinians inside Israeli jails, the systematic torture of prisoners, house demolitions, and many other routine Israeli practices—violates international humanitarian law. But because of US protection, Israel has been immune from suffering consequences for its wanton criminality.

Israeli newspaper *Ha'aretz* reported in February 2006 on a meeting of top Israeli officials shortly after the Palestinian elections. Dov Weisglass, a top advisor to Israeli Prime Minister Ehud Olmert told those assembled: "It's like an appointment with a dietician. The Palestinians will get a lot thinner but won't die." Among those who reportedly "rolled with laughter" at this grotesque "joke" were Israeli Foreign Minister Tzipi Livni, the army chief of staff and the head of the secret police.[108] For the next nearly three years, Israel severely restricted and often completely blocked supplies and people from coming into Gaza, while also blocking commodities and people from going out. Because it is a tiny area with a large refugee population, food, medical supplies, and other necessities must be brought into Gaza continually. The United Nations Relief and Works Agency trucks in food, medicine, and educational materials.

Since it supposedly ended the occupation of Gaza, the Israeli military has regularly carried out targeted assassinations and other attacks inside Gaza by means of F-16 fighter-bombers, "Apache" attack helicopters and special operations forces. Responding to the blockade, bombings, and killings, Palestinian fighters fired homemade rockets from Gaza into Israel. Again, only the Palestinians actions were labeled as "terrorism" in the US and European corporate media. Not once were Israel's grave crimes called acts of state terrorism.

A six-month ceasefire agreement was negotiated in Cairo on June 19, 2008, between the Hamas-led government in Gaza and the Israeli government. Israel regularly violated the agreement by continuing the blockade, and on November 4, Israel killed six people inside Gaza. It followed this attack by sealing off Gaza altogether. The resistance forces inside Gaza resumed rocket fire. The Bush administration and Democratic Party leaders, including Senate leader Harry Reid and House Speaker Nancy Pelosi, condemned the Palestinians and proclaimed their full support for Israel. This sequence of events should be understood for what it was: a worked-out war plan again using Israel's favorite pretext of "retaliation"—the word that magically transforms the aggressor into victim and vice-versa.

One month later, on December 27, Israel launched massive air strikes all over Gaza, which intensified over the next three weeks. Israel also initiated a massive land invasion of Gaza. In the assault, 1,417 Palestinians were killed and over 5,500 wounded.[109] The casualties were overwhelmingly civilian. The Israeli military used some of the most horrific anti-personnel weapons—such as white phosphorous and the new Dense Inert Metal Explosive—in one of the most crowded areas of the planet. These weapons cause death and severe disfigurement in exceedingly cruel ways. Physicians noted the pattern of wounds they were treating during the assault on Gaza often were unusual. Patients came to them with severed limbs that showed signs of extreme heat at the point of amputation, but no metal shrapnel.[110]

Destitute before the Israeli assault, Gaza suffered over $2 billion in damage. Tens of thousands of homes, along with hospitals, schools, and food warehouses, including UN facilities, were targeted for destruction. The sheer scale of destruction forced the mass media, spearheaded by Arab-language and European outlets, to document some of the atrocities being committed by the Zionists and endorsed by their US backers. But Israel refused to allow reporters into Gaza; thus, most of the damning footage came out after the assault ended. Still, the reports coming out of Gaza helped reveal to the world the war crimes and crimes against humanity committed by the Israeli state. On the Israeli side, there were 13 people reported killed, and 120 wounded. But while Israel suffered far fewer casualties than it had in Lebanon in 2006, the Gaza war also failed to achieve its real objective—the destruction of Hamas and other Palestinian resistance forces. All throughout the Gaza assault, resistance fighters continued to fire rockets into Israel and defend the civilian population as best they could. It was a lesson of courage to the world. The resolve of the Palestinian people did not waver in the face of a most powerful and brutal enemy.

US-ISRAELI RELATIONS AFTER BUSH

With all the death, misery, and destruction it caused, the Bush regime clearly failed to achieve its strategic objective of pacifying and reshaping the Middle East. And Israel—the recipient of massive US financial, military, and diplomatic support—failed in its key strategic tasks: the destruction of the popular resistance movements in Lebanon and Palestine. Over the past four decades and more, collaboration has been the central feature of the US-Israeli relationship. Generally speaking, mainstream politicians and the corporate media have nothing but positive things to say about Israel. The aid, collaboration and political proclamations can make it appear that the interests and outlook of Washington and Tel Aviv are one and the same.

While the aims of the two countries' leaders may appear identical, they are not. The effort of the Obama administration to resurrect the "Oslo Peace Process" of the 1990s, or something like it, brought to the forefront some key differences between US and Israeli leaders. As the last sixty-plus years have irrefutably demonstrated, Israel's leaders, whether on the "right" or the "left," are united in seeking to expand the country's territory at the expense of the Palestinians. Israel also continues its illegal annexation of Syria's Golan Heights and a piece of Lebanese territory known as Shebaa Farms.

The Israeli government formed in the spring of 2009, led by the extreme right-wing prime minister Benjamin Netanyahu and his fascistic foreign minister Avigdor Lieberman, adamantly refused to even pay lip service to the creation of a viable Palestinian state. In order to avoid global isolation due to its far-right makeup, Netanyahu brought former prime minister Ehud Barak, leader of the misnamed Labor Party, into his government. The payoff for Barak was being allowed to retain his post as defense minister. The bloc between Netanyahu, Lieberman, and Barak could appear to be an unholy alliance, since Barak is supposedly from the Israeli left. But when Barak was prime minister in the late 1990s through early 2001, settlement expansion in the West Bank reached record levels. As Barak was allegedly seeking a "peace" agreement with the Palestinians in 2000, he was working to undercut the minimum basis for an accord based on two states by expanding settlements.

When US envoy George Mitchell traveled to Israel to meet with Netanyahu and Lieberman in April 2009, he expressed the official US position of support for two states. What Mitchell and the United States mean by this is a demilitarized and dependent Palestinian state covering most, but not all, of the West Bank and Gaza.[111] Under US proposals going back more than a decade, Israel would retain major settlement blocs in the West Bank and the roads connecting them to pre-1967 Israel. The Israeli army would patrol the settlements and roads. That would mean a Palestinian "state" without contiguous territory. Instead, the state would consist of several separated pieces of land, reminiscent of the tiny bantustans apartheid South Africa attempted to impose on the African people in the name of "self-determination." Israel would also retain control over the borders, airspace, water, and mineral rights of the Palestinian state. Under this plan, Palestine would be a weak and divided neocolonial entity under the economic, military, and political domination of its neighboring mini-superpower. Palestinian aspirations for self-determination are not part of this equation.

These were the terms offered to the late Palestinian Authority President Yasser Arafat in 2000 in the Camp David negotiating session with then-Israeli Prime Minister Ehud Barak and US President Bill Clinton. Arafat and the Palestinian Authority leadership could not accept the deal, which would also have entailed renouncing the Palestinian right of return. But the new Israeli leaders oppose even this deal. When Netanyahu and Lieberman met with Mitchell in April 2009, they refused to utter the word "state" in relation to the Palestinians. Instead, they launched into complaints about how earlier so-called concessions had allegedly damaged Israel.[112] After considerable pressure from Washington, Netanyahu delivered a "major" speech about "peace prospects" with the Palestinians. Although he mentioned the creation of a Palestinian "state," there were so many preconditions and restrictions that the possibility of talks was rendered impossible.[113] Washington recognized this, although the White House called the hard-right speech an "important step forward." It is clear that the Netanyahu government had no intention of accepting even the idea of a Palestinian state at this time.

From 1967 until the 1991 Gulf War, the United States also had opposed the creation of anything called a Palestinian state. The fear in US ruling circles during those years was that any Palestinian state, even a very small one, could quickly become a center of revolutionary activity for the entire Arab world. But as explained previously, the 1987–1991 Intifada and Israel's inability to crush it, forced a policy reevaluation by Washington. Another key factor in the US reassessment was the understanding that—based on the changed international situation after the overthrow of the Soviet Union—it might be possible to bring the central PLO leaders, including Arafat, into the US orbit.

The Bush I and Clinton administrations understood the centrality of the Palestinian issue to the conflict in the Middle East. Without in any way altering the long-established US strategic objective of dominating the Middle East, Washington made a tactical shift in 1991–1993 and accepted the idea of establishing some sort of very weak Palestinian state. The Bush I and Clinton administrations pressured Israel to go along with them, but not without strong protests. The second Bush administration reversed this course in 2001–2008. It gave the Israeli government of Ariel Sharon a blank check. No amount of Israeli violence toward the Palestinians was considered "too much." All US administrations since have continued this policy of Bush II.

Obama: Imperialism's 'Softer' Approach?

After taking over the presidency in 2009, Barack Obama, who had a history of rhetorical sympathy for the Palestinian cause, made some moves raising hopes among his supporters that actions might be forthcoming which would match his earlier words. His first call to a world leader was to the president of the Palestinian Authority, Mahmoud Abbas, and his first overseas trip was to Egypt where he spoke of the "intolerable conditions" of the Palestinian people.

Barely months into his presidency, Obama was awarded the highly politicized Nobel "Peace" Prize. But nothing of substance changed. US diplomatic and political support for Israel continued throughout the Obama administration and military aid was raised to $3.8 billion annually for ten years.

The setbacks suffered by the Pentagon in Iraq and Afghanistan had made the Israeli military even more important to US hegemonic aims in a key strategic region. Moreover, the Obama administration was beginning the "pivot to Asia," the start of shifting large-scale military forces to prepare for a new war with the People's Republic of China. In 2011, the administration joined with NATO allies and reactionary Arab regimes in supporting a multi-faceted rebellion aimed at overthrowing the government of Syria, a key ally of the Palestinian struggle. In early 2013, the administration prepared for an all-out war on Syria. It only pulled back at the last moment when faced with the prospect of a worldwide rebellion against a new US war in the Middle East. The goal of "regime change" was blocked by the Syrian Arab Army aided by Iran, Russia and the Lebanese Hezbollah movement, but Syria suffered a massive loss of life and material damage. Parts of Syria remain occupied today by US and other hostile foreign forces.

The same year, Obama and his neo-con Secretary of State, Hillary Clinton, succeeded in violently overturning the nationalist Libyan government of Muammar Gaddafi. Gaddafi himself was tortured and murdered. Speaking on national television, Clinton laughingly proclaimed, "we came, we saw, he died." Libya remains devastated and divided between two reactionary governments. The huge toll of migrants drowning in the Mediterranean while fleeing Libya is due in large part to the US-sponsored counterrevolution of 2011.

Throughout Obama's terms in office, 2009–2017, the US continued to shield Israel from international sanctions, regardless of the latter's crimes. In 2014, Israel launched what it called "Operation Protective Edge," a massive air assault on Gaza, which then as now had no anti-aircraft defenses. An August 2, 2014, the French press agency AFP reported:

> The war between the Islamist Palestinian movement Hamas and Israel has caused the deaths of close to 1,800 Palestinians . . . the destruction of thousands of homes,

and ruined an economy which was already weakened
. . . As of Saturday at midday the Israeli offensive had
killed 1,712 Palestinians and injured 8,900 . . . UNICEF
counted at least 296 dead minors . . . The United Nations
estimates . . . some 58,900 persons homeless in the Gaza
Strip . . . Ten of the 32 hospitals were closed and another
11 damaged.

Commenting on this report, the Cuban leader, Fidel Castro, reflecting
the predominant global sentiment, asked: "Why does the government
of this country (Israel) think that the world will be impervious to this
macabre genocide that is being committed today against the Palestinian people?" By the end of the seven-week war, more than 2,300 Palestinian had been killed and over 10,000 wounded. Immense damage
was done to Gaza housing and infrastructure. Israeli casualties were
73 killed and 469 injured. As usual, Washington blocked the passage
of any resolution at the UN Security Council critical of Israel, while
Congress voted to send $225 million in additional military aid to the
Israeli war machine.

Later the same year, the US engineered the rejection by the Security
Council of a resolution calling for the establishment of a Palestinian
state within three years in the West Bank, Gaza, and East Jerusalem.
Taking cynicism to new heights, Samantha Power, US ambassador to
the UN, said she was voting no because "peace must come from hard
compromises that occur at the negotiating table," knowing full well
that Israel had no intention of making any such compromises. Since
1972, the US has vetoed thirty-four UN Security Council resolutions
critical of Israel and blocked many more from ever coming to a vote.

Obama's two-term presidency dashed any earlier hope that his rhetorical sympathies with Palestine, or his early meeting with Mahmoud
Abbas would make for any tangible improvement for the lives of Palestinians. The opposite was true, as suffering under occupation and
apartheid only increased in both the West Bank and Gaza during his
presidency, as did blank-check funding for Israel.

Trump: Escalating Israeli Apartheid

Donald Trump dropped any pretense of even-handedness even before
taking office as President, announcing in December 2016 that his

ambassador to Israel would be an extreme right-wing Zionist and his bankruptcy lawyer, David Friedman. In the announcement of his appointment, Friedman was quoted as saying he looked forward to "doing his job from the US embassy in Israel's eternal capital, Jerusalem." At the time, the US and nearly all other countries that had diplomatic relations with Israel recognized Tel Aviv, not Jerusalem, as its capital. But a year later, Trump announced that the US was officially recognizing Jerusalem as Israel's capital. The Trump administration and its Israeli counterparts were hoping that the US designation would lead to a rush by other countries to do likewise, but only three other countries—Guatemala, Honduras, and Kosovo—have joined in.

Following the US recognition of Jerusalem as the Israeli capital, a reactionary plan was cooked up by Trump advisers, self-referred to as the "Deal of the Century," which sought to improve Israel's relations in the region while isolating the Palestinians. The key contributors, in addition to the governments of the United States and Israel, were a number of reactionary Arab regimes, particularly Saudi Arabia, the United Arab Emirates, and Bahrain. These absolute monarchies, while sometimes posing as supporters of the Palestinian cause, have long feared the Palestinian liberation struggle and all other popular movements in the region. Washington also sought to bring into the "Deal" other allies and dependencies from Europe and the Middle East, as well as major financial institutions.

While exact details remained unpublicized, core elements of the plan were widely known. Its architects were a trio of arch-Zionist supporters of Israel: Trump's son-in-law, fellow real estate developer and "special advisor" Jared Kushner; Trump's former bankruptcy attorney Jason Greenblatt; and newly-appointed US ambassador to Israel David Friedman. As Sami Wassef, a Palestinian living in the US described the "Deal" at a 2020 Los Angeles rally:

> It's an imposition of continuing occupation, making the occupation legal, making the settlements legal, putting all of the Palestinians in big cities, in Bantustans the way apartheid South Africa tried to do with what they called homelands for the Africans, what America in its founding tried to do with Native Americans, putting them on

reservations, and now they want to do that with us in our own country.[114]

The creators of the "Deal," along with the president, share utter contempt for the Palestinians. Friedman repeatedly stated his view that Israel has the "right" to annex part or all of the West Bank, an assertion which is in complete contradiction to international law and international opinion.

The Trump administration never pretended to be interested in Palestinian input. From moving the US embassy to Jerusalem, to recognizing Israeli "sovereignty" over the Golan Heights (Syrian territory), to cutting off funding for the United Nations agency that provides health, education, housing, and other services to millions of Palestinian refugees, Trump and his operatives offered nothing but unlimited hostility to the Palestinian people. Their racist disdain was highlighted by Kushner's comments in an HBO interview. When asked: "Do you believe the Palestinians are capable of governing themselves without Israeli interference?" Kushner replied in true colonizer fashion: "I think that's a very good question. I think that's one we'll have to see. The hope is that over time they can become capable of governing."

Emboldened by the Trump administration's actions, in July 2018, the Israeli parliament ratified into law an apartheid system that has long been a reality. "Israel as the Nation-State of the Jewish People," was the approved Basic Law in a country where such laws take the place of the constitution Israel has never had. The "nation-state law" had been under consideration for many years, but even many ardent Zionists had been opposed, not because they disagreed with its provisions but because it would remove all doubt worldwide about the apartheid character of the regime. For the same reason, many pro-Israel organizations and leaders in the United States spoke out against the law. Apartheid is a crime against humanity under the International Convention on the Suppression and Punishment of the Crime of Apartheid.

The Great March of Return

On March 30, 2018, a major Palestinian initiative was launched in Gaza, the world's largest open-air prison. "The Great March of

Return" demanded that Palestinian refugees be allowed to return to their lands—lands that had been seized and ethnically cleansed to make way for the state of Israel's creation in 1948. Massive protests erupted in cities across Gaza, and the date was of no small significance: March 30 is also Land Day, a commemoration of a 1976 Palestinian demonstration against the ongoing confiscation of their lands inside the 1948 borders of Israel. Six Palestinians had been killed by Israeli troops and many others wounded in the 1976 protest.

Despite being a nonviolent demonstration, The Great March of Return was met with extreme violence from the Israeli state. Israeli occupation forces murdered at least 15 Palestinians and injured more than 1,400 using live ammunition, rubber-coated steel bullets, and huge quantities of tear gas against tens of thousands of protesters. They also carried out tank and air attacks against the unarmed demonstrators, all of whom were carrying out the protest inside the fence that surrounds Gaza and posed no threat to the Israeli snipers shooting them. The actions were initially set to continue for six weeks, culminating on May 14, 2018, the day the US embassy moved to Jerusalem, as well as the seventieth anniversary of Al-Nakba (the Catastrophe) which commemorates the dispossession of the Palestinian people. Instead, the demonstrations continued every Friday for twenty months.

According to the Palestinian Health Ministry, on the first day alone, 1,416 people were wounded: 758 from live fire, 148 from rubber-tipped bullets, 422 from inhaling tear gas, and 88 from other causes. Palestinian officials said that 1 was killed and 237 were wounded in Rafah; 4 were killed and 345 wounded in southern Gaza; 5 were killed and 286 wounded in northern Gaza; 2 were killed and 197 wounded in central Gaza; and 3 were killed and 351 wounded in Khan Yunis. Many others were wounded in solidarity actions in the West Bank. On May 14, 62 demonstrators were killed.

Almost three months later, a UN General Assembly resolution condemned Israel's use of deadly force against a fenced-in people. Kuwait proposed two UN Security Council statements condemning Israel's deadly actions, but, predictably, both were blocked by the US, which called for "investigations" into Israel's killing of Palestinian protesters—as if there were any doubt as to who did all the shooting. In February 2019, a UN Human Rights Council independent commission found that of the 489 cases of Palestinian deaths or injuries analyzed, only 2 could possibly be justified as responses to danger by Israeli security forces. The investigation also showed that a total of 233 Palestinians were killed and 9,204 wounded in the Great March of Return protests. In all of the Great March of Return protests only one Israeli soldier was wounded and his injury was officially ruled "moderate."

Meanwhile, an Israeli military tweet proudly proclaimed "We knew where every bullet landed," only proving that the casualties were deliberately inflicted. More than 1,400 protesters suffered between three and five bullet wounds each.[115] The lethal Israeli response to the Great March of Return protests proved beyond any doubt that all of Palestine remains under brutal occupation.

Biden: More of the Same, More of the Worst

In 2020, Joseph Biden was elected president, after a campaign in which he repeatedly proclaimed, "I am a Zionist." As Biden took office, a major struggle was underway in East Jerusalem. In response to the mobilization of tens of thousands of Palestinians to defend the right to live in the Palestinian neighborhoods including Sheikh Jarrah and Silwan, and the right to worship at the Al-Aqsa mosque, Israel unleashed murderous terror all across occupied Palestine. Al-Aqsa is an iconic national symbol of the Palestinian people and one of the holiest sites in Islam. It has been repeatedly targeted by Zionist extremists who want to demolish and replace it with a synagogue.[116]

The Israeli government responded in May 2021 by carrying out a violent and desecrating attack on Al-Aqsa which left more than 400 Palestinians wounded, with 250 suffering injuries serious enough to require hospital treatment. Israeli police fired volleys of plastic-covered steel bullets, tear gas, and other munitions indiscriminately into crowds of protestors. This included flash-bang grenades launched into the mosque itself. In response, Palestinian forces fired hundreds of rockets into Israel from Gaza. Israel launched hundreds of air strikes on Gaza.

For the first time in many years, rebellions broke out in Palestinian areas of cities and towns inside the 1948 borders of Israel. Solidarity demonstrations were held in many other countries. A ship carrying Israeli cargo was blocked from unloading in Oakland, California; Seattle, Washington; and other West Coast cities.

Recent years have seen the rapid growth of openly fascist settler gangs who roam the West Bank and East Jerusalem at will, brutalizing

Palestinians and burning homes, shops, crops, and cars. The settler bands, whose favorite chant is "Death to the Arabs," are protected by Israeli army forces who often join in the assaults. In December 2022, two of the leaders of the fascist settlers, Itamar Ben-Gvir and Belazel Smotrich, were elected to the Israeli parliament and allotted key ministries by the prime minister, Benjamin Netanyahu. Ben-Gvir is using his newly created position as "minister of national security" to build a heavily armed vigilante militia as well as having control over the police and prisons. Smotrich has been awarded another new position that gives him special powers over the West Bank.

Dominated by fascist and extreme right-wing religious parties, the current Israeli government has initiated a series of "reforms" that undermine civil liberties for Israelis, which resulted in the emergence of a mass opposition in the streets. The glaring—and likely fatal—weakness of this movement is its refusal to take up the issue of the apartheid system that oppresses half the population of occupied Palestine.

In Jenin, Nablus, Hebron, and other West Bank cities, new Palestinian armed self-defense organizations have been formed in recent years. While the cities are supposedly under Palestinian security control, all are regularly raided by the Israeli army. Covering a confrontation in Jenin in May 2022, the well-known Palestinian journalist, Shireen Abu Akleh was murdered by an Israeli sniper, causing widespread international outrage. She was one of more than twenty journalists killed by the Israeli military over the past two decades. In defiance of evidence, the Biden administration statement said there was "no sign" it was an intentional killing. The statement sparked widespread outrage among Abu Akleh's family and journalists around the world.

Even before the launching of the Israeli assault on Gaza in October, 2023 was already the "deadliest year for Palestinians" in the West Bank since the Al-Aqsa intifada ended in 2005. For example, on July 3–4 of 2023, Israeli forces again stormed the Jenin refugee camp, killing at least twelve Palestinians in a single night and wounding over a hundred more.[117] The bombing of Gaza that began in October 2023, following the "Al-Aqsa Flood" Palestinian military operation, is the most intense ever. In just a few weeks, many thousands have been killed, tens of thousands wounded, hundreds of thousands homeless, and over a million displaced. It is clear that the Israeli aim in this new round of "ethnic cleansing," is to drive out the population from all or part of Gaza. It is an extension of al-Nakba that started seventy-five years ago. As of the end of October 2023, with no end in sight, more than 8,500 Palestinians had been killed, among them 3,400 children. In addition to the relentless bombing, Israel has cut off food, water, medical supplies and fuel to the besieged population. This is collective punishment of an entire population, a war crime and a crime against humanity.

In time-worn fashion, US leaders have restated their cynical upside-down refrain, "Israel has the right to defend itself," as if Israel, with the most powerful military in the region, is the victim and the oppressed Palestinian people are the aggressors. Biden and his top officials have all expressed full support for Israel's latest genocidal assault and promised $14 billion in new military aid. The latest war, like all its predecessors, is truly a US/Israeli war. It is up to the people of the United States, in partnership with the people of Palestine and the people of world, to stop it.

To the shock of US and Israeli leaders, millions of people around the world, including hundreds of thousands in cities, towns and campuses across the United States have responded by holding militant protests demanding an end the bombing and siege on Gaza. There has never been a time when international solidarity with the Palestinian people was of greater importance. As a sign at one recent protest rightly put it: "The cause of Palestine is the cause of humanity."

SECTION IV:
NO JUSTICE,
NO PEACE

IS ISRAEL AN APARTHEID STATE?

The term "apartheid" has wide acceptability as a way to describe the situation facing Palestinians living in historic Palestine. It is, of course, accurate. The success of the Palestinian resistance, the people's will to exist despite seemingly insurmountable odds, and the growing international solidarity movement for Palestine have successfully brought the true facts to light for nearly the whole world. But in the United States, the veil of silence about Israeli apartheid is just beginning to be lifted.

Clarity is required when using the term—Palestinians face apartheid not only in the West Bank and through the siege of Gaza, but inside the Israeli state as well. This began in 1948, not 1967 or at some later date. And the contradictions of the apartheid conditions are becoming more acute by the day.

An important document describing Israeli apartheid is former President Jimmy Carter's 2006 book *Palestine: Peace Not Apartheid*.[118] It caused a huge controversy upon its release. Pro-Israel organizations, politicians, academics, and media went into a frenzy about the book and its author. Carter was hit with bogus charges of "anti-Semitism"—the routine response to anyone in the United States who criticizes Israel. Carter's great sin, from much of the US ruling class' point of view, was that he had pulled back the curtain on a subject generally treated as taboo in this country: the systematic, colonial oppression of the Palestinian people at the hands of the Israeli state. The book only touches on the brutal reality of occupation and the abuse of the population in the West Bank and Gaza—particularly in the chapter titled "The Wall as a Prison." He uses the term "apartheid" to describe conditions in those areas. That it is discussed at all is a major departure for an author of Carter's mainstream standing. This reality is something that most of the world knows about. It is only in the United States and Israel where the undeniable is denied.

What really got under the skin of Israel's leaders and defenders was the word "apartheid" in the book's title. Apartheid was the form of institutionalized racist rule practiced in South Africa for many decades. Its literal translation is "apartness." Under apartheid, all people in South Africa were categorized as either "White," "Colored," "Indian," or "Black" in their identification papers. While apartheid supposedly provided rights for all four groups, it was a system of legalized white supremacy, much like the "separate but equal" Jim Crow system that existed in the United States for a century after the Civil War. Both the openly racist South African and US systems used legal and extralegal forms of terrorist violence against the oppressed—like Israel uses against the Palestinians today. It is not just the negative association with the hated South African apartheid system that so upset Israel's supporters. Apartheid is an international crime. The International Convention on the Suppression and Punishment of the Crime of Apartheid was ratified and became international law November 30, 1973.

That an apartheid system exists today in Palestine is beyond question. Anyone who travels to the West Bank and Gaza immediately confronts the blatant suppression of the Palestinians under Israeli occupation. Occupation and its attendant racist practices permeate every aspect of life. In 2008, a delegation of South African veterans of the anti-apartheid struggle visited the West Bank. They concluded that the apartheid system forced on the Palestinians is even more brutal and shocking than what had existed in South Africa. The July 10, 2008, *Ha'aretz* published an article about the delegation, entitled "Worse than apartheid." In it, South Africa's *Sunday Times* newspaper editor, Mondli Makhanya, is quoted:

> When you observe from afar you know that things are bad, but you do not know how bad. Nothing can prepare you for the evil we have seen here. It is worse, worse, worse than everything we endured. The level of apartheid, the

racism and the brutality are worse than the worst period of apartheid.

> The apartheid regime viewed the [B]lacks as inferior; I do not think the Israelis see the Palestinians as human beings at all. How can a human brain engineer this total separation, the separate roads, the checkpoints? What we went through was terrible, terrible, terrible—and yet there is no comparison. Here it is more terrible.[119]

In the West Bank, the approximately five hundred thousand illegal Israeli settlers live in relative luxury, with their own separate modern housing, roads, schools, and hospitals. The two million Palestinians there live under harsh military occupation. Their cities, towns, and villages are isolated from each other by hundreds of Israeli military checkpoints. The Israeli apartheid wall has annexed large chunks of Palestinian land to Israel and separated many Palestinian villagers from their farmlands, schools, and jobs. The killing and wounding of Palestinians by the Israeli occupation forces is a daily occurrence. Torture of Palestinian detainees and prisoners by the Israeli police is commonplace, as are home demolitions, of which there have been tens of thousands. As of 2006, the annual per capita gross domestic product for Israelis has risen to around $25,000, and per capita income is around $20,000. For Palestinians in the West Bank and Gaza, per capita gross domestic product has fallen to $1,200, and per capita income in Gaza has fallen to $700.[120]

In addition to the tens of thousands of Israeli occupation troops, armed Zionist settlers constitute a Ku Klux Klan-like paramilitary force. They are allowed to attack and harass the Palestinian population with impunity. The lowest-ranking Israeli army soldier can detain, question and abuse the highest-ranking Palestinian official with impunity. To paraphrase racist Chief Justice Roger B. Taney in the US Supreme Court's infamous 1856 *Dred Scott v. Sandford Fugitive Slave Act* decision: "Palestinians have no rights that Israelis are bound to respect."

Former Israeli Education Minister Shulamit Aloni wrote an opinion piece in the January 9, 2007 edition of *Yediot Aharonot*, Israel's largest circulation newspaper, at the height of the controversy over

Carter's book. It was entitled, "Indeed there is apartheid in Israel."
Interestingly, her column was posted initially on the newspaper's
Hebrew website, but not on its English-language site. Aloni described
the "Jewish only" roads in the West Bank:

> Wonderful roads, wide roads, well-paved roads, brightly
> lit at night—all that on stolen [Palestinian] land. When a
> Palestinian drives on such a road, his vehicle is confiscated
> and he is sent on his way.[121]

She goes on to recount an incident she witnessed between a Palestinian stopped for driving on one such segregated road and an Israeli
occupation soldier. Aloni asked the soldier why he was confiscating
the Palestinian's car. The soldier replied, "It's an order—this is a Jews-
only road." Aloni continued:

> I inquired as to where was the sign indicating this fact
> and instructing [other] drivers not to use it. His answer
> was nothing short of amazing. "It is his responsibility to
> know it, and besides, what do you want us to do, put up a
> sign here and let some anti-Semitic reporter or journalist
> take a photo so that he can show the world that apartheid
> exists here?"[122]

Not Just the West Bank and Gaza

Carter has fervently denied that he is referring to pre-1967 Israel
with the explosive word "apartheid." He defends the state of Israel—
although Israel has been a racist and apartheid-style state since its
formation in 1948. Palestinians, who comprise about 20 percent of
the population inside the 1948 borders, are allowed to vote in Israeli
elections. But in every other respect—from jobs to benefits to mar-
riage and other civil, national, and economic rights—they are treated
as third-class citizens. It is virtually impossible for Palestinians, who
are technically citizens of the Israeli state, to buy or lease land.

Inside the 1948 borders, Israeli government ministries in 2002
allocated just 7 percent of their budgets to the Arab population. That
same year, the Ministry of Education appropriated 3.1 percent of its
budget to Arab schools. There are generally separate school systems

and curricula for Arab and Jewish students. The Palestinian unemployment rate is twice the Jewish rate; salaries on average are less than 60 percent of what Jews earn.[123] The foundation of Israel's apartheid system is grounded in who has the right to live inside the pre-1967 borders and who does not. Nothing is more fundamental than who has and does not have the right to live in a society. Here, the apartheid character of Israel is clear and indisputable.

Israel's basic law defines the country as a "state of the Jewish people." The law accords the "right of return" to any Jewish person living anywhere in the world. The overwhelming majority of Jewish people have lived outside of Palestine for nearly twenty centuries. At the same time, Israel has blocked the return of the 750,000 Palestinians driven out of their homeland in 1948–1949 and their more than six million descendants. Their homes, farms, orchards, shops, and other property were seized without compensation. They have been denied the right of return despite scores of UN resolutions upholding that right.

Israel has a number of basic laws, yet sixty-one years after its "Declaration of Independence," it does not have a constitution. The reason for this is that a constitution presumably would have to guarantee equal rights for all citizens. Such a guarantee would be in contradiction with the idea of Israel as a "Jewish state." Palestinians and others, mostly "guest workers," comprise around a quarter of the Israeli population.

"Israeli Arabs" is the designation used by Israeli authorities for the Palestinian population inside the 1948 borders. But mass protests in 2000 in solidarity with the Intifada that erupted the same year affirmed once again the unity of the Palestinian people. The Israeli police killed thirteen Palestinian demonstrators in October 2000, the month after the start of the Al-Aqsa Intifada. During that same period, there were many violent, anti-Arab demonstrations by Israelis, including numerous attacks on Palestinian mosques, shops, homes, and individuals. No Israelis were killed. Over the next two years, Israeli security forces "mistakenly" killed fourteen more Palestinians inside 1948 Israel. In that same period, no Israelis were reported killed by the police, including in criminal situations.[124]

Racism and discrimination are intensifying inside Israel, at both official and societal levels. One example at the official level was a vote in late 2008 by the Central Election Commission of the Knesset to ban parties based in the Palestinian community from running candidates in the February 2009 election. This ban was later overturned by the Israeli High Court—at least in part due to concern for Israel's international standing. But it was an unmistakable sign of the increasingly unconcealed racism that pervades Israeli society.

In May 2009, the extreme right-wing cabinet and Knesset approved a law making it a crime punishable by one year in prison for anyone with Israeli citizenship to deny that Israel is a "democratic and Jewish state." There is an obvious and glaring contradiction between the state being both "democratic" and "Jewish," in that one part of the population is granted standing that is denied to the rest. Under the law, any Palestinian—or other non-Jewish citizen—can be jailed for demanding a state based on equal rights for all. Another 2009 law makes it a crime punishable by up to three years in prison to commemorate al-Nakba, the forced dispossession of the Palestinian people. The equivalent here would be to demand that African Americans, Latinos, Native Americans, Asians, Arabs, and everyone else recognize the United States as a "white and democratic" state. Public events about the history of anti-Indian genocide, slavery, land theft, legalized discrimination, lynching, and so on—without which the United States as we know it could not have come into being—would be outlawed.

Hajo Meyer, an anti-Zionist Jew and survivor of the Nazi Auschwitz concentration camp, responded to the law against commemorating al-Nakba:

> It is so racist, so dreadful. I am at a loss for words. It is an expression of what we already know. [The Israeli Nakba commemoration organization] Zochrot was founded to counteract Israeli efforts to wipe out the marks that are a reminder of Palestinian life. To forbid Palestinians to publicly commemorate the Nakba . . . they cannot act in a more Nazi-like, fascist way. Maybe it will help to awaken the world."[125]

Deepening Racism, Fascism inside Israel

The reality of Israeli apartheid is least understood in the United States, which is somewhat ironic. US support and aid, now totaling hundreds of billions of dollars, has been crucial to Israel's very survival over the past six decades.

The colonial character of Zionism, Israel's history as an occupying power, and its institutionalized racism have all laid the foundation for the deepening racist and fascist tendencies manifesting in Israeli society in the twenty-first century. Israel was founded as and remains a colonial-settler state. The effect of this fact on Israelis—no matter the class to which they belong—has been to infuse their consciousness with a colonial mentality. This will continue so long as Israel remains a Zionist state, so long as the Palestinians lack self-determination.

Much like the French settlers in Algeria or the British, Dutch, and others in southern Africa, the settlers in Israel are not merely immigrants, they are necessary agents—knowingly or not—of the colonizing power and, in the case of Israel, its imperialist backers. That the Israelis receive preferential treatment over the Palestinians in all ways is a requirement of maintaining their rule over the indigenous Arab inhabitants. In 1971, Matzpen, a Marxist political current formerly active in Israel, described the factors that have shaped Israeli consciousness:

> This society, including its working class, was shaped through a process of colonization. . . . The permanent conflict between settlers' society and the indigenous, displaced Palestinian Arabs has never stopped and it has shaped the very structure of Israeli sociology, politics, and economics.[126]

The Zionist colonial reality has cast a homogenizing effect over the entire culture at all levels of society. This material fact underscores the profoundly unscientific view held by some on the US left that the only way for justice to prevail is for Palestinian and Israeli workers to unite and overthrow the Israeli government and the Palestinian Authority. It is a shortsighted view that misses the crux of the Palestinian liberation struggle. The struggle is against colonialism, imperialism, and for national liberation. One cannot ignore the sense of colonial privilege that Zionism has used to infect the consciousness of the Israeli working class and other class strata.

Other more liberal sectors of the US left cast their hope in the so-called Israeli peace movement and human rights organizations. This argument also fails, but mainly because these Israeli "peace" organizations, like Peace Now, adhere to a liberal variant of Zionism, but Zionism nonetheless. They believe that Israel can exist as a "Jewish state," and also grant equal rights, at least formally, to its Arab citizens. They believe Israel can and should give Palestinians a state in the West Bank and Gaza—the two-state solution. In essence, they agree with the Obama peace plan. It is a chauvinist view of the struggle, because it puts "what's best for Israelis" above winning self-determination for the Palestinians. Bowing even one inch to Zionism cannot lead to a just solution to the occupation of Palestine. Believing in the efficacy of the liberal Zionist peace movement is a road to nowhere. Auschwitz survivor Hajo Meyer explained the problem:

> Of course it is positive that parts of the Jewish population of Israel try to see Palestinians as human beings and as their equals. However, it disturbs me how paper-thin the number is that protests and is truly anti-Zionist. We get worked up by what happened in Hitler's Germany. If you expressed only the slightest hint of criticism at that time, you ended up in the Dachau concentration camp. If you expressed criticism, you were dead. Jews in Israel have democratic rights. They can protest in the streets, but they don't.[127]

Moreover, liberal Zionism is a minority view among Israelis. Even mildly liberal ideas contradict the aims of the Israeli state and the ideology that sustains it. The current makeup of the government is an expression of the deeply racist convictions held by increasing numbers of Israelis.

In December 2007, the mainstream Association for Civil Rights in Israel released a seventy-page report documenting the growth of racist views among the Israeli population. The report's findings included:

- A 26 percent rise in anti-Arab incidents in the past year.
- Less than half of Jewish Israelis believe that Jews and Arabs inside Israel should have equal rights.
- 55 percent think Arabs, who constitute about 20 percent of the 1948 Israel's population, should be "encouraged" to emigrate.
- More than 75 percent of Jewish Israelis said that they would not want to live in the same building or neighborhood with Palestinian Arabs.

- 74 percent of Jewish Israeli youth polled stated a belief that "Arabs are unclean."
- Palestinians inside Israel are regularly denied entry into bars, face unfair treatment at airports and discrimination in job markets.[128]

In the aftermath of the murderous twenty-three-day Israeli assault on Gaza in December 2008 through January 2009, *Ha'aretz* published a lengthy and startling article on the preferred attire of Israeli army soldiers, entitled "Dead Palestinian babies and bombed mosques—IDF fashion 2009." Military service in Israel is mandatory for all men and women, with exceptions only for the most religious Jews. The article speaks for itself:

> Dead babies, mothers weeping on their children's graves, a gun aimed at a child and bombed-out mosques—these are a few examples of the images Israel Defense Forces soldiers design these days to print on shirts they order to mark the end of training or of field duty. The slogans accompanying the drawings are not exactly anemic either:

> A T-shirt for infantry snipers bears the inscription "Better use Durex [a condom]," next to a picture of a dead Palestinian baby, with his weeping mother and a teddy bear beside him. A sharpshooter's T-shirt from the Givati Brigade's Shaked battalion shows a pregnant Palestinian woman with a bull's-eye superimposed on her belly, with the slogan, in English, "1 shot, 2 kills."

> A "graduation" shirt for those who have completed another snipers course depicts a Palestinian baby, who grows into a combative boy and then an armed adult, with the inscription, "No matter how it begins, we'll put an end to it."

> There are also plenty of shirts with blatant sexual messages. For example, the Lavi battalion produced a shirt featuring a drawing of a soldier next to a young woman with bruises, and the slogan, "Bet you got raped!"

A few of the images underscore actions whose existence the army officially denies—such as "confirming the kill" (shooting a bullet into an enemy victim's head from close range, to ensure he is dead), or harming religious sites, or female or child non-combatants.

In many cases, the content is submitted for approval to one of the unit's commanders. The latter, however, do not always have control over what gets printed, because the artwork is a private initiative of soldiers that they never hear about. Drawings or slogans previously banned in certain units have been approved for distribution elsewhere. For example, shirts declaring, "We won't chill 'til we confirm the kill" were banned in the past (the IDF claims that the practice does not exist), yet the Haruv battalion printed some last year.

The slogan "Let every Arab mother know that her son's fate is in my hands!" had previously been banned for use on another infantry unit's shirt. A Givati soldier said this week, however, that at the end of last year, his platoon printed up dozens of shirts, fleece jackets and pants bearing this slogan.

"It has a drawing depicting a soldier as the Angel of Death, next to a gun and an Arab town," he explains. "The text was very powerful. The funniest part was that when our soldier came to get the shirts, the man who printed them was an Arab, and the soldier felt so bad that he told the girl at the counter to bring them to him."

Does the design go to the commanders for approval?

The Givati soldier: "Usually the shirts undergo a selection process by some officer, but in this case, they were approved at the level of platoon sergeant. We ordered shirts for 30 soldiers and they were really into it, and everyone wanted several items."[129]

The 2018 passage of the Nation-State Law and the appointment of openly fascist ministers to Netanyahu's cabinet in 2022, detailed in the introduction of this edition, makes what has long been reality an incontestable truth: Israel is an apartheid state no less vicious than its South African counterpart. In fact, the Israeli state has only become increasingly racist, Jewish supremacist, and fascistic.

How can such extreme, institutional racism be overcome? Only the victory of the Palestinian struggle and the achievement of true self-determination can undercut the material basis for the colonial mentality so pervasive in Israeli society. A just and lasting resolution of the colonial issue starts with full, unqualified support for the Palestinian liberation struggle. It is not simply about "democracy" or "coexistence"—although both of those things can happen. What first must happen is a dismantling of the Israeli apartheid system and all of its racist mechanisms and institutions. The imperialist domination of the region also must become a relic of the past.

THE PALESTINIAN RIGHT OF RETURN

Another key issue in the Palestinian struggle today is the right of return for refugees. The two-state solution explicitly leaves the fate of millions of Palestinian refugees up in the air. While it is clear that the United States and Israel will not stand for its implementation, the struggle for return is at the center of Palestinian consciousness.

The war that established the state of Israel in 1948 also led to the expulsion of more than three-quarters of the Palestinian population, or close to 750,000 people. Israel's 1967 Six-Day War, when it seized the remainder of historic Palestine—the West Bank and Gaza—created 300,000 more refugees, many of them second-time exiles. None of those driven out in 1948 and 1967, or their descendants, now numbering more than six million people, have ever been allowed back. None have been compensated for their loss, despite the passage of UN General Assembly Resolution 194 on December 11, 1948:

> Article 11. Resolves that the refugees wishing to return to their homes and live at peace with their neighbors should be permitted to do so at the earliest practicable date, and that compensation should be paid for the property of those choosing not to return and for loss of or damage to property which, under principles of international law or in equity, should be made good by the Governments or authorities responsible;
>
> Instructs the Conciliation Commission to facilitate the repatriation, resettlement and economic and social reha-

bilitation of the refugees and the payment of compensation, and to maintain close relations with the Director
of the United Nations Relief for Palestine Refugees and,
through him, with the appropriate organs and agencies of
the United Nations.

Despite the clear and unambiguous language of Resolution 194, and
its reaffirmation many times over the years, Israel and the United
States have ignored its provisions. Although Iraq was blockaded and
starved for years, supposedly for not adhering to UN resolutions, no
sanctions have ever been imposed on Israel for defying Resolution 194
or any other resolution. Adding insult to injury for the Palestinians,
the new Israeli state proclaimed that any person living anywhere in
the world who could prove that he or she had one Jewish grandparent
regardless of whether they or their family ever stepped foot in the
Middle East, had the "right of return" to Israel and would be granted
citizenship in the new exclusivist state.

More than six decades after al-Nakba, the right of return remains a
central demand of the Palestinian people's struggle. It is obvious why
this issue is so vital to the Palestinian cause. If a people are deprived of
their land, their very existence as a people is threatened. Defending the
right of return is a key element in the struggle to maintain the unity of
the Palestinian people between those who remain inside historic Palestine and those who have been illegally and unjustly expelled. Why
Israeli leaders and their US backers are so opposed is another matter
altogether. It is not because there is "no room" for the Palestinians in
Palestine. That argument is blatantly racist. It has been debunked by
the Palestinian demographer Dr. Salman Abu-Sitta, who has pointed
out that most of the more than 530 demolished Palestinian towns and
villages remain unoccupied today.[130] They were destroyed and their
residents driven away in 1948 for political purposes—to create an
exclusivist, settler state.

Nor is this some long-resolved issue buried in the sands of time.
Hundreds of thousands of people forcibly exiled in 1948 and 1967
are still alive today. Many hold among their dearest possessions keys
to their homes in Palestine. Some of those houses, particularly in the
demolished villages, were bulldozed into the ground. Many others,
especially in cities like Haifa, Jaffa, Jerusalem, and elsewhere were

expropriated and turned over to Zionist settlers. Today, 88 percent of the more than six million Palestinian refugees either live: (1) inside historic Palestine—with 46 percent in 1948 Israel, the West Bank, or Gaza; or (2) within 100 miles of its borders in Jordan, Lebanon, and Syria.[131] Put another way, nine out of ten Palestinian refugees could be home in the time it takes many people in the United State to commute to work. Hundreds of thousands of Palestinian families live in extreme poverty in fifty-nine refugee camps. For them especially, the right of return is a vital everyday issue. The situation is especially dire in the camps of Lebanon and Gaza, which are home to more than one million people.

'The Refugees Will Return'

The return of the exiled Palestinians would not mean that the Jewish population would be forced to leave. This is a common claim made by the supporters of Israel. But it would mean that Israel could not continue as an apartheid state with special rights for one group. This goes to the heart of why both Israeli and US ruling circles are so adamantly opposed to basic justice and the right of return for the Palestinians. In December 2003, Benjamin Netanyahu stated:

> If the Arabs in Israel form 40 percent of the population, this is the end of the Jewish state. . . . But 20 percent is also a problem. . . . If the relationship with these 20 percent becomes problematic, the state is entitled to employ extreme measures.[132]

The words of Netanyahu, who returned to Israel's top office in 2009, were strikingly similar to ones spoken nearly six decades earlier by the country's first prime minister. From Ben-Gurion to Netanyahu, all Israeli governments have shared a common aim: to maintain and expand an exclusivist, racist state that denies the rights of the indigenous population. The Israelis want to maintain their domination of Palestine and its land.

The significance of and intransigence to the right to return was highlighted in no greater demonstration than the 2018–2019 Great March of Return, the organized attempt of thousands of Gazans to peacefully cross the border wall to their ancestral homes. This was of course met with brutal repression by Israeli forces, who assassinated hundreds of unarmed protesters and wounded thousands more.

US leaders care much less about Israeli expansionist aims, but they too oppose both the Palestinian right of return and one state with equal rights for all in Palestine. The United States wants to maintain Israel as an instrument of imperialist domination in the entire Middle East region. Israel's role could be negated if it ceased to be a colonial, apartheid state. As an implanted settler entity, Israel is locked in unending conflict with neighboring states and their peoples—even those with which it has made "peace"—as well as with the Palestinians it has dispossessed. This reality makes it highly dependent on its one true "friend" in the world, the United States.

When the apartheid system was dismantled in South Africa in the early 1990s, it ceased to play the role of imperialism's cop in southern and central Africa. Israel is far more important to the US strategic aim of global supremacy than was the former South African apartheid regime. The return of the exiled Palestinians and an end to apartheid Israeli-style would likely also end Israel's role as a regional enforcer.

The imperialists and the Zionists alone are not the writers of history. Over more than sixty years, even longer, the world has witnessed how the Palestinian masses have intervened, drafting their own narrative of resistance and unbending struggle. The central message has been clear: The Palestinian right of return is inalienable, it is possible, and it will happen. From refugee camps in Beirut, to Ramallah, Gaza City, and Haifa; from Damascus to Los Angeles—the phrase that most often rings out at political meetings, protests and rallies is also one of the truest: "The refugees will return!"

SUBSIDIZING OCCUPATION: US AID TO ISRAEL

Over the past several decades, the United States has provided the state of Israel with vast military and economic aid—far surpassing that granted to any other country. US governmental aid to Israel has taken the form of a mix of grants, loans, and military hardware, cumulatively valued in the hundreds of billions of dollars. The Congressional Research Service (CRS) report in 2008, "US Foreign Aid to Israel," states in its summary: "Israel is the largest cumulative recipient of US foreign assistance since World War II."[133] With just 0.01 percent of the world's population, Israel has been the recipient of over 30 percent of all US foreign assistance in that period. This aid is not because Jewish people have acquired a special place in the hearts of US policy makers. Rather, it is an indication that Israel is seen as an extension of US power in the Middle East, an area so strategic that three of the four top recipients of US foreign aid are located there.[134]

In addition, the US government has allowed and encouraged private fundraising for Israel unlike that permitted for any other foreign state. This private aid has included the sale of tens of billions of dollars in Israel Bonds, which have been purchased by labor unions, universities, other institutions, and private investors. Annual fund appeals from pro-Israel organizations in the United States have raised additional billions in tax-deductible donations. Such tax-deductible support is not allowed for any other country.

The official figures for US aid are misleading in a number of respects. Unlike grants and loans to other countries, which are generally disbursed quarterly, aid to Israel is turned over as a lump sum at the beginning of each fiscal year. It goes into Israel's general fund budget, and what happens after that is a mystery. This has added billions of dollars in hidden additional interest costs to the US Treasury, and allowed Israel to reap billions of additional dollars in interest earnings on the money delivered upfront. There is also significant military and other government aid to Israel that is not officially listed. To mention just one example, when Israel launched its devastating aerial war on Lebanon in 2006, many of the bombs it dropped were "on loan" from the Pentagon. The Pentagon has also paid out billions for so-called joint projects with the Israeli military. But in cases such as the Arrow, Arrow II and "David's Sling" anti-missile defense systems, the US military has no intention of acquiring the technology for itself. Thus, these and other similar programs are just another form of concealed subsidy.

Supporters often boast that "Israel has never defaulted on a US government loan." But that claim has to be viewed in light of the reality that many—if not all—of the "loans" are later forgiven by acts of Congress. In other words, they are converted after the fact into grants.[135] The astonishing level of US-taxpayer aid to a relatively well-to-do country—Israel's per capita income, approximately $27,000 annually in 2008, on par with a number of European states—is rarely discussed in any depth in the corporate media. Even when it is reported, the actual magnitude of US aid to Israel over the past half-century is customarily downplayed by failing to translate the grants and "loans" from earlier years into current dollars. For instance, the 2008 CRS report includes charts showing a total of $101.2 billion in US government aid to Israel from 1949 to 2007. That is the official total of aid not adjusted for inflation. In 1952, for example, reported US aid to Israel totaled $86.4 million. Adjusted for inflation, however, that amount is actually $695.2 million.

According to basic economics, the presence of inflation requires an upward adjustment to obtain meaningful figures comparable to the present. A dollar in 1952 or 1967 or even yesterday is worth more than a dollar today. Expressing US aid flows to Israel in constant 2009 dollars helps ensure that these figures mean something to us today. In 1979, as part of the payoff for signing the Camp David Accords that brought Egypt firmly into the US sphere of influence, Israel received nearly $4.9 billion. In 2009 dollars, that equals a staggering $14.36

billion—nearly $4,000 for every person living in the Israeli state at the time. Expressed in 2009 dollars, official US aid to Israel from 1949 to 2007 is more than double the generally cited amount of $101.2 billion. The true amount is over $206 billion.

Even this sky-high figure does not tell the whole story—far from it. It does not include loan guarantees. In 1997, the listed figure for US aid is $3.13 billion in 1997 dollars ($4.16 billion in 2009 dollars). But in that year alone, Israel received an additional $400 million in assistance from US taxpayers and $2 billion in loan guarantees, so that total aid received came to approximately $5.53 billion in 1997 dollars. For perspective, US aid to Israel between 1949 and 1996 was greater than the total assistance to all the countries of Latin America (including the Caribbean) and sub-Saharan Africa, which together have a population of more than one billion people.

A 2023 congressional report reiterated that "Israel is the largest cumulative recipient of U.S. foreign assistance since World War II." In 2016, during Obama's final year in office, his administration approved a record $38 billion military aid package to last a decade. For this generous gift, Netanyahu sent a personal thank you message to president Obama—supposedly a great friend of the Palestinian people—for the "historic deal" which came only two years after the murderous bombing of Gaza and its civilians. The package included "$500 million a year for Israeli missile defense funding, the first time this has been formally built into the aid pact" and "a phasing-out of a special arrangement that for decades has allowed Israel to use 26.3 percent of the U.S. aid on its own defense industry instead of on American-made weapons." A historic deal for both sides of the colonial arrangement.

Since the unprecedented genocidal bombing of Gaza began in October 2023, Joe Biden has proposed, and the House of Representatives has approved, a record $14 billion dollar aid package to Israel for its continued massacre of civilians. This is in comparison to the measly $100 million it offered in humanitarian aid to Gaza.

It is nearly impossible to find all aid to Israel above and beyond the officially stated figures in the official US budget. Much of it is very artfully concealed. As part of the proposed October 2023 package, the Biden administration has asked for military aid deals with Israel to be done without congressional disclosure or approval. This is despite the fact that Israel already possesses one of the most well-funded and well-equipped militaries in the world and that its "enemies"—the stateless, exiled, occupied, and blockaded Palestinians—do not even possess an army. Even neighboring states such as Lebanon and Syria are resourced with a fraction of what the Israeli military possesses, exacerbated by Israel's constant bombing and occupation of them.

The unprecedented and ever-increasing subsidies to Israel are illustrative of the Zionist project's importance to US imperialism, and a stark reminder of its vulnerability in the region in spite of this support.

PALESTINE AND
THE US ANTI-WAR MOVEMENT

There has long been a global movement in solidarity with the Palestinian people's struggle. For decades, left groups in countries throughout the world have organized mass actions in solidarity with Palestine. The movement started in response to the Palestinian resistance movement in the Middle East. It has only grown and intensified over the years.

In the United States, the issue of Palestine had been a source of undue controversy on the left, especially in the mass anti-war movement emerging at the turn of the century. Some forces deliberately sidelined the issue, thereby bowing to Zionism and racism and tacitly supporting the official US government line on the issue. Other organizations, allied with Palestinian and Arab American groups, have consistently pushed Palestine to the forefront of the movement. These groups have demonstrated that the issue of Palestine is inextricably linked to the struggle against imperialism in the Middle East.

Progressives in the United States have a special duty to raise the issue of Palestine and demand self-determination, justice, and the right of return for Palestinians. The US government has provided hundreds of billions of dollars to prop up the Israeli state. Israel is its watchdog in the region. Washington has done nothing but wage wars and support proxy wars against the people of the Middle East. One of its main stumbling blocks to regional domination is the Palestinian struggle.

Putting the issue of Palestine in its correct place in the movement against US imperialism has been a fierce struggle. It is worth recounting how far we have come. The mass anti-war movement in the 1960s and 1970s did not embrace the Palestinian issue. Organizations in the United States, mainly revolutionary Marxists and leftists in the national liberation movements, championed the cause of Palestinian liberation. It was viewed as part of the worldwide struggle against colonialism and for revolution. But the more liberal sectors of the US movement refused to incorporate it into their agitation and political program. This was displayed shamefully in the early 1980s.

On June 12, 1982, more than one million people gathered in New York City at the largest rally in US history for nuclear disarmament. The same day marked the start of the second week of Israel's invasion and relentless bombing of Lebanon. As the rally got under way in Central Park, US-supplied Israeli warplanes were raining down cluster bombs on the Lebanese and Palestinians in Beirut. But the organizers of the rally—representing the main liberal/pacifist forces in the anti-war movement—banned any mention of the bloodbath unleashed on Lebanon. Why? Because talking about Lebanon at all would have required criticism of Israel's brutal assault. That would have upset the pro-Israeli forces in the "peace movement," perhaps to the point of some withdrawing their support. By their disgraceful decision, the June 12 action organizers said, in effect: "We protest the threat to the lives of people in the United States posed by a potential future war; we remain silent about those dying in the present war being waged by the United States and Israel."

The June 12 rally was the most egregious example in a pattern of excluding Palestine from the mainstream peace/anti-war movement, a pattern that persisted—with very few exceptions, from the time of the Vietnam War until the early 2000s. Many of the liberal leaders—and some claiming to be socialists and communists—justified this exclusion on the grounds that support for the Palestinian cause would be "divisive," and dramatically shrink the turnout for anti-war demonstrations. The same leaders would often explain that while they, "of course," personally supported the Palestinian struggle, the broader movement was "not there yet."

This type of chauvinist thinking was an attempt to prevent what needed to happen most—have the US movement against war come out decisively for Palestine, countering the official government and corporate media lies. Instead of having one million workers and progressives from all backgrounds hear about the criminality of the US-backed Israeli onslaught, and the justice of the Arab resistance, by their deafening silence, the leaders who supposedly championed "peace" justified the most aggressively militaristic regimes in the world. But people in the United States needed to know the truth. They needed to know that everyone who cares about social justice should take up the struggle of the Palestinian people.

What finally broke this reprehensible pattern was a struggle in spring 2002 over the April 20 anti-war protests that took place in Washington, DC, and San Francisco. Two coalitions, the ANSWER Coalition[136] (Act Now to Stop War and End Racism) and the A20/ United We March Coalition—which later that year evolved into United for Peace and Justice (UFPJ)—agreed, after considerable negotiations, on a joint call for the April 20 demonstrations, opposing the "Bush program of war, racism and poverty."

On March 29, the Israeli government, with the full backing of the Bush administration, launched a massive assault and full reoccupation of the Palestinian cities and refugee camps in the West Bank and Gaza. The Israeli occupation forces rounded up, beat and imprisoned thousands of Palestinian activists, and carried out a massacre and wholesale destruction in the Jenin refugee camp in the West Bank. This was at the height of the Al-Aqsa Intifada. The ANSWER Coalition responded to the offensive by calling for the reorienting of the April 20 demonstrations to protest the US-backed Israeli war on the Palestinians. The A20 Coalition opposed this reorientation, resurrecting the old argument that raising the Palestinian struggle would predetermine a small turnout at the protests.

In fact, the opposite turned out to be true. On April 20, 2002, a myth was shattered. More than one hundred thousand people marched in Washington, the largest anti-war protest since the 1991 Gulf War. It was clear that the majority of demonstrators came because of, not in spite of, the focus on the Palestinian struggle. Each coalition had its own starting rally, before merging together in a joint march. The vast majority of participants that day joined the ANSWER opening rally, which focused on Palestine. There was an especially strong turnout from the Arab American and Muslim communities.

Similar struggles were repeated in the lead-up to demonstrations on March 20, 2004—the first anniversary of the US invasion of Iraq, and September 24, 2005. Both of these were demonstrations that, after considerable struggle, ended up being co-sponsored by UFPJ and ANSWER. Initially, UFPJ opposed both unity with ANSWER and the inclusion of any demand related to Palestine. In both 2004 and 2005, campaigns by ANSWER and Arab American, Muslim, and other organizations prevailed. Unified protests took place with demands calling for an end to colonial occupation in Palestine as well as Iraq. On September 24, 2005, more than 300,000 people marched in Washington. These struggles helped bring an end to the demonization of the Palestinian cause within the anti-war and other progressive movements.

When Israel launched its murderous assault on Gaza in late December 2008, tens of thousands of people were in the streets within days. Such a response would have been hard to imagine even a decade earlier. The wave of protests not only in cities in the Middle East and Europe but also in cities and towns throughout the United States was unprecedented. It showed a growing understanding that many people who seek justice are tied to the Palestinian struggle.

Another positive development inside the United States was the rise of the boycott, divestment, and sanctions (BDS) movement aimed at targeting businesses, schools, and institutions that do business with apartheid Israel, along with the movement for an academic and cultural boycott of Israel. Originally called by Palestinian organizations, the movement has grown in size and scope, becoming international and a positive component of the overall Palestine solidarity movement in the United States.[137]

In February 2009, Hampshire College in Amherst, Mass., divested from more than two hundred companies in violation of its "socially responsible investment policy." This included divestment from companies involved in the Israeli occupation of Palestine. The campus group Students for Justice in Palestine initiated the review of Hampshire's investments that resulted in divestment. It was the first college or university to take such action.[138] However, by 2019, due to BDS' growing popularity, the capitalist ruling class had in turn passed anti-BDS laws in 27 states, covering over 250 million Americans.[139]

Support Growing

As this new edition goes to print, the US has recently witnessed the largest demonstration in support of Palestine in its history. On November 4, 2023, over 300,000 gathered in a National March on

Washington organized by the ANSWER Coalition, Palestinian Youth Movement, US Palestinian Community Network, Al-Awda: The Palestine Right to Return Coalition, and The People's Forum, among many other endorsing organizations. It is likely that many more national and local demonstrations will continue for weeks, if not months and more to come.

But why has it been so difficult historically for the anti-war and progressive movement in the United States to take a clear stand in support of the Palestinian national liberation movement? What has caused much of the movement's reluctance to recognize that the Palestinian struggle is as clearly anti-colonial as those in South Africa, El Salvador or Vietnam?

Without taking into account the colonial character of Israel's oppression of the Palestinian people—and the key role of the United States as Israel's prime sponsor—it is not possible to really understand the struggle that rages inside Palestine. To describe the struggle as one of resistance to colonial occupation, however, immediately calls into question the legitimacy of the Israeli state, as Israeli leaders themselves are all too aware. Questioning Israel's legitimacy draws the wrath of the establishment here—liberal and conservative alike—as few, if any, other political positions can.

In the movement against the occupation of Iraq, the organizations and individuals that had advocated side-stepping the Palestinian struggle were misguided at best. Artificially separating the US occupation of Iraq from the US-backed Israeli occupation of Palestine—geographically, only a few hundred miles away—does violence to reality. It ignores what the US ruling class is trying to accomplish in the Middle East. Washington seeks to turn Iraq into a permanent colony and control its rich oil resources. But that is not all. The US ruling class aims to subjugate and remold the entire region to fit neatly into its expanding empire, as its 2011 interventions in Libya and Syria most clearly highlight.

"Washington" refers to the Republicans and Democrats in equal measure. Both are parties of the rich, parties of imperialism. No matter which one is running the executive branch and international affairs at a particular time, they both view Israel as a critical instrument in their quest for regional domination. For the Democratic Party establishment, as for the Republicans, support for Israel is

nonnegotiable, because it is nonnegotiable for the imperialist establishment as a whole. Leaders of the anti-war movement who rest their
hopes for the future on the Democrats are under heavy pressure to
withhold support for the Palestinian struggle, or preferably, to keep
it off the movement's agenda altogether.

Counting on the Democrats is counting on an illusion, as the
outcome of the 2008 election has shown. After running a perceived
"anti-war" campaign, the Obama administration made vague and
hedged promises of withdrawing US troops from Iraq by the end of
2011. This still has not happened, as US bases are currently being
shelled by Iraqi resistance forces in acts of solidarity with the Palestinian resistance. Despite these promises, Obama instead deployed tens
of thousands of troops to Afghanistan, with the US not withdrawing
troops until 2020. While there are conflicts between the Washington
and Tel Aviv governments, the Obama, Trump, and Biden administrations have all sent Israel tens of billions in military aid throughout
their presidencies combined, without hesitation.

The larger US objective in the Middle East is predicated on destroying all opposition in the region. At the top of their list of targets are
the Palestinian and other resistance movements and independent
states in the area. The Palestinian resistance, despite heavy losses
suffered in decades of struggle against overwhelming odds, remains
undefeated and deeply rooted in the population.

The Palestinian cause, moreover, is central to the overall struggle in the Middle East. Defeating the Palestinians would be a great
victory for imperialism and a big setback for the Arab people as a
whole. Conversely, a victory for the Palestinians would be a step
forward for Palestinians, Arabs, and all working-class and progressive
people in the world. As Elias Rashmawi of the Free Palestine Alliance
and the ANSWER Coalition put it:

> Those who are clear on national and class interests, the
> intersecting interests of the Palestinian people with the
> struggling people of the world, whether it be the Filipinos,
> the Cubans, the Colombians, or the different oppressed
> communities within the United States, who realize that
> a victory, or even an advance in Palestine, is not only
> an advance for the Palestinian people, but is in fact an

advance for all. The vast majority of those struggling in the world know that they are fighting for their dignity, everybody's dignity, fighting for a better society, for a better social structure, for control of our resources. We are fighting for an international solidarity that can actually bind us together. We are fighting for a better future. We are not fighting because we love to fight. On the contrary, we are fighting because we want a better life.

The ANSWER Coalition has been anchored in the real needs of not just Palestinians but people in the United States—the working class, the poor, the unions. Why is that? Because it sees the connection and it knows that the empire should not just be beautified and made into a gentler empire. The empire must be defeated. That is precisely the genuine aspiration for most people in the world.[140]

The issue of Palestine, as Rashmawi pointed out, is not just about the just struggle of one people. It has long been a dividing line in the anti-war and progressive movement between reformists and revolutionaries, between those who want a "gentler empire" and those who know that the only answer is to defeat imperialism. This is an ongoing struggle.

Due first and foremost to the determined resistance of the Palestinian people, and with the work of anti-imperialist forces here, support for Palestine is broader and deeper in the US anti-war movement than at any previous time.

THE 'IRRECONCILABLE CONFLICT' AND THE FUTURE

The irreconcilable contradiction in the Middle East remains as real today as it has been throughout the past century. At its core is not a "clash of civilizations," as reactionaries like Samuel Huntington and Bernard Lewis have asserted. It is not a "clash" between religions or peoples. It is instead a struggle between imperialism and its allies on the one hand, and the peoples of the region—Arab, Iranian, Kurdish, and others—who seek true liberation on the other.

There have been fourteen US presidential administrations since World War II—half Democratic, half Republican. Middle East policy has taken on different titles: the Truman Doctrine, the Eisenhower Doctrine, the Nixon Doctrine, the Carter Doctrine, "Dual Containment," and more. While the tactics have changed over time, the central, fixed objective has not: US domination of the region. This imperialist goal cannot be reconciled with the aspirations of the peoples of the Middle East. Another and key irreconcilable conflict within the broader struggle in the Middle East is that between the apartheid state of Israel and the Palestinians. Israel is not just a state that occupies Palestine or a part of it. Israel's aim is the negation, the destruction of the Palestinian people.

"Irreconcilable" does not mean "unsolvable." But it does mean that the contradiction cannot be reconciled within the presently existing structures of society. In this regard, it is similar to another irreconcilable contradiction, that between the capitalists and labor. The relationship of forces between capitalists and workers can shift in the course of the ongoing struggle, but class conflict can never be resolved within the framework of capitalism. The capitalists will always seek to maximize their profits at the expense of the workers. That will only end with the end of capitalism and its replacement by a new socialist system.

In spite of its powerful military, European-style standard of living, and the support of the world's lone superpower, Israel and its supporters are perpetually haunted by the idea that Israel could disappear as a state. What haunts them is not a ghost, but a living people who have refused to fade quietly into the mists of history. Countless Israeli leaders have tried to make them disappear, maintaining as Golda Meir did that "there is no such thing as a Palestinian people." A remarkable statement from a former Israeli prime minister and self-proclaimed terrorist, Menachem Begin, explains why erasing the name "Palestine" is such a critical issue for the Zionists. Begin spoke to a member of an Israeli kibbutz in 1969:

> My friend, take care. When you recognize the concept of "Palestine," you demolish your right to live in Ein Hahoresh [the kibbutz]. If this is Palestine and not the land of Israel, then you are conquerors and not tillers of the land. You are invaders. If this is Palestine, then it belongs to a people who lived here before you came.[141]

There is nothing ambiguous about his statement. If you accept that there is such a place as Palestine, said Begin, then there must be a Palestinian people. He admitted candidly that the very existence of the Palestinians makes Israel an illegitimate, colonial state. The greatest threat to Israel—an existential threat in the most literal sense of the word—is that the Palestinian people exist.

The Israeli response to this threat has been to find every possible means over the past six decades to drive the Palestinians out: expulsion, massacres, torture, house demolitions, the Apartheid Wall, economic strangulation, endless checkpoints, and every other conceivable form of harassment. Israel's fundamental problem is that the Palestinians have not gone away. On the contrary today, for the first time since 1948, the Palestinian population inside British Mandate Palestine exceeds the Israeli Jewish population.

So, what now? Much of the territory for a two-state solution—always of very dubious viability—now sits under Israeli settlements.

If the Israelis seek to annex the West Bank, or most of it, what will happen to the Palestinian population? The Palestinians will not accept a bantustan. If it is imposed, the resistance will continue. Would Israel try to carry out another mass expulsion from the West Bank and perhaps inside the 1948 borders? Since October 7, 2023, the Israeli government has waged a massive ethnic cleansing campaign in Gaza, displacing over a million civilians through maniacal airstrikes and a ground invasion which very well may end in defeat. However, Israeli leaders have issued contradictory statements on what it hopes to achieve in Gaza aside from "eliminating" Hamas, a task it has thus far failed mightily in achieving. The more openly fascist and genocidal officials call for a second nakba and a permanent annexation of Gaza, while others express either caution or uncertainty. An Israeli ministry has announced plans to forcibly displace two million Gazans into a "tent city" in Egypt's Sinai Peninsula financed by Qatar, but this proposal has yet to be accepted by any party, most importantly the US. Without US support, Israel would be completely isolated in the world. Neither US leaders, nor the rest of the world, could accept the official legalization by Israel of an apartheid system, and it remains to be seen what their reaction will be to a clear campaign of ethnically cleansing the Gaza Strip. The recent acts of the Israeli state highlight what many have long known: the two-state solution remains an impractical and undesirable "resolution" to the issue of colonialism, occupation, and apartheid.

There is, of course, another alternative: one state, secular and democratic, with equal rights for all. While politicians in both Israel and the United States treat this outcome as "unthinkable" or "a catastrophe," it is the one that holds the greatest possibility for resolving the "irreconcilable contradiction."[142] Many Palestinians support this alternative and so do a small but significant number of Jewish Israelis. According to imprisoned general-secretary of the PFLP, Ahmed Saadat, the one-state solution is the only acceptable outcome:

> Some have argued that the current reality is pushing towards a two-state solution—an Israeli state next to a Palestinian state based on the pre-1967 borders. Of course, this solution involves ignoring the right of return, or replacing it with reparations. We in the PFLP argue that

forcing such a solution on the Palestinian people will not end the struggle. The two-state solution that is based on the racist notion of "a national, homogeneous Jewish state" totally disregards the fact that over 1.3 million Palestinians—20 percent of the entire population—live inside "Israel." This will continue to permit the causes of conflict to remain inside Israel. Therefore, the solution based on two states is a myth.

Our people's quest, like any other people, is a democratic and free society. This democratic state—the only state form that can produce social and economic development—cannot be led or dominated by the parasitic and comprador bourgeoisie, but by a unity of the popular forces that share structural interests in national independence, return to the homeland, popular democracy and economic development. This is, simply, our view in the PFLP, and the view of the national, democratic liberation movement.[143]

Throughout most of recent history, the prospects for the Palestinian cause have looked bleak. Again and again, the Palestinians have been counted out—in 1948, 1967, 1971, 1982, 2002, 2008, 2014, 2018, 2020, and still as of this writing. After the defeat of Iraq in the first Gulf War and the overthrow of the Soviet Union, both Bush I and Clinton believed they could end the Palestinian struggle through the "peace process." Both were wrong. The Palestinians have confronted seemingly overwhelming power aimed at destroying them. The triple alliance of US imperialism, Israel, and the reactionary Arab regimes has always wished—for separate but related reasons—to liquidate the Palestinian resistance once and for all.

Unable to crush the Palestinians using strictly military means, the United States and its allies in the region had sought to divide in order to conquer. Since the beginning of the Oslo process, Washington has promoted civil war among the Palestinians. Militarily, the bombing of Libya and subsequent US-led overthrow of Muammar Gaddafi, as well as the destabilization of Syria and attempts to overthrow the Assad government have severely weakened the historic allies of

Palestine. Diplomatically, the US and its allies have sought to drive a wedge between Palestine and the Gulf monarchies, highlighted by the Abraham Accords. Economically, it has waged war against anti-imperialist governments such as Iran with unrelenting sanctions. Today, the US government continues to support the Palestinian Authority led by Mahmoud Abbas, which has tenuous control in small parts of the West Bank, while opposing the Hamas government in Gaza. Despite doing great damage, neither repression nor division has succeeded in destroying the Palestinian resistance. It has intensified it.

That the Palestinian people still stand and resist is testimony to what a courageous, determined, deeply rooted, and heroic resistance movement can accomplish. The Palestinians have long suffered, and continue to suffer greatly today. But they have not been defeated, and the Israelis are not winning. Above all, it is the steadfastness of the Palestinian and other resistance movements in the region that has forced the leaders of the US Empire to rethink their tactics once again. Resistance has reaffirmed the truth—the imperialists and their lackeys are not invincible.

While the Palestinians have not been defeated, they cannot achieve victory by themselves. They have fended off the combined forces of great powers, but cannot completely overcome them alone. The prospects for victory inside Palestine are indissolubly linked to revolutionary developments in neighboring Arab states and other countries around the world—and nowhere more than in the United States.

APPENDICES

ISRAEL: BASE OF WESTERN IMPERIALISM

Pamphlet by Abdel Wahab el-Messiri, published by the Ad Hoc Committee on the Middle East in May 1969. Slight stylistic changes have been made to the original.

About the Author

Abdel el-Messiri was born in Egypt in 1938. He received his BA at Alexandria University in 1959 and his MA at Columbia University in 1963. Mr. el-Messiri taught American literature at Rutgers University, where he received his PhD in 1969.

He is the author of several articles on American and Western literature, which appeared in Arab and American periodicals.

Israel: Base of Western Imperialism was originally published in *Arab Journal, Special Summer issue,* 1968. The *Journal* is the English-language magazine of the Organization of Arab Students in the United States and Canada.

The author has somewhat expanded and revised his article for the present publication.

Mr. el-Messiri has focused on two historical aspects of the Zionist state which will be of special interest to those concerned with the question of self-determination in the Middle East. One deals with Israel as a jumping-off point for imperialist control, and documents that this was indeed the orientation of Zionist leaders in concert with colonial expansionists.

The second aspect of his analysis is particularly relevant to current developments in this country as well as in the Middle East: a discussion of the relations between Israel and the Afro-Asian and developing nations, it puts into its global context the solidarity that has begun to be expressed with the Palestinian guerrillas in the ranks of American anti-imperialist militants.

Palestine as a Jumping-off Point

Many people in the Western world blame Arab belligerence for some of the peculiar traits of the state of Israel. One such trait is its failure to be an integral part of the cultural and economic structure of the region. Although the Arab struggle against the Zionist state has no doubt helped isolate Israel and contributed to the development of its peculiar, unnatural character, it is also true that the peculiarities of the present Zionist state are inherent in Zionist ideology. The execution is a faithful fulfillment of the idea.

The idea was conceived in nineteenth-century Europe. When the Austrian journalist Herzl attended the Dreyfus trials in Paris, he was disturbed by what he saw. There in Paris he decided that a place, any place, in the backward continents of Asia and Africa, would provide a solution for the problems of European Jewry. Indeed, in a nineteenth-century imperialistic Europe haunted with its own dreams of the white man's burden, it was quite customary "to export European tensions" to Africa and Asia. For example, overproduction of commodities could be solved through the Indian market, and lack of raw materials for British factories could be solved by converting Egypt into a cotton plantation. It was all simple and civilized—for the exploiters. So in this context the Jewish Question could be solved by applying the same magic formula.

Herzl discovered the formula and spent the rest of his life shuttling from one imperial power to another. He first approached the Turkish sultan and the German kaiser. Later, he tried to contact the king of Italy and was granted audience with the anti-semitic Russian Interior Minister Von Plehve.

In a journal entry dated September 23, 1902, Herzl gives a detailed list of the colonialists he thought he was relentlessly manipulating:

> The figures in my chess game now are Cecil Rhodes (with whom I am to meet after his return from Scotland); Roosevelt, the new President (through Gotthiel), the King of

England (through the Bishop of Ripon); the Czar (through General Von Hess), etc.[144]

Writing to one of the chess figures of his game, Sir Cecil Rhodes, Herzl said:

> You are being invited to help make history. That cannot frighten you, nor will you laugh at it. It is not in your accustomed line; it doesn't involve Africa, but a piece of Asia Minor, not Englishmen but Jews. But had this been on your path, you would have done it by now.
>
> How, then, do I happen to turn to you . . . ? Because it is something colonial.[145]

Like many colonialists of ninteenth-century Europe, Herzl thought of the Jewish state as a partial fulfillment of the white man's burden. In a letter sent, in 1896, to the grand duke of Baden, Herzl wrote:

> If it is God's will that we return to our historic father-land, we should like to do so as representatives of Western civilization and bring cleanliness, order and the well-established customs of the Occident to this plague-ridden, blighted corner of the Orient.[146]

As an outpost of European progress, the Zionist state held great promise for Europe. Apart from restoring cleanliness to that "plague-spot of the Orient," the Zionists also planned to "build rail roads into Asia—the high-way of the civilized peoples."[147] The Zionist state was designed to be a fortress against Asia, "a vanguard against barbarism."[148]

This viewing of the Zionist state as an extension of the West and as an outpost for Western imperialism, was not solely Herzl's. Many Zionists tend to identify themselves with European colonizers. Ben-Gurion, in *Rebirth and Destiny,* evoked the image of the conquis-tadors to describe the Zionist settlers: "We were not just working—we were conquering, conquering, conquering a land. We were a company of conquistadors."[149]

The image of the French colons in Tunisia or British settlers in Canada and Australia was Weizmann's favorite. In a conversation with Lord Cecil in April 1917, Weizmann once reminisced, "I ventured the opinion that the Zionist Organization had—even then—done more constructive work in Palestine than the French in Tunis."[150]

This same tendency to draw a sharp line of demarcation between a technologically advanced "European" community and backward natives is evident in a note sent by Weizmann to President Truman on November 27, 1947. Describing the Zionist community in Palestine, Weizmann said that it consisted mainly of "an educated peasantry and a skilled industrial class living on high standards." To this bright image he contrasted the bleak one of "illiterate and impoverished communities bearing no resemblance to the Zionist community."[151]

While Weizmann and Ben-Gurion use imagery that gilds and somewhat purifies reality, Jabotinsky, like his disciple Begin, embarrasses the Zionists by his frankness. (Jabotinsky was the leader of the right-wing "Revisionist" movement. His follower Begin led the Irgun terrorists in the 1942 fighting and was brought into the Israeli cabinet prior to the June war—ed.) In a language that smacks of racism, he wrote to [US] Sen. O. Grusenberg declaring that he did not admire oriental culture. "We Jews are Europeans. . . . What do we have in common with the 'Orient?' And everything that is 'oriental' is doomed."[152] Therefore, he did not hesitate to assert:

> I willingly confess that we have no Arab policy and doubt whether such a policy is at all practicable. History teaches that all colonizations have met with little encouragement from the native on the spot; it may be very sad but so it is, and we Jews are no exception.[153]

Therefore Jabotinsky wanted the Zionists to train themselves in the arts of self-defense just as "in Kenya (where) every European was obliged to train for the Settlers' Defense Force."[154]

Even after the establishment of Israel, the Zionist state and Israeli masses still view themselves in the same way. Mr. Ben-Gurion learned Spanish to read *Don Quixote* and ancient Greek to read the *Iliad,* but never Arabic to understand his environment. *Ha'aretz,* the Israeli magazine, in the April 30, 1958, issue, reported that Mr. Ben-Gurion refused to carry an Israeli identification card because it contains a few Arabic words. Mr. Ben-Gurion gave the reasons for his refusal elsewhere. He greatly fears that Israel might "degenerate into another mere Levantine state."[155] This would be tantamount to disaster, from his European point of view.

Mr. Abba Eban, in *Voice of Israel* with his customary eloquence, defines his concept of the ideal relationship that should exist between Israel and her neighbors:

> The idea should not be one of integration. Quite the contrary: integration is rather something to be avoided. One of the great apprehensions which afflict us when we contemplate our cultural scene is the danger lest the predominance of immigrants of Oriental origin force Israel to equalize its cultural level with that of the neighbouring world.

> So far from regarding our immigrants from oriental countries as a bridge toward our integration with the Arabic-speaking world, our object should be to infuse them with Occidental spirit, rather than to allow them to draw us into an unnatural orientalism.[156]

If Ben-Gurion evoked the image of the conquistadors and Weizmann that of the colons, Eban evokes that of the Yankee in Latin America.

> What we aspire to is not the relationship which exists between Lebanon and Syria, it is far more akin to the relationship between the United States and the Latin American continent.[157]

General Itzak Rabin, after the June 5 war, evoked the image of the crusaders coming to liberate the holy land, apprehensive of Arab or Muslim cultural engulfment.

Israelis, in general, prefer to look at their country as an outpost of progress and as an oasis of Western democracy in a desert of Afro-Asian backwardness. In the May 13, 1968, issue of *Newsweek*, an Israeli citizen was reported as saying: "I'm perfectly happy being a foreign body in the Middle East." The Zionist state, in other words,

since its birth as an idea, and after its realization as an aggressive structure considers itself an extension of Western imperialistic dreams and
ideals. Israel is its own jailer.

Now that the intellectual or psychological framework has been
treated, more specific details will be presented. It was previously stated
that exporting European tensions to Africa or Asia was quite customary. The Zionists actually negotiated for the acquisition of the
following places: the Sinai Peninsula, Al-Arish region, a part of Kenya,
the whole of Malagasi, a slice of Cyprus, and a portion of Uganda. All
of these places are not suburbs of Paris or London, or even Columbus,
Ohio. They are all parts of Africa or Asia. The Zionists, however,
settled for Palestine, the whole of Palestine including Trans-Jordan, for
the obvious reason that it would be easier to mobilize the Jewish masses
behind such a project due to the area's mythical and sentimental appeal.

The not so obvious reason, however, is that the Zionists felt that
by choosing Palestine they could enlist the unqualified support of
the colonial powers. Many of them wanted a base of operation in the
Afro-Asian continent.

The dream of a Jewish state as a jumping-off point was discovered
by the first European invader of the East in modern times: Napoleon
Bonaparte. On April 20, 1799, the French commander issued an
appeal to all the Jews of Asia and Africa asking them to follow the
French command so that their "lost glory" and "usurped rights" may
be restored. Behind the appeal were Napoleon's imperial dreams and
desire to block Britain's route to India.

The dream was later rediscovered by Colonel George Gawler,
one-time governor of South Australia. Throughout the 1840s he
pressed the claims for Jewish resettlement in Palestine in order that
the British might ensure her unbroken lines of communication.[158] In
1879, Sir Laurence Oliphant, a notorious anti-Semite, was one of the
most active British advocates of Jewish resettlement in Palestine. He
visited Palestine, and discovered that the scheme of a Jewish state in
this region would ensure "the political and economic penetration of
Palestine by Britain."[159]

One of the members of the British war cabinet, Sir Herbert Samuel,
developed an interest in Zionism and the British Empire. He placed a
memoir before the cabinet proposing that Palestine should be made

a home for Jews. He argued that apart from humanitarian motives Britain needed to have friendly inhabitants in the region.[160]

The colonial secretary of England in 1902, Mr. Joseph Chamberlain, because he was trying to get possession of places near Palestine to be used as an assemblage center and a jumping-off point, welcomed Herzl's idea.[161]

These are some of the views of the colonialists. Some socialists, who now urge the Arabs to accept Israel as a fact, knew of the jumping-off point theory and its importance for the colonialists.

The Leeds Conference of the British Socialist Party held at Easter 1918 warned in its resolution that the Balfour Declaration of 1917 had been a "veiled attempt at the annexation of Palestine" (the British Mandate was imposed in 1923) "and also a means to enlist the assistance of the Jews the world over for the imperialist ends of Great Britain and its allies." Wolfe, the mover of the resolution, warned: "The conversion of Palestine into a Jewish state would mean that the Jews would be used as a tool by the capitalists all over the world."[162]

The Zionists were only too happy to be the tools of the colonialists. The ultimate goal of Herzl's chess game was neither the spread of civilization in "barbaric" Asia nor was it the fulfillment of the ancestral dream of the Jewish people. As he himself bluntly admitted in one of his letters, the idea of the Zionist state is not merely a "theological matter"; it is rather a political factor which "English policy in the Orient could and should reckon with." "England's advantage," Herzl added, "would be that a railroad would immediately be built across Palestine from the Mediterranean to the Persian Gulf."[163] The presence of the implanted Zionist state in this strategic point will serve to protect it from the incursions or revolution of the "natives." After a meeting with Mustafa Karnil, the Arab nationalist leader, the shrewd Herzl wrote the following words in his diary:

> I feel that it would be good for our cause if the English were forced to leave Egypt. For then they would have to seek another road to India in place of the Suez Canal, which would be lost to them or at least rendered insecure. At that point a modern Jewish Palestine would be an expedient for them—the railroad from Jaffa to the Persian Gulf.[164]

Two years before his death, Herzl was still thinking of the colonialist role the Zionist state could play. He wrote to Lord Rothschild of England indicating to him the advantages that would accrue to him if he were to support the Zionist idea:[165]

> You may claim high credit from your government if you strengthen English influence east of the Mediterranean by a great colonization of our people at a middle point of Egyptian and Indo-Persian interests.[166]

Weizmann, the leading Zionist of his time, endorsed the view of the Zionist state as a jumping-off point, He told the British assistant secretary of state for foreign affairs that a "Jewish Palestine would be a safeguard to England, in particular in respect to the Suez Canal."[167]

Jabotinsky, embarrassingly frank as usual, said:

> I need not dwell on the well-known truism of Palestine's importance from the viewpoint of British imperial interests; I have only to add that its validity depends on one paramount condition. namely that Palestine should cease being an Arab country.

> The defect of all England's "strongholds" in the Mediterranean roots in the fact that (with the only exception of little Malta) they are all of them inhabited by populations whose national magnetic centers lie elsewhere and who are therefore organically and incurably centrifugal.

> England governs them against their will, and this is a precarious hold under modern conditions. There will inevitably come a day when Gibraltar will revert to Spain, Cyprus to Greece, Egypt is already "gone" for Egypt is politically if not racially Arab.

> Should Palestine remain Arab, Palestine would follow the orbit of Arab destinies—Federation of Arab countries, and elimination of all traces of European influence. But a Palestine predominantly Jewish, Palestine as a Jewish

State, surrounded on all sides by Arab countries, will, in the interests of its own preservation, always seek to lean upon some powerful Empire, non-Arab and non-Mohammedan. . . . This is an almost providential basis for a permanent alliance between England and a Jewish (but only a Jewish) Palestine."

Ben-Gurion also accepted the definition of the Zionist state as a jumping-off point. The conquistadors conquered the land so that "England will have bases of defense on sea and on land in the Jewish state and in the British corridor."[168] Ben-Gurion was speaking in his capacity as a member of the World Zionist Organization.

As a base or outpost of Western "progress," Israel needs the friendship and defense of big Western powers. Consequently, later as a prime minister, Ben-Gurion recognized that "from the point of view of our existence and security . . . the friendship that we (in Israel), arrived at with European countries . . . is more important than the sentiment that prevails now among the Asian people."[169]

The interest of imperialistic powers in Israel has never slackened. The "jumping-off point" theory is now advocated by some militarists and imperialists in the US State Department. James Landes, "economic representative" to the Middle East and later head of the Civil Aeronautical Authority, said in *Fortune*, September 1945: "[O]ur rights to fly and land, even to use what we have built, rest everywhere on the most tenuous of war-time easements. Moreover, to reach around the world, or to reach eastward to China, and the Pacific . . . we require free and untrammeled access to the Mediterranean and the Red Sea."[170]

Walter Lippman on November 15, 1945, in the *New York Herald Tribune*, recommended American presence in the Middle East "for example, at the port of Haifa—exercising not only influence from the distance of Washington, but influence radiating from some local point of actual American power!"[171]

In the view of US Senator Riley, Israel is indeed such a local point. At a mass rally held for Israel on March 29, 1953, he said that the United States regards the Zionist oasis as the main base for its military and economic efforts in the Middle East. In 1968 the imperialist's view of Israel has not undergone any radical change. The *New York Times* Jerusalem correspondent, James Feron, reported on June 11,

1966, some conversations with Israeli officials. The following excerpt is highly instructive:

> This is the way a Foreign Office official put it: The United States has come to the conclusion that it can no longer respond to every incident around the world, that it must rely on a local power—the deterrent of a friendly power— as a first line to stave off America's direct involvement.

In the Israeli view Defense Secretary Robert S. McNamara outlined this approach last month just a few days before the Skyhawk deal was announced. In a major address in Montreal, one that attracted considerable attention in high quarters here, Mr. McNamara reviewed American commitments around the world and said: "[I]t is the policy of the United States to encourage and achieve a more effective partnership with those nations who can, and should, share international peacekeeping responsibilities."

Israel feels that she fits this definition and the impression that has been conveyed by some government officials is that Foreign Minister Abba Eban and Mr. McNamara conferred over Skyhawk details in the context of this concept when the Israeli diplomat was in Washington last February![172]

The Zionist state is determined to be an oasis of peace under the aegis of the burning napalm.

The Oasis and the Afro-Asian Countries

Israel, a foreign, alien body, was not welcomed by the countries of Africa and Asia. The original 1947 recommendation to create a "Jewish State" in Palestine was approved on the first vote, only by European, American, and Australasian states.

Every Asian state and every African state (with the exception of the Union of South Africa) voted against it. When the vote was cast in plenary session on November 2, 1947, American and Zionist pressures succeeded in prevailing only upon one Asian country (the Philippines) and one African country (Liberia), both of which had special vulnerability to American pressures, to abandon their declared opposition. In other words, the "Jewish State" was planted at the point of intersection of Asia and Africa without the free approval of any

Middle Eastern, Asian, or African country except the Union of South
Africa, a white supremacist settler state.[173]

Israel was created by white racism, and as a state it has remained
basically a white and racist entity. This may partly account for the
refusal of the colored of the desert to welcome the oasis. Whenever a
colored, oppressed people achieve a measure of freedom and independence they usually take a pro-Arab position.

This is clearly demonstrated by the attitude of the heroic
Afro-American people. In the forties, when the Partition Plan was
being considered in the United Nations, American Zionist organizations pressured the NAACP to try to influence the Liberian vote in
favor of the Partition Plan. Liberal, compromising, integrationist elements have always been, and still are, staunch supporters of the racist
state of Israel. But like all the ancient regimes of Afro-Asian countries,
the integrationist leaders are becoming increasingly irrelevant. The
new radical leadership, which represents a new spirit of pride and
independence among Afro-Americans, is avowedly pro-Arab.

In the last two years, the Arab cause was propagated and defended
by Afro-Americans with amazing historical intuition and in the face
of cheap Zionist propaganda and smear tactics. White America, for
the first time, was forced to hear about the Deir Yassin massacre and
Israeli land robbery. The Black Power convention at Newark in the
summer of 1967, the Black caucus of the New Politics Convention at
Chicago, the SNCC [Student Nonviolent Coordinating Committee –
ed.] newsletter about Zionist atrocities in Palestine, all made headlines
and reminded the dormant American conscience of the displaced Palestinians. They made it a long hot summer for the Zionist imperialists.

A good example of the attitude of Afro-Americans on the Arab-
Israeli conflict is the statement by the national liberation leader Stoke-
ley Carmichael. When asked by a *National Guardian* reporter on September 16, 1967, about the basis of SNCC's stand on the Arab-Israeli
conflict, Carmichael answered:

We reason that the Jews have been mistreated for centuries
and centuries. . . . There is no need (however) for the Jews
to turn around because the white man persecuted them,
and persecute the Africans and especially the Arabs. If the
Jews want a state of their own it seems to me that what they

should have done after the war when the white Western powers were dividing up Germany was to demand that they be given a part of Germany. . . . But for the Jews to use the extermination of the Jews in Germany by Germans as an excuse to take land from the Arabs is clearly unjust.

The NAACP supports Israel, while the militants champion the Arabs. The same pattern could be traced in Latin America. While the satellites and the police states agree with the American imperialists and back Israel, the revolutionary forces and independent countries take a pro-Arab position. The Cuban government, in a statement on June 7, 1967, accused Israel of collaboration with the imperialists. "For this reason," the statement went on to say:

> The Cuban Revolutionary Government, fully aware of the principles formulated in this declaration (of June 2) of our party, reiterates its strongest solidarity with the Arab nations facing imperialist aggression today, and condemns this aggression.

Che Guevara, in a message to the Tricontinental spoke in similar terms. He charged that Israel collaborated with the imperialists in its attack against "the progressive countries of the Zone." In addition, other progressive and revolutionary parties back the Arabs in their fight against the oasis.

In the Afro-Asian continents, Israel has remained, ever since its inception, a total stranger.[174] It has been refused admission to any inter-state conference of Asian, African, Afro-Asian, or Non-Aligned States ever held. In the first Afro-Asian Conference held at Bandung on April 18, 1955, the Afro-Asian countries declared their "support of the rights of the Arab people of Palestine, and called for the implementation of the United Nations resolutions on Palestine and the achievement of the peaceful settlement of the Palestine questions."

Other Afro-Asian conferences that proclaimed similar positions are:

1) The (First) Conference of Independent African States held at Accra, April 15, 1958;

2) The Casablanca Conference of the Heads of African States, held at Casablanca, Morocco on January 3, 1961;

3) Conference of the Ministers of Foreign Affairs of the States of the African Charter of Casablanca, held in Cairo in April 1961;

4) The (First) Conference of the Heads of State or Governments of Non-Aligned Countries held at Belgrade in September 1961.

This list is highly selective, and is not meant to be exhaustive by any means. What is even more important than the official conferences, are the conferences held by revolutionary parties or organizations in the Afro-Asian continents.

Again a partial list of such conferences may give some idea about the solid base of support for the Arab Palestinian people in the Afro-Asian continents, and the opinions the peoples of these continents hold about Israel.

1) The First, Second, Third and Fourth Conferences for the Solidarity of Afro-Asians held respectively in Egypt in 1958, Ghana 1960, Tanganyika (now Tanzania) 1963 and Ghana 1965. The Fourth Conference was attended by delegates from 70 countries.

The resolutions of these conferences are quite representative of the attitudes of the Afro-Asian peoples. The conferees stated that Israel was a base of Western imperialism as a jumping-off point to dominate the emerging Afro-Asian countries. The resolutions of the Third Conference specified that Israel was founded to protect the petroleum interests of the imperialists and to halt Arab socialist and nationalist reconstruction as well. The Second Conference described Israel as an agent of neocolonialism and international corporations. After reviewing Israel's role in Afro-Asian countries, the Third and Fourth Conferences asked all revolutionary forces and parties to fight against Zionist penetration on the Afro-Asian continents. All conferences condemned the forcible eviction of the Palestine people in order to found the alien state of Israel. Therefore the conferees (in the Second and Third Conferences) condemned Jewish immigration to occupied Palestine, upheld the right of the Palestinian people to go back to their land and praised their heroic determination to achieve this goal.

The Fourth Conference asserted that "the Palestine issue cannot be solved except as a part of a general plan for the liquidation of imperialism. Any solution that does not include a liquidation of the aggressive imperialistic base Israel is nothing but an imperialistic compromise:

2) Conference of Afro-Asian Youth held in the UAR in 1958.

3) Conference of the Solidarity of Afro-Asian Women held in the UAR, 1961.

4) First and Second Conferences of Afro-Asian writers held in Japan in 1961 and in the UAR in 1962.

5) Conference of African Peoples held in the UAR in 1961.

6) First, Second, and Third Conferences of Afro-Asian Journalists held in Indonesia during 1963 and 1964.

7) The First Intercontinental, held in Havana, Cuba in January 1966 and in which 82 countries participated. The resolutions of this conference concerning Israel were quite comprehensive. Here is a very brief summary of the main points:

The conference, after reviewing the resolutions of the Afro-Asian solidarity conference, and after familiarizing itself with the circumstances under which Israel was imposed on the Palestinian people and the role Israel is playing in serving the interests of the imperialists against the forces of progress and peace in the region, resolved: that world Zionism is an imperialistic movement, expansionist in its goals, racist in its structure, and fascist in its methods; that Israel, the settler state, is a base of imperialism and one of its tools; that the right of the Palestinian people to liberate their homeland is a natural extension of their right for self-defense; that the presence of Israel in occupied Palestine is illegitimate; and that all progressive forces and political parties and committees should sever relations with Israel. The conference denounced America's backing of Israel, Jewish immigration to Palestine, and the military aid given by Israel to satellite governments in Africa. The conference also warned against the so-called Israeli technical and financial aid and considered it a new disguised form of American imperialism. The conference finally called for the backing of the Palestinian people in their fight against Zionism.

If the revolutionary forces back the Palestinian people, some Afro-Asian Western satellites or white-settler states support the oasis.

There is a great deal of sympathy for Israel in South Africa and Rhodesia because the Afrikaners and Rhodesians believe that the Zionists of Israel, like them, are a white people surrounded by hostile, non-white neighbors. The *National Review* in its November 30, 1965, editorial, exhorted that Rhodesia, South Africa and Israel must all be defended as outposts of Western civilization. One oasis Rhodesia (occupied Zimbabwe), is intensely interested in lending a helping hand to Israel. The Rhodesian government extended all possible facilities for Rhodesian Zionists to transfer funds to Israel, the Israeli paper *Ha Yom* reported in its January 4, 1968, issue. The paper then added, "Zionist activity in Rhodesia is not inferior to that in South Africa. There are Zionist Youth movements working with the assistance of Israeli missionaries."

Another oasis, South Africa, does its best to keep Israel green. The relationship between South Africa and Israel, however, have deep roots and a well-entrenched tradition.

Because of the similarity between the South African experiment in apartheid and Zionist ideals, South Africans have always been able to appreciate the aims and objects of the Zionist movement.

> From the beginning of Union, the leaders of the new South African nation showed a deep understanding of the great adventure of the Jewish people to build their own land. There was Botha the first prime Minister of the Union of South Africa. . . . There was Smuts, who played a part in securing the Balfour Declaration, and whose name is written imperishably into Zionist history because of all

he did to help the Jewish people. There was Hertzog . . .
who gave his blessing to the Zionist Movement. There was
his lieutenant, Tielman Roas who was the chief architect
of the Pro-Zionist Declaration which the Government of
General Hertzog issued in 1926.[175]

Zionist leaders also flocked to the white-settler state to receive inspiration. Chaim Wetzmann, later first president of Israel, visited South
Africa and received an honorary degree from the Witwatersrand
University. He was warmly welcomed by the South Africans.[176] When
the 1948 war broke in Palestine, Jewish youth in South Africa, living
in an atmosphere conducive to the understanding of Zionist ideals,
went gladly to fight.[177] Once Israel was established, the South African
prime minister, Daniel F. Malan, was the first head of government of
any country to visit Israel. He went back to the apartheid state with a
message that Israel could offer inspiration to South Africa.[178]

During the last war between Israel and the Arab people [1967],
the racist government of South Africa announced that it had given
permission to the Zionist Federation in Pretoria to send half a million
pounds in aid to Israel. The ministry of finance of the Union declared
that it would allow the Zionist Federation to remit annually a similar
amount to Israel for the coming five years.[179] *The South African
Sunday Times* of June 11, 1967, editorialized:

> South African Jews can thank the Prime Minister for per-
> mitting the transfer of funds from South Africa to Israel.
> A statement issued last night by the South African Zionist
> Federation (Second, in strength to the Zionist Organiza-
> tion of America) and the South African Board of Deputies
> says it greatly appreciates the sympathy given by the Prime
> Minister to the delegation, representing the entire Jewish
> community of South Africa, which recently called on him.

Commenting on the outcome of the war, the South African magazine *Sondagstem* of June 11, 1967, congratulated Israel on its
amazing achievement. *Die Oosterlig* of June 12, 1967, said that
the June events in the Middle East proceeded "to the advantage of
South Africa." If one oasis triumphs, the others share in the fruits.

A totally independent Egypt that helped Algeria and other African national liberation movements is indeed a menace and a threat to other white-settler states.

Other reactionary forces in the Afro-Asian continents support Israel and have strong relationships. Right-wing parties in India who, like the Zionists, tend to think of the Arab-Israeli conflict as racial and religious, back Israel. Some of them in the '40s volunteered to fight for the Zionist invaders. During the June 5 war, they opposed the stand of the Indian government and advocated full support for Israel.

The states of Nepal and Thailand, notoriously pro-Western, have full diplomatic relations and have signed various trade and cultural agreements with Israel. Israel is also on very good terms with Australia and New Zealand.

During the June 5 war, Ho Chi Minh issued a statement supporting the Arabs and condemning the United States and Britain. The Saigon regime, on the other hand, throws what little weight it has behind Israel. Premier Ky, who wanted four or five Hitlers in Vietnam, said, "I'm for Israel." He need not worry at all, Israel is for him, too. The December 6, 1967, issue of *Newsweek* reported that Israel may go so far as to officially recognize the South Vietnamese government. However, if diplomatic recognition has not come as yet it could take many other forms. The January 22, 1968, issue of *Newsweek* reported that Premier Levi Eshkol, during his visit to the United States to get military aid, insisted to Jewish leaders, including critics of LBJ's Vietnam policy, that "what Johnson does in Vietnam is right."

The polarity of a Western oasis and an Afro-Asian desert is very well exemplified by the fact that the Palestine Liberation Army sent representatives to "stand by the Vietnam Liberation Front in its struggle against US imperialism." In contrast, Moshe Dayan, shortly to become Israeli defense minister, at the same time was making a trip to Vietnam which was financed by the USIS. He conferred with McNamara, Taylor, and Rostow both before and after the trip. The imperialists wanted his advice and needed his help. He was only too willing to gratify.

What Does the Oasis do to the Desert?

Israel is loyally discharging its function as a loyal oasis. Many Western capitalists send their capital to Israel so that it may acquire a little tan and some Afro-Asian veneer. In this way, the capital is made more acceptable to emerging nations.

Many Israeli companies and organizations which invest money in the African states and grant loans are either completely or partly owned by Western monopolies. American, British, French and West German monopolies own over 400 of the important projects in Israel.

The Afro-Asian institute, in Tel-Aviv, was established to train Afro-Asian trade union leaders and to generate in them a genuine love for "democracy" and free enterprise. The AFL-CIO, well-known for its subversive activity against revolutionary movements in the under-developed world, contributes 50 percent of the institute's expenses.

Israel backed American intervention in Korea. It opposed and still opposes China's admission to the United Nations. It also voted against many anti-colonial resolutions. The most notorious votes are those cast against the independence of Tunisia and Algeria. The colons of Israel did not like the idea of seeing another community of colons disappear. Some of the French generals in Algeria, who tried to set up a Franco-type government-in-exile, confessed during their trials in Paris that they had obtained promises from some countries to recognize their government once it was established. Those states were the governments of South Africa, Portugal, and Israel!

The same pro-Western, pro-colonial policy is manifested in Israel's support for the atomic tests conducted by France in the African Sahara. The tests enraged the African peoples because the nuclear radiation was a definite menace to life on the continent. The collaboration between Israel, France, and England in the Suez affair of 1956 marked the climax of the aggressive activism of the outpost.

This was the climax, but not the conclusion. When the US Marines landed in Jordan and Lebanon and threatened the 1958 Iraqi revolution, Israel endorsed the intervention. In 1961, Israel supported Tshombe's secession movement in Katanga. Israel also provided Portugal with arms to exterminate African nationalists in Angola and Mozambique. The November 29, 1961, *Haolam Hazeh* reported that Israel not only sold Portugal machine guns, but also supplied her with planes to destroy African villages in Angola. Very recently, a *Guardian* correspondent asked Spartacus Monimambu, commander of the Angolan Peoples Liberation Movement, about the sources of military aid for Portugal, the latter pointed out that they were NATO and

Israel.[180] It seems that Israel is entirely committed to aiding colonial powers. Furthermore, in 1967, Israel voted against the independence of Aden. (It is an open secret in the United Nations that the Israeli delegation always gives aid and comfort and valuable advice to the imperialists.) When the issue of Aden was being considered in the United Nations the Israeli delegation, I was told, lobbied against the passage of a resolution favoring the independence of Aden even more than did the American and British delegations. Radio Israel still backs the Yemeni royalists in their reactionary war against the republican regime.

One of the latest acrobatic accomplishments of Israel was the Ben Barka affair. The leftist Arab trade unionist was kidnapped and murdered in Paris under very mysterious circumstances. An article in the December 11, 1966, issue of the Israeli magazine *BUL* implies that Israeli intelligence was responsible for the kidnapping and assassination of Ben Barka. The editor of the Israeli weekly and his assistant were arrested and convicted of having violated state security regulations. The Israeli court that tried the two editors ordered that the verdict not be published. The revealing issue of *BUL* was swiftly confiscated and suppressed. Four hundred copies, however, had already been circulated.

Hostile as it is to the colored of the desert, Israel had consistently refused to vote in the United Nations against the apartheid regime of South Africa. In the last few years, however, Israel—in order to better serve the interests of the neocolonialists in the virgin continents—is trying to change its appearance. It has built up a new façade and tries to pass for a vigorous, energetic emerging state, anxious to help others. For this reason, Israel now votes against South Africa in the United Nations, and Zionists in the apartheid state apologize for the misdemeanor and point out that apart from this little, nasty voting, everything is fine and dandy.

Yet the volume of trade between the two outposts is always increasing. It is bound to remain at its present level or even increase because most of the Zionist funds, collected by Zionist groups for Israel, have to be spent in South Africa due to the foreign exchange regulations. (A similar situation occurred in America after the dollar crisis. Israel promised President Johnson to spend the money for Israeli bonds in the United States, which will lead to a deepening of the relations between the oasis and the metropolis.)

The outpost of progress in Asia is helping defend other outposts. An earlier reference mentioned Israeli support of American intervention in Korea. Its support of the Saigon regime and of American intervention in Vietnam, however, assume more subtle forms.

The *Near East Report*, a pro-Zionist publication, reported in its March 1966 issue that the South Vietnamese ambassador to Washington announced that his government "had accepted a 1965 Israel invitation to send South Vietnamese agricultural experts for training in Israel." The term "agriculture" may sound a little innocuous, but it should be remembered that the Israeli Nahal are both farmers and soldiers. The ambassador also told the *Jewish Telegraphic Agency* that the Saigon government was negotiating with Israel for the dispatch of Israel's Nahal instructors to his country.

The degree of Israeli involvement in Vietnam can also be measured by the admission of an Israeli foreign office spokesman that Israel had sent "humanitarian" aid to the Saigon government in November 1961. During his trip to Asia in 1967, Mr. Abba Eban did not denounce, in his communiques, American raids on Hanoi. When asked by the Knesset on April 12, 1967, for an explanation, he gave the very pragmatic answer that such a denunciation sharply conflicted with the official policy of all the countries he visited. The minister, it seems, confined his visits only to oases!

On the same day, a communist member in the Knesset, Meir Vilner, sponsored a motion that revealed beyond any doubt, Israeli involvement in Vietnam. Excerpts from this motion, because of its extreme importance are translated below:

1) The Knesset censures the decision of the governments to receive missions (of farmer-soldiers or diplomats—text unclear) sent by the pro-American government and asks for the cancellation of such missions.

2) The Knesset asks the government to order Israeli shipping companies to stop the transport of supplies and fuel from the USA, and Japan to Vietnam.

3) The Knesset asks the government to join other governments that support the cessation of raids on

the Democratic Republic of North Vietnam and the
withdrawal of American troops.

In the discussion that followed, not a single member of the Knesset
contested the truth of the statements in the motion. One deputy,
though, suggested that Mr. Vilner should send this motion to Cairo.
When the motion was put to the vote it was opposed by such "leftists"
as the Mapam and Ahdut Havoda deputies.[181]

Israel as an outpost of Western capital and neo-colonialist ideol-
ogies fulfills the prophecies and aspirations of the imperialists. On
the day that the nineteenth-century European Zionist ideologue
Theodore Herzl started formulating his plans for a Jewish state, Israel
began to assume its present unnatural form.

That the Afro-Asian peoples, including the Arabs, oppose Israel
is only logical and human. The history of these peoples in modern
times is one of revolution against Western imperialism and Western
cultural dominance. They are trying to pull down imperialism and
all that it stands for: military bureaucracies, dictatorships, feudal and
reactionary regimes, and white-settler states. Israel is an integral part
of this disintegrating structure.

Conclusion

When I told a pacifist member of the Mapam Party, a student at
Rutgers University, of the attitude of his party to the war in Vietnam,
his answer was, "Israel has to defend itself." This confirms all the fears
of Afro-Asian socialists and nationalists. Israel was implanted by the
imperialists as an isolated entity so that it might evolve interests which
are in sharp conflict with those of the inhabitants of the region.

By virtue of this isolated existence, the Israelis will not only alien-
ate themselves from the inhabitants' aspirations but, in preservation
of this isolation, they will move in an opposite direction.

The repatriation of the Palestinian refugees and the creation of a
new socialist democratic multi-ethnic, multi-religious state, an ideal
advocated by the Palestinian freedom fighters, could help liquidate a
racist political structure which has served imperialist interests in the
Afro-Asian continents.

AUSCHWITZ SURVIVOR HAJO MEYER: 'I CAN IDENTIFY WITH PALESTINIAN YOUTH'

Interview with Hajo Meyer by Swiss human rights activist Adri Nieuwhof, published online by Electronic Intifada, *June 2, 2009.*

Hajo Meyer, author of the book *The End of Judaism,* was born in Bielefeld, in Germany, in 1924. In 1939, he fled on his own at age fourteen to the Netherlands to escape the Nazi regime, and was unable to attend school. A year later, when the Germans occupied the Netherlands, he lived in hiding with a poorly forged ID. Meyer was captured by the Gestapo in March 1944 and deported to the Auschwitz concentration camp a week later. He is one of the last survivors of Auschwitz.

Adri Nieuwhof: What would you like to say to introduce yourself to EI's readers?
Hajo Meyer: I had to quit grammar school in Bielefeld after the Kristallnacht [the two-day pogrom against Jews in Nazi Germany], in November 1938. It was a terrible experience for an inquisitive boy and his parents. Therefore, I can fully identify with the Palestinian youth that are hampered in their education. And I can in no way identify with the criminals who make it impossible for Palestinian youth to be educated.

AN: What motivated you to write your book, *The End of Judaism*?
HM: In the past, the European media have written extensively about extreme right-wing politicians like Joerg Haider in Austria and

Jean-Marie Le Pen in France. But when Ariel Sharon was elected [prime minister] in Israel in 2001, the media remained silent. But in the 1980s I understood the deeply fascist thinking of these politicians. With the book I wanted to distance myself from this. I was raised in Judaism with the equality of relationships among human beings as a core value. I only learned about nationalist Judaism when I heard settlers defend their harassment of Palestinians in interviews. When a publisher asked me to write about my past, I decided to write this book, in a way, to deal with my past. People of one group who dehumanize people who belong to another group can do this, because they either have learned to do so from their parents, or they have been brainwashed by their political leaders. This has happened for decades in Israel in that they manipulate the Holocaust for their political aims. In the long-run the country is destructing itself this way by inducing their Jewish citizens to become paranoid. In 2005 [then Prime Minister Ariel] Sharon illustrated this by saying in the Knesset [the Israeli parliament], we know we cannot trust anyone, we only can trust ourselves. This is the shortest possible definition of somebody who suffers from clinical paranoia. One of the major annoyances in my life is that Israel by means of trickery calls itself a Jewish state, while in fact it is Zionist. It wants the maximum territory with a minimum number of Palestinians. I have four Jewish grandparents. I am an atheist. I share the Jewish socio-cultural inheritance and I have learned about Jewish ethics. I don't wish to be represented by a Zionist state. They have no idea about the Holocaust. They use the Holocaust to implant paranoia in their children.

AN: In your book you write about the lessons you have learned from your past. Can you explain how your past influenced your perception of Israel and Palestine?
HM: I have never been a Zionist. After the war, Zionist Jews spoke about the miracle of having "our own country." As a confirmed atheist I thought, if this is a miracle by God, I wished that he had performed the smallest miracle imaginable by creating the state fifteen years earlier. Then my parents would not have been dead.
I can write up an endless list of similarities between Nazi Germany and Israel. The capturing of land and property, denying people access to educational opportunities and restricting access to earn a living to

destroy their hope, all with the aim to chase people away from their land. And what I personally find more appalling than dirtying one's hands by killing people, is creating circumstances where people start to kill each other. Then the distinction between victims and perpetrators becomes faint. By sowing discord in a situation where there is no unity, by enlarging the gap between people—like Israel is doing in Gaza.

AN: In your book you write about the role of Jews in the peace movement in and outside Israel, and Israeli army "refuseniks." How do you value their contribution?

HM: Of course it is positive that parts of the Jewish population of Israel try to see Palestinians as human beings and as their equals. However, it disturbs me how paper-thin the number is that protests and is truly anti-Zionist. We get worked up by what happened in Hitler's Germany. If you expressed only the slightest hint of criticism at that time, you ended up in the Dachau concentration camp. If you expressed criticism, you were dead. Jews in Israel have democratic rights. They can protest in the streets, but they don't.

AN: Can you comment on the news that Israeli ministers approved a draft law banning commemoration of the Nakba, or the dispossession of historic Palestine? The law proposes punishment of up to three years in prison.

HM: It is so racist, so dreadful. I am at a loss for words. It is an expression of what we already know. [The Israeli Nakba commemoration organization] Zochrot was founded to counteract Israeli efforts to wipe out the marks that are a reminder of Palestinian life. To forbid Palestinians to publicly commemorate the Nakba... they cannot act in a more Nazi-like, fascist way. Maybe it will help to awaken the world.

AN: What are your plans for the future?

HM: [Laughs] Do you know how old I am? I am almost eighty-five years old. I always say cynically and with self-mockery that I have a choice: either I am always tired because I want to do so much, or I am going to sit still waiting for the time to go by. Well, I plan to be tired, because I have still so much to say.

THE US, ISRAEL, AND THE 'PROJECT TO END PALESTINE'

Interview with Elias Rashmawi, a leader of the Free Palestine Alliance and the ANSWER Coalition (Act Now to Stop War and End Racism), by Richard Becker, published in the October 2004 issue of Socialism and Liberation, *the magazine of the Party for Socialism and Liberation.*

Richard Becker: September 28 is the fourth anniversary of the Intifada. How do you assess the Palestinian struggle at this point? Elias Rashmawi: I'm glad you called it the Intifada not the "second Intifada." That's a common misconception, because people assume that the first uprising of the Palestinian people was the one that occurred in the late 1980s. However, there were many uprisings before that, most notably the 1936 general strike and the associated uprising with it. Before that, during the 1920s, there were several others.

When one assesses the current situation of the Palestinian struggle, one cannot only assess it in terms of the "second Intifada" or what is happening today. One must assess it in terms of what has taken place over about a hundred years or so: the Palestinian people's struggle for national liberation.

I would say that the main issue right now is: How does one assess the success of what we refer to as the "Project to End Palestine" (PEP)? I believe that we need, as progressives, as people in the movement, to look at Palestine not in terms of the dichotomy between the Israelis or the Zionist forces on one side and the Palestinian people on the other, as if this is a dichotomy between two isolated parties. We need to look at it in the larger context.

There is a need by the imperialist forces, particularly the US, and Western Europe to a lesser degree, to in fact eliminate Palestine. Not just to eliminate Palestine the people, Palestine the land, Palestine the cause—but to eliminate Palestine in the context of the overall international struggle for national liberation, for a better society, and for a different vision for the future.

I think the PEP is definitely not doing too well. In order for the US and Israel to succeed, they would need to do several things. First would be to eliminate actual elements that make Palestine what it is: the land, the people, and the context of liberation.

In terms of the land, the idea was to conquer the land and transfer it to the state of Israel. In terms of the people, it was to fragment and segment the Palestinian people into different entities—most importantly to cut them out or to remove them from the larger Arab struggle and the larger struggle for national liberation. That has not been too successful. The third aim is against the actual context of liberation and what that means. The PEP has in fact attempted to transform the Palestine movement for liberation into a Palestine movement for quasi-statehood, for a bantustan,[182] so that it would be transformed into a junior servant—not even a junior partner—within a globalized Middle East.

On all three points, the PEP has had some successes and some great failures.

We need to assess some of these issues as to where we are now, the status of the current leadership, the uprising, the status of the people, the political manifestation of the different political parties, how the state of Israel is proceeding and the United States is proceeding. If we in fact are tied to, and are part and parcel of the Arab people's march, we need to assess the Arab regimes and what is taking place in terms of the Arab masses.

The first issue that needs to be looked at in my opinion is the Palestinian factor. Let's look at that in three separate, but intricately connected elements. First, let's look at the people. The PEP has had as a main objective to isolate, fragment, and segment the Palestinian people into different entities. The means include the assimilation of Palestinian refugees into other states such as Jordan, Lebanon, Syria, Iraq, and others. Or, Palestinians are segmented into "1948 Palestinians,"[183]

"1967 Palestinians,"[184] "refugees," and so forth. The thread connecting all of these segments of the Palestinian people is the cumulative historical national identity that developed most sharply through the struggle of the hundred years or so that we have talked about.

The ultimate goal that the US and the state of Israel have for the Palestinian people is fragmenting and totally disuniting them. This goal has failed, in the sense that the most important issue for Palestinians—and a key anchor for the liberation struggle—continues to be the right of return.[185] Today the Palestinians who are refugees, or dispossessed, or in the diaspora, not only have not dropped their demand for return, they have strengthened it.

Now the right of return is not some sort of emotional, hypothetical or theoretical demand. We as a people require a return to our homeland so that we can continue the most important part of our struggle—the unification of our people in a place where we can control our destiny, control our resources and control our future in an egalitarian sort of society. Equality is a must. Had we dropped the demand for return, as called for by the US, Israel and the Arab regimes, we would have lost the possibility of ever looking forward to a unified Palestinian Arab people. But the demand has not been dropped.

RB: Let me just ask one question for clarification. When you said that the right of return is not theoretical or subjective, can you just explain that a little bit more?
ER: As years went by and as the dispossession of Palestinians continued, there were three conflicting views on the right of return. The first was that we should just forget it. According to this view, we will stay where we are—Jordan, the US, Syria, Lebanon, Egypt, Iraq, anywhere we are—and just continue our lives. Those who have remained, that is the 1967 Palestinians, would eventually have some sort of statehood under some framework, be it under a Jordanian federation or under the Israeli state. That was one wing, which basically said the right of return is really nonsense, that nobody can actually ever imagine it.

Some of those now in the Palestinian Authority secretly hold this point of view, but are unable to express it publicly. Publicly, what they express is a second point of view: it is good to have a right to return, but it is a theoretical right. All we really need, this wing says, is to have the state of Israel issue a public apology that says it is sorry for what it has done. Then we would have a reconciliation commission, and we Palestinians would stay in exile and they would maintain the theocratic nature of the Israeli state.

The third view is that held by the vast majority of the Palestinian people. It says that the right of return is not a theoretical, or ethical, or subjective right. It is in fact a material right that is a prerequisite of self-determination. It means the return of Palestinian refugees in exile or in the diaspora to their original towns and homes. Many researchers, most notably Dr. Salman Abu-Sitta, have conducted extensive research in terms of the actual viability and practicality of the return of Palestinian refugees to their original homes, villages and towns. What was found, to the astonishment of many, was that this is not only a possibility politically, but practical and viable from the standpoint of the individual and the collective right of return.

RB: What do you think that the Israeli strategy is right now? What are they hoping to achieve in a strategic sense over, say, the next couple of years?
ER: I would say the most important part for them right now, and for the US, is to fashion the Palestinian Authority in a certain way so that it can accept responsibility for governing a bantustan.

The Israelis and the US are seeking to eliminate Palestinian political organizations, completely gut or remove any Palestinian leadership and political formations that are capable of standing up to this newly fashioned Palestinian Authority. At the same time, they want to sanitize the Authority, so that the voices and faces would be Palestinian, but all aspects related to the real national aspirations of the Palestinian people would be removed. They are seeking an Authority that would have the façade of being Palestinian, but would at the same time be their functionary. You will find that the main demand by the US and Israel is for the Palestinian Authority to transform and to be an "acceptable" authority, so that it can take leadership as a functionary apparatus that they are trying to set up for that entire region.

RB: Do you think that the Israeli leaders hope that, due to the massive repression in every sphere of life, large numbers of Palestinians will give up and leave?

ER: Well, I think that in order to achieve that there are certain pre-requisites. In order to achieve that, there would have to be at a certain point a transformation in the makeup of the people.

The Israelis are trying to create a situation where those who remain must accept the dictates of the occupation. Those who do not, they hope, will pack up and leave. The Palestinians who cannot do either, because they are unable to leave—most of them are not willing to leave and want to fight to the very end—would just be erased. The project of simply erasing the Palestinians, literally and physically, is not new and is not an aberration. The Israelis use bulldozers, erasing the homes of Palestinians and making roads, and later set up a settlement. They have done it before, in 1948, when they destroyed over 450 villages. They also did it right after the June 1967 war.

They tried it between 1948 and 1967, as well. In fact, Ariel Sharon himself went very close to a neighborhood where I used to live in Gaza. He went to the Shate [Beach] refugee camp and removed a very large number of homes with bulldozers in order to make room for areas where the Israeli army can enter and maintain its own operations, unchallenged by Palestinian commandos that were very prevalent in the 1970s in Beach camp and much of Gaza.

They are doing it right now in Rafah; they are doing it now in Jabaliya, Beit Hanoon, everywhere in the Gaza strip. They've done it in Jenin, Nablus, and certain areas of Ramallah in the West Bank. They are transforming Palestine as a land into a Zionist settler entity. That is their goal—not just by erasing the homes of Palestinian refugees, who in most cases are third-time or fourth-time refugees—but by actually building on top of those homes. Now there are so many settlements that the vast majority of the land of Gaza and the West Bank has now been transformed into settled areas.

RB: Given the fact that the Palestinian resistance clearly cannot hope, within the present relationship of forces, to militarily defeat Israel at this time, what are the present objectives of the movement?

ER: Well, there are several stages that Palestinians are trying to chart for themselves. In the current stage, the primary concern is to maintain the viability of the Palestinian political manifestation that exists. Not only do we need to maintain its viability, but to involve and incorporate as large a sector of the population within the political manifestation as possible. That is one of the key successes of the Palestinian struggle. Palestine is one place where the political manifestation reflects the vast majority of the people.

In Palestine, it is critical to make sure that the Palestinians are not only invested in the political struggle, but in the contradiction with the Israeli state. That is key. It means that every Palestinian himself or herself becomes a project for liberation. If Palestinian political organizations succeed, and they appear to be succeeding tremendously in this, that means the continuity of Palestinian liberation will be sustained.

It is also necessary to thwart the formation of a standardized, fashioned, and groomed Palestinian Authority that would in fact become even more of a functionary for the state of Israel. To do that, the Palestinian political organizations have to succeed in mobilizing the vast majority of the Palestinian people in the ranks of these organizations to thwart the development of a Buthelezi-style, puppet government.[186]

And we must take care that none of the anchoring slogans and the anchoring political programs for the Palestinian people are compromised. That means first, the Palestinian right of return; second, for the Arab identity and the Arab character of Palestine; third, that we do not accept the theocratic and exclusionary state of Israel, regardless of whether it de facto exists. We as Palestinian Arabs do not accept that. If we hold fast on these issues, and these are the most important issues right now, then we can continue to wage the liberation movement for years to come.

RB: Do you believe that the prospect of a two-state solution, Israel and a Palestinian state side-by-side, is a viable one?
ER: The prospect of a two-state solution is inherently flawed. It is impossible to achieve regardless of whether or not the Palestinian people even agreed to it. The reason is that the two-state solution would require the following to happen. First, within ten to fifteen years the state of Israel would transport thousands upon thousands of Palestinian out of Israel in order to maintain demographic superiority within their state. Right now there are 1.2 million Palestinians inside the 1948 borders.[187]

Within twenty years, if current trends prevail, Palestinians would become at least 50 percent of the population within the state of Israel.

Their vote would become not only a determining vote, which it is increasingly becoming, but it would become the dominant vote. Now if the state of Israel is to maintain itself in the façade that it wants to, as a state where voting is the primary issue, then it would have to remove the Palestinian Arabs from its borders.

Another point: In the long term, let's assume for the sake of discussion that the Project to End Palestine succeeds completely. Let's assume that the United States succeeds, in fact, in maintaining or constructing a new Middle East according to its own image. Let's assume all of that actually takes place and Israel emerges as a victorious state.

A couple of things would need to happen. First, it would need to normalize relations with its surroundings. But in the way that it was formed, Israel is a foreign entity outside the realm of that part of the world, the Arab nation or what people in the US call the Middle East. If Israel continues as a separate state, it cannot normalize relations.

So in the long run, say twenty or thirty years from now, what are we looking at? We are looking at the demographic problem of the Palestinians who are threatening the demographic makeup of that state. We are looking at non-acceptance by its surroundings. Not only that, we are looking at an increasingly militarized state that must remain so in order to maintain itself.

Now, the other state, the Palestinian state that is supposed to come into existence, would require that all the Palestinian refugees be assimilated into the countries where they are now residing. There would have to be a major change in the makeup of Lebanon, Syria, and Jordan in order for those states to absorb and to maintain permanently the Palestinians living there.

That means the actual character of the Indigenous people, the Arab people, of those states would have to now be transformed in order to accept a new dictate from the state of Israel and the US It would also require that the Palestinians abandon their national aspirations for unity and not only cede or accept the existence of the state, but in fact give up their own rights.

There is a difference between the two. You can say, "Fine, you are de facto reality, I accept your existence, but I still want to secure my rights." But in this case you have to also give up your own rights and most importantly it would mean that the Palestinian "state" we are talking about would be constructed on somewhere between 50 and 70 percent of the remaining part of Palestine, the West Bank and Gaza—if that—which together comprise 22 percent of historic Palestine. That would mean about 10 to 11 percent of the land for the Palestinian "state."

That small part of the land is geographically impossible to be able to develop as a nation state in terms of continuity. Given the extreme turbulence that is slowly developing within the Arab nation as a whole and among Arab peoples in their different countries or nation states, I would suggest the viability of these two states is not only improbable, but I think it is impossible. It will not happen.

RB: So if the two-state solution is out, then the solution or the outcome will be one state in Palestine?

ER: Well, it is an inevitable outcome. It is not what will happen because we want it to happen. It is what is going to happen simply because Israel now is creating bantustans. They are going to at some point call it a Palestinian state—there is no question about that. Within five or ten years, they will create some sort of homeland very much like the homeland Buthelezi had in apartheid South Africa. It will be the same for the Palestinians and they will have their own Buthelezi. But that will be in the short run.

In the long run, in order to in fact create a viable situation that can exist in that part of the world in the heart of the Arab nation—the Arab nation being all the Arabs together—the natural process of political contradictions will develop into a one nation state. I would go further than that. I would say that at some point in time, be it fifty years or a hundred years from now, Jordan, Syria, Lebanon, Palestine, and perhaps Iraq will have to find points of unity between them. Those nation states will eventually have some sort of manifestation of unity within a short period of time. Not necessarily because the leaders want it, but because the makeup of the peoples and the geographic continuity and the economic stability and the aspirations of the region as a whole are in fact leading towards that. The only thing that prevents it from getting there are the client regimes, the US construct that is imposed on that region and the presence of the state of Israel in its current theocratic exclusionary Zionist entity.

RB: Can you comment on the relationship between the US and Israel? There are some, including in the anti-war movement, who

have the view that US foreign policy is directed from Tel Aviv, or directed through the Zionist lobby, for the benefit of Israel?

ER: I disagree with that. I think that is not a correct reading of history, and also not a correct reading of politics. Politics is all about power. It is all about control of resources, control of geopolitical strategic locations, peoples, lands, power groups and so on. It is not about a lobby, it is not about a conspiracy that ten, twenty, fifty, a hundred, or ten thousand people sit behind closed doors or in smoke-filled rooms and decide what the policy is. It is not like that.

I think we need to be more objective and honest with ourselves and our movement in order for us to move ahead. We need to look at the interests of the US in that part of the world. The number one factor is that from the Gulf to the Atlantic Ocean, the twenty-two Arab states control extremely vital and strategic points of interest, not just for the United States but for the world at large. They control energy resources like natural gas and oil. They control land masses, airspace and waterways that provide the connection to Africa, Asia, and much of southern Europe. They control the passage through the Mediterranean Sea. They are the northern flank of Africa. They are the western flank of Asia and the southern flank of the former Soviet republics. These are extremely crucial factors.

Now imagine if there was some sort of Pan-Arab unification. Imagine the power and prosperity that the Arab masses would have if they in fact had control over these aspects of their lives, control over the various geostrategic aspects that we have mentioned. If that actually existed, the Arab people would possess one of the most critical locations in the world in terms of economic wealth, trade, military power, and so forth.

It is not the state of Israel that is the only or primary entity directly invested in the maintenance of a fragmented Arab world. Primarily, it is the US and Western Europe that are directly vested in what we have just talked about.

It is the US and Western Europe, but mostly the US, that is vested in what develops with Japan and China in terms of trade, the routes of commerce from southeastern Asia through the Indian Ocean up to the Red Sea, to the Mediterranean Sea and into Europe. It is the US that is invested in what happens in the former Soviet republics. It is the US multinational and transnational corporations that have transformed their character to become larger than most countries in that part of the world economically.

It is the United States now, as an economic and military power, as an emerging unilateral empire in the world, that is hinged on the fragmentation of the Arab part of the world. The region possesses factors that could threaten the viability of the project of empire.

Within this whole construct, Israel becomes like most other states, except with a special symbiotic relationship because of its colonial nature. It has a critical dependency on imperial power. It is not like, for instance, Turkey or Egypt or any of the Indigenous states in the region. In those states, a transformation in politics would change the social character; the social and economic relationships between the people and those in power would change, while the state itself would remain.

Israel would not remain without its Zionist character, its Jewish exclusivist character, because it is a settler colony very much like apartheid South Africa. It is a settler colony that cannot be maintained except as an apartheid state. It can only really be sustained as part and parcel of its surroundings. In the case of South Africa, that was as an African state. In the case of the state of Israel, well, that part of the world is Arab.

Israel plays the part of a unique functionary. But I do not think that when we consider all of the various players and interests, be they corporate interests, or the military-industrial complex, or the centers of political power in the US and Western Europe, that the interests of the state of Israel rise above the rest. That could not be the case unless we believed that all interests are subject to Zionist interests. That would not be a correct and materialist reading of history.

We read history in terms of the interests of those in power and how they go about achieving their interests, the processes they employ, the mechanisms that they employ, the plans and the constructs that they propose. The state of Israel fits in to that but it is not what determines those plans.

RB: There has been a big struggle in the US anti-war movement during the last three years over Palestine. Can you comment on this and its significance?
ER: I think movements in general, and the anti-war movement in the US in particular, do not exist in isolation from what happens politi-

cally in the world. I think we all represent the interests of where we come from. In the US, the ANSWER Coalition, United for Peace and Justice, MoveOn.org and all of these different formations that exist, whether in virtual space or in the streets, reflect a certain view.

The reason Palestine is such a sharp contradiction is because Palestine is the anchoring point for the Arab nation, and the Arab nation is an anchoring point for national liberation worldwide. Thus Palestine becomes a gate to something very big. The issue is that those who lead liberal movements in the United States have interests in maintaining the overall modality of the world that sees Palestine as a hurdle.

They have sought over the years to either defeat it or to contain the issue. When they could not defeat it or contain it, they tried to transform it and marginalize it. The reason is not because they don't like Arabs or they don't like Palestinians or they don't like brown people or they don't like people who are darker in shade. That is not the case.

We are really looking at two models in the world, and the anti-war movement in the US is broken down along these lines. The liberal view looks at an empire that needs to be beautified, that needs to become gentler and kinder and nicer but is still empire. This is the movement that supports John Kerry.

On the other hand, those who are clear on national and class interests, the intersecting interests of the Palestinian people with the struggling people of the world, whether it be the Filipinos, the Cubans, the Colombians, or the different oppressed communities within the US, who realize that a victory, or even an advance in Palestine, is not only an advance for the Palestinian people, but is in fact an advance for all. The vast majority of those struggling in the world know that they are fighting for their dignity, everybody's dignity, fighting for a better society, for a better social structure, for control of our resources. We are fighting for an international solidarity that can actually bind us together. We are fighting for a better future. We are not fighting because we love to fight. On the contrary, we are fighting because we want a better life.

The ANSWER Coalition has been anchored in the real needs of not just Palestinians but people in the US—the working class, the poor, the unions. Why is that? Because it sees the connection and it knows that the empire should not just be beautified and made into a gentler empire. The empire must be defeated. That is precisely the genuine aspiration for most people in the world.

AHMED SAADAT ON THE PALESTINIAN STRUGGLE: 'LIBERATE THE PEOPLE FROM THE OCCUPATION'

Interview with Ahmed Saadat, secretary general of the Popular Front for the Liberation of Palestine, by Julien Versteegh of the Belgian weekly Solidaire, *newspaper of the Workers Party of Belgium. The interview was conducted February 11, 2006, in Saadat's prison cell in the West Bank city of Jericho. Saadat was detained for four years in a Palestinian Authority prison guarded by 18 US and British soldiers.*

On March 14, 2006, Israeli troops stormed the Palestinian prison of Jericho, where Saadat and four other PFLP members were being held for their alleged implication in the execution of the racist Israeli tourism minister Rehavam Zeevi in 2001. Israel's blatant and illegal act of aggression in Jericho was widely condemned worldwide. Saadat and his comrades are still political prisoners in the hands of Israel. Solidaire was one of the last media outlets to interview Saadat before his capture by Israel. This interview was also published in the May 2006 issue of Socialism and Liberation, *the magazine of the Party for Socialism and Liberation. What follows is an introduction by author Versteegh followed by his interview with Saadat.*

Introduction by Julien Versteegh

Saturday February 11, 7 a.m. I start my journey to the prison in Jericho and that is no mean feat. The trip to Jericho, a city in the eastern part of the West Bank, is the biggest challenge. After Bethlehem, you have to pass at least two checkpoints of the Israeli army. On my way back, I had to pass four of them.

All visitors have to undergo a body search by Palestinian security personnel under supervision of a US soldier in civilian clothes. Cameras and mobile phones are forbidden. I have to go through two doors and a metal detector before I enter the courtyard that is surrounded by the prison cells. They lead me to one of these cells. Inside it is quite comfortable and I am offered tea, coffee, and cookies. Ahmed Saadat welcomes me. He looks tired and talks about his four children who are permitted to visit him once in a while. His wife, on the other hand, was recently placed under house arrest by Israel for at least six months. We talk for four hours, frequently interrupted by visiting friends.

Julien Versteegh: For Europeans, it is hard to understand that a prisoner can be elected to the parliament. How did that happen?
Ahmed Saadat: My story is not different from those of many other freedom fighters who fight for national liberation. But I have also been detained because I'm the secretary general of the PFLP. The Palestinian Authority has arrested and detained me because of Israel's pressure on American and European governments. They have issued an international arrest warrant and have pressured the Palestinian Authority to arrest me and other comrades.

It is not surprising that the United States and the European Union have put the PFLP on their lists of terrorist organizations: It serves to brand the whole Palestinian resistance as terrorists. It is part and parcel of the American policy to impose its hegemony on the rest of the world.

JV: The PFLP was able to have three of its candidates elected to the Palestinian Legislative Council. What's your assessment of this result?
AS: Of course, we are not satisfied with this result and we are doing our best to grow in strength. Definitely, the result does not accurately reflect the PFLP's real influence on the terrain. The elections have been overshadowed by the contradictions between Fatah and Hamas and the people's desire to oust Fatah, which has been dominant in the Palestinian Authority. The people thought that possibly Hamas could change the current situation.

JV: What does the PFLP stand for?

AS: The PFLP is a legal Palestinian party that aims to liberate the people from the occupation. Like Hamas, we want to continue the Intifada. We reject the Oslo Agreement (the so-called peace agreement signed in 1993 by Israel and the Palestine Liberation Organization) and the Roadmap (the so-called peace agreement imposed by the United States, the European Union, Russia and the United Nations in 2003). Just like Hamas, we refuse to recognize Israel as long as our national rights are not recognized.

There is no hope in negotiations with Israel, because they refuse to negotiate with the Palestinians. The new Israeli party Kadima (established by Sharon) has built its program around the current state of affairs in order to impose its Zionist territorial program: 60 percent of the West Bank has to be confiscated, evicting its Palestinian population, and a purely Jewish state has to be established. The Roadmap is leading us to the situation before the Intifada and wants to impose a compromise about the UN resolutions that are recognizing our legitimate rights. We don't need any negotiations about these resolutions. We want to see them implemented.

The United States is applying double standards when it is about international resolutions. On the one hand, they are using their military power to chase Iraq from Kuwait (in 1991), to occupy Iraq, to force Syria out of Lebanon, to demand an end to Iran's nuclear program. On the other hand, they agree with Israel's aggression against our people, and they refuse to use their power to make Israel apply the UN resolutions on the Palestinian problem (for fifty-eight years). They pretend not to know that Israel has three hundred nuclear warheads.

JV: But the conflict between the Israelis and the Palestinians has to end some day, doesn't it?
AS: The only livable solution for the historic conflict between Israel and the Palestinian people is the establishment of one democratic state in the historic Palestine that existed before 1948. That is currently not realistic and therefore we have to anticipate an intermediate stage with an independent Palestinian state within the borders of 1967: the whole West Bank and the Gaza Strip with Jerusalem as its capital. In this intermediate stage the Palestinian refugees' right to return has to be guaranteed.

The PFLP is using several methods in the liberation struggle. It is a people's party with several people's organizations for the workers, the women, the students, and the intellectuals. Moreover, we organize social services to help the people in the field of health care, agriculture, education, arts, and human rights.

JV: What does your economic and social program look like?
AS: It is based on the strengthening of democracy in all its aspects: the establishment of an independent economy, according to our legitimate right to resistance, our right to create the objective conditions for our people that enable the liberation and national independence.

Our program tries to serve the interests of the whole people and aims to improve the living conditions of the peasants and the poor. It wants to solve the massive unemployment and ensure equal opportunities for everyone to develop professional skills. Therefore, the institutions of the Palestinian Authority will have to be rehabilitated.

In the field of the economy, our program highlights in the current phase the unification of the public and the private sectors in order to create the basis for the national and self-reliant Palestinian economy.

JV: How do you assess the recent victory of Hamas?
AS: It is the logical result of the struggle that has, in the past few years, opposed Hamas to the Palestinian Authority. Hamas is much stronger on the terrain than the other organizations. The people have therefore put their hope in Hamas to change the political system that is ruling the Palestinian Authority nowadays.

JV: Is an alliance with Hamas possible?
AS: We are not afraid of an alliance with Hamas, but we are also open for an alliance with other Palestinian organizations in order to create a national front against the occupation. We need a genuine national government. There is a big chance for an alliance with Hamas if it remains firm on the position that the Oslo Agreement and the Roadmap have to be rejected.

In the meantime, the PFLP tries to build a left Palestinian project with all Palestinian organizations that claim to be left and especially with the Democratic Front for the Liberation of Palestine. This project is based on a clear vision and on our Marxist identity, our struggle for independence and class struggle, linked with the national struggle at the regional, Arab level, with the international people's struggle, and the international revolutionary movements.

JV: Which are points of divergence with Hamas?
AS: There are differences between our political programs but also between our social programs. Hamas wants to establish an Islamic state in Palestine, with institutions according to Islamic law. On the other hand, the PFLP tries to build a democratic state with respect for freedom of opinion and religion and guarantees for the respect for human rights, and with respect for the separation between state and religious structures.

Hamas knows that it cannot implement its program today. We have asked them about their plans, and they answered that the implementation of their Islamic program is impossible as long as the occupation lasts.

Also in the field of the economy we have our differences with Hamas. They try to build a liberal, capitalist economy while we are advocating an integrated economy with unity between public and private sectors as a first step towards a socialist economy and a basis for an independent and strong national economy.

The development of Islamic organizations throughout the world is a direct consequence of the collapse of the Soviet Union. It weakened the organizations of the left that fought against imperialism in the Arab world. The communist forces in the Arab world have applied the viewpoints of the Soviet Union by the book and have never developed their own theoretical and political "flavor." That would have enabled them to analyze the contradictions in the Arab world. After the collapse of the Soviet Union, most left parties were shocked and confused and started to quarrel. They lost their confidence in Marxist-Leninist theory. Their weakening left a gap that is being filled by the Islamist movements. The victories of the Iranian Islamic revolution and of the anti-Soviet Afghan resistance fighters have encouraged the development of Islamic movements in the Arab world and Palestine, among others.

JV: You said that it is important to wage a national struggle on the basis of class struggle. What do you mean?

AS: Since its foundation, the Palestinian Authority has paved the way for new social divergences among the Palestinian people. In this new context, we are fighting for social reforms within the Palestinian Authority while continuing our struggle for national liberation. We have to build a new society already while continuing the struggle against the occupation.

Currently, there are two big contradictions. The most important contradiction is about the occupation, between our people and the state of Israel. The second contradiction is within the Palestinian people, between the people and the bourgeoisie of the Palestinian Authority and the PLO.

The Palestinian bourgeoisie wants to end the struggle against the occupation and is willing to agree to any compromise with Israel in order to defend its own economic interests. Here in Jericho, for example, the Palestinian Authority has built a casino with financial support from Ariel Sharon's son, Omri!

ENDNOTES

Overview

1   "President Obama delivers remarks to State Department employees," *Washington Post,* January 22, 2009.

2   "US House passes Republicans' Israel-only aid bill, faces dead end in Senate," Reuters, November 2, 2023. https://www.foreignassistance.gov/cd/israel/ February 5, 2008.

3   Abdel Wahab el-Messiri, *Israel: Base of Western Imperialism* (New York: Committee to Support Middle East Liberation, 1969). See Appendix A for the complete text.

Does the Israel Lobby Control US Policy?

4   John J. Mearsheimer and Stephen M. Walt, *The Israel Lobby and US Foreign Policy* (New York: Farrar, Straus and Giroux, 2007).

5   Mearsheimer and Walt, *The Israel Lobby and US Foreign Policy,* 185.

6   Palestinian American activist Muna Coobtee discussed the Israel lobby question at the Seventh Annual Convention of Al-Awda, Palestine Right to Return Coalition, in Anaheim, CA, in May 2009. Coobtee said: "The rulers of this empire do not take orders from their underlings. This is a point on which so many people, even in the US-based Palestine solidarity movement, are confused. Bending to overly simplistic and non-political arguments about the role of the Zionist lobby gives a real basis to otherwise baseless charges of "anti-Semitism." And our movement is not anti-Semitic. We do not hate Jewish people, many of whom work with us against Zionism. This is a point upon which we on the left cannot waver." Coobtee spoke on behalf of the ANSWER Coalition (Act Now to Stop War and End Racism).

7   Mearsheimer and Walt, *The Israel Lobby and US Foreign Policy,* 49.

8   See Appendix A, *Israel: Base of Western Imperialism,* for details of Israel's support for US imperialism's wars against the anti-colonial movements in Asia, Africa and Latin America.

9   The Iran-Contra affair was a major political scandal that came to light in November 1986, during the Reagan administration. It was discovered that senior US officials— led by Marine Lt. Col. Oliver North and the National Security Council—agreed to facilitate the sale of arms to Iran to secure the release of hostages in Lebanon and to get money to fund Nicaraguan Contras. Iran was at war with Iraq at the time. The anti-communist Nicaraguan Contras were fighting a proxy war on behalf of US imperialism against the revolutionary Sandinista government in Nicaragua. Israel acted as the intermediary, shipping arms to Iran. Fourteen US officials were charged with crimes and eleven were convicted, including then-Secretary of Defense Caspar Weinberger. The next president, George H. W. Bush, who served as vice president under Reagan, pardoned them all.

Dividing the Middle East

10   Lawrence, an agent of British imperialism, was canonized in the racist Hollywood epic *Lawrence of Arabia*. It should be noted that neither Lawrence nor the British ever intended to grant the Arabs a truly independent state. This would become clear to the Arab world very quickly.

11   The treaty was named after the British and French foreign diplomats Sir Mark Sykes and François Georges-Picot.

12   Balfour Declaration, *Encyclopedia Britannica*, http://www.britannica.com (accessed June 15, 2009).

13   Ismail Zayid, "Palestine: Fifty Years of Ethnic Cleansing and Dispossession," *Dossier on Palestine* (Halifax, Nova Scotia 2002).

14   Ibrahim Abu-Lughod, *The Transformation of Palestine* (Evanston: Northwestern University Press, 1971), 58, quoting "Syrian Protests Against Zionism," *Literary Digest,* No. 66 (July 3, 1920), 31.

15   Albert Bushnell Hart, ed., *Selected Addresses and Public Papers of Woodrow Wilson* (New York: Modern Library, 1918), 249.

16   Ibid.

17   Ibid., 272.

Zionism: A Colonial Project

18   *The Jewish Bulletin*, July 31, 1998, quoted in Jews for Justice in the Middle East, *The Origin of the Palestine-Israel Conflict* (Berkeley: If Americans Knew, 2002), 3.

19   Ilene Beatty, *Arab and Jew in the Land of Canaan* (1957), quoted in *The Origin of the Palestine-Israel Conflict*, 3.

20   *The Origin of the Palestine-Israel Conflict*, 18.

21   The Rothschilds are a family of European Jewish origin that established worldwide operations in oil, banking, and finance. Several Rothschild men were ennobled by Austria and Britain in the late 1800s. They were principal financial backers of the colonial settlement of Palestine by Europeans in the early 1900s, and have been major benefactors of the state of Israel.

22   Avi Shlaim, *The Iron Wall: Israel and the Arab World* (New York: W.W. Norton & Co., 2000), 3.

23 Ghada Karmi, *Married to Another Man: Israel's Dilemma in Palestine* (London: Pluto Press, 2007).

24 John B. Quigley, *Palestine and Israel: A Challenge to Justice* (Durham, NC: Duke University Press, 1990).

25 Don Peretz, *The Arab-Israeli Dispute* (New York: Facts on File, 1996), 9.

26 Albert T. Clay, "Political Zionism," *Atlantic Monthly*, February 1921.

27 Peoples Press Palestine Book Project, *Our Roots Are Still Alive: The Story of the Palestinian People* (New York: Peoples Press, 1977), 24, quoting Theodore Herzl, *The Diaries of Theodore Herzl* (1956).

28 Theodore Herzl, vol. 4 of *Complete Diaries of Theodor Herzl,* ed. Raphael Patai, trans. Harry Zohn (New York/London: Herzl Press and Thomas Yoseloff, 1960), 1525.

29 Lenni Brenner, *The Iron Wall* (London: Zed Books, 1984), Chapter 2.

30 Ibid.

31 V.I. Lenin, "The Position of the Bund in the Party," *Iskra,* No. 51, October 22, 1903, vol. 7 of *V.I. Lenin Collected Works*, 4th English Edition (Moscow: Progress Publishers, 1964), 92–103.

32 Letter to C.P. Scott, editor of the *Manchester Guardian*, November 1914, quoted in *Our Roots are Still Alive*, 29.

Building a Settler State American-Style

33 Tom Segev, *One Palestine, Complete: Jews and Arabs Under the British Mandate* (New York: Metropolitan/Holt Paperbacks Books, 1999), 194.

34 Winston Churchill, "Zionism versus Bolshevism: A struggle for the soul of the Jewish people," *Illustrated Sunday Herald,* February 8, 1920.

35 The King–Crane Commission was an official investigation conducted in 1919 by the US government into the circumstances and conditions existing in certain parts of the former Ottoman Empire, in order to inform US policy with regard to partitioning the Ottoman Empire. The commission visited Palestine, Syria, Lebanon and Anatolia. President Woodrow Wilson wanted an American mandate in the area. The commission did recommend a mandate with two provisions: (1) That the unity of Greater Syria be preserved; and (2) they recommended "serious modification of the extreme Zionist program." The findings of the King–Crane Commission were ignored by all the imperialist powers vying for regional domination—the United States, Britain and France. "King–Crane Commission Report," quoted in *The Origin of the Palestine-Israel Conflict*, 6. Read the entire report here: http://www.hri.org/docs/King-Crane/.

36 From two articles in Jabotinsky's newspaper, *Razsvyet*, November 4 and 11, 1923, quoted in John W. Mulhall, CSP, *America and the Founding of Israel: An Investigation of the Morality of America's Role* (Los Angeles: Deshon Press, 1995), 90.

37 Joseph Schectman, *Fighter and Prophet: The Vladimir Jabotinsky Story* (New York: Thomas Yoseloff, 1961), 324, quoted in *Israel: Base of Western Imperialism*.

38 V.I. Lenin, "Critical Remarks on the National Question," vol. 20 in *V. I. Lenin, Collected Works,* 4th English Edition (Moscow: Progress Publishers, 1964), 34–35.

39 Such thinking is what imperialists like Churchill so feared.

40 Fayez Sayegh, "The 'Non-Colonial' Zionism of Mr. Abba Eban," *Middle East Forum* 42, (1966): 50.

41 Zeev Sternhell, *The Founding Myths of Israel* (Princeton, NJ: Princeton University Press, 1998), 35–36.

42 See Appendix A.

43 *New York Times,* December 4, 1948. Read the full text of the letter here: http://www.yayacanada.com/einstein_ltr_fascism.html.

44 This is the thesis that the Israeli historian Avi Shlaim has convincingly documented in his book, *The Iron Wall: Israel and the Arab World.*

The Revolution of 1936–1939 in Palestine

45 Ghassan Kanafani, *The Revolution of 1936–1939 in Palestine* (New York: 1804 Books, 2023), 48–49

46 Ibid., 74.

47 Simha Flapan, *Zionism and the Palestinians* (Lyndhurst, NJ: Barnes & Noble Books, 1979), 141.

48 Benny Morris, *Righteous Victims: A History of the Zionist-Arab Conflict, 1881–2001,* (New York: Knopf Publishers, 1999), 676, citing Flapan, 141. Ben-Gurion said this in 1938. Morris is one of the first "new historians" living in Israel, who helped demolish Zionist myths. He later moved into the camp of the extreme right wing.

49 Naseer Hasan Aruri, *Palestinian Refugees: The Right of Return* (London: Pluto Press, 2001).

50 Simha Flapan, *The Birth of Israel: Myth and Realities* (New York: Pantheon, 1987), 22.

World War II: Anti-Semitism and Genocide

51 Michael Bar-Zohar, *Ben-Gurion: The Armed Prophet* (1968), 69, quoted in *Our Roots Are Still Alive,* 52.

52 Michael J. Bennett, *When Dreams Came True: The GI Bill and the Making of Modern America* (McLean, VA: Brassey's Inc., 1999), 256.

53 Morris, *Righteous Victims,* 162.

54 Arthur D. Morse, *While Six Million Died: A Chronicle of American Apathy* (Woodstock, NY: Overlook Press, 1968); David S. Wyman, *The Abandonment of the Jews: America and the Holocaust 1941–45* (New York: Pantheon Books, 1984), 300.

55 US Secretary of the Treasury, Henry Morgenthau Jr., "Report to the Secretary on the Acquiescence of this Government in the Murder of the Jews," January 13, 1944.

56 Rita Freed, *War in the Mideast,* (New York: World View Publishers, 1972), citing a New York Times poll.

57 Alfred Lilienthal, *What Price Israel?* (Chicago: Institute for Palestine Studies 1953), 194–96, quoted in *Our Roots Are Still Alive,* 62.

Illegal UN Partition

58 Those in the US left that do not reject Zionism outright essentially are "liberal" Zionists. Their position is one where any consistent anti-imperialist stand is undermined.

59 Nur Masalha, *Expulsion of the Palestinians: The Concept of "Transfer" in Zionist Political Thought, 1882–1948* (Chicago: Institute for Palestine Studies, 1992), 176.

60 Ibid., 180–81.

61 The Haganah was controlled by the Labor Zionists; the Irgun was controlled by the Revisionists. Both were used expressly for terrorist operations.

62 Ilan Pappe, *The Ethnic Cleansing of Palestine* (Oxford: Oneworld, 2007), Chapter 4.

Born of Massacres and Ethnic Cleansing

63 Pappe, *The Ethnic Cleansing of Palestine,* 90.

64 Sharif Kanani and Nihad Zitawi, *Deir Yassin, Monograph No. 4, Destroyed Palestinian Villages Documentation Project* (Bir Zeit, Palestine: Documentation Center of Bir Zeit University, 1987), 55.

65 Jacques de Reynier, "A Jerusalem un Drapeau Flottait sur la Ligne de Feu," quoted in *Our Roots Are Still Alive,* 70.

66 *Our Roots Are Still Alive,* 71.

67 Article 11 of UN General Assembly Resolution 194 reads as follows: "[T]he refugees wishing to return to their homes and live at peace with their neighbors should be permitted to do so at the earliest practicable date, and that compensation should be paid for the property of those choosing not to return and for loss of or damage to property which, under principles of international law or in equity, should be made good by the Governments or authorities responsible." The full text of Resolution 194 can be accessed here: http://www.un.org/documents/ga/res/3/ares3.htm.

68 Walid Khalidi, *All That Remains: The Palestinian Villages Occupied and Depopulated by Israel in 1948* (Beirut: Institute of Palestine Studies, 2006). Many personal testimonies about al-Nakba, the Palestinian dispossession can be found at the website: http://palestineremembered.com/.

69 Benny Morris, *Israel's Border Wars 1949-56* (London: Oxford University Press, 1997), 12.

70 As translated from Arabic, fedayeen means "self-sacrificers."

71 Morris, *Righteous Victims,* (Vintage edition), 277–78.

Watchdog for the West

72 West Germany was the inheritor state of Hitler's regime. While the socialist German Democratic Republic carried out a thorough purge of former Nazi

elements, in West Germany most of the industrialists, bankers, scientists and government and military officials who had participated in the Third Reich were "rehabilitated."

73 *Ha'aretz*, September 30, 1951, quoted in *Our Roots Are Still Alive*, 92.

74 The French Socialist Party was only socialist in name. Their true ideology was and is social democracy within the confines of capitalism. In France, they partnered with imperialism, promoting the continued colonial rule of the Algerian people.

75 Shlaim, *The Iron Wall*, 172.

76 Ibid., 181.

Fortifying the US-Israeli Alliance

77 The name "Israel Defense Forces" is a complete misnomer. The IDF cannot be described as a "defensive" force in any sense of the word. Throughout Israel's existence as an expansionist state, the IDF has operated as an offensive dagger aimed at any resistance movement or progressive government in its or Washington's path. A primary function has been to carry out and expand the occupation of Palestinian lands. As such, it is more appropriately known as the IOF, the "Israel Occupation Forces."

78 Linguist and political writer Noam Chomsky described the role of the ADL in his 1989 book *Necessary Illusions:* "The ADL [is] . . . 'one of the main pillars' of Israeli propaganda in the US, as the Israeli press casually describes it, engaged in surveillance, blacklisting, compilation of FBI-style files circulated to adherents for the purpose of defamation, angry public responses to criticism of Israeli actions and so on. These efforts, buttressed by insinuations of anti-Semitism or direct accusations, are intended to deflect or undermine opposition to Israeli policies." In truth, the ADL has made its central task the defamation of Israel's critics in the United States. Noam Chomsky, *Necessary Illusions: Thought Control in Democratic Societies* (Toronto [Ont.]: House of Anansi Press, 2003), 317.

79 "Address by Prime Minister Begin at the National Defense College, Aug., 8 1982," Israel Ministry of Foreign Affairs.

80 *Ha'aretz,* March 19, 1972.

81 *New York Times,* May 11, 1997.

82 Freed, *War in the Mideast, 57.*

83 Ibid.

84 Federal Research Division, *Syria, A Country Study* (Whitefish, MT: Kessinger Publishing, LLC, 2004), 60.

85 Freed, *War in the Mideast,* 51.

86 The estimate of "hundreds of billions" is measured in 2009 dollars.

87 The figures are adjusted for inflation using 2009 dollars.

The Palestinian Struggle Takes Center Stage

88 *Fortune* magazine, September 1967.

89 In the PFLP's founding document, the organization said: "The slogan of our masses must be resistance until victory, rooted inthe heart, with our feet planted on the ground in deep commitment to our land. Today, the Popular Front is hailing our masses with this call. This is the appeal. We must repeat it every day, through every breakthrough bullet and the fall of each martyr, that the land of Palestine today belongs to all the masses. Every area of our land belongs to our masses who have defended it against the presence of the usurper, every piece of land, every rock and stone, our masses will not abandon one inch of them because they belong to the legions of the poor and hungry and displaced persons. In order to liberate this land, and for our steadfast people, our fighters today fall with their heads lifted." Read the full document here: http://www.pflp.ps/english/.

90 *Palestine: Crisis and Liberation,* (Havana: Tricontinental, 1969), 147–49, quoted in *Our Roots Are Still Alive,* 121.

91 Karameh means "dignity" in Arabic.

92 Gerard Chaliand, *The Palestinian Resistance* (Middlesex, England: Pelican Penguin, 1972), 74, quoted in *Our Roots Are Still Alive,* 122.

93 Seymour Hersh, *The Samson Option: Israel's Nuclear Arsenal and American Foreign Policy* (New York: Random House, 1991).

94 Arafat wore a pistol holster during his UN address. Read the full speech here: http://www.monde-diplomatique.fr/cahier/proche-orient/arafat74-en.

Lebanon: Civil War and Occupation

95 *Our Roots Are Still Alive,* 164-5.

96 Lou Cannon, *President Reagan: The Role of a Lifetime* (New York: Simon & Schuster, 1991), 420.

97 The Palestine National Charter is the constitution of the PLO.

Intifada, 'Peace Process,' Intifada

98 Under international law, it is forbidden for an occupying power to imprison nationals of the occupied country inside the jails of the occupier. Thanks once more to the shield provided by its protector, the United States, Israel ignores this prohibition with impunity.

99 This book's writer was one of many protesters arrested blocking the gates of the Federal Labs plant in 1988.

100 Muna Coobtee, "Yasser Arafat and the Palestinian freedom struggle," *Socialism and Liberation,* January 2005.

101 *Christian Science Monitor,* May 28, 2009.

102 Richard Curtiss, "On May 4 Palestinians Can Turn Oslo Accord Lemons Into Lemonade," *Washington Report on Middle East Affairs,* March 1999, 13-15.

103 "Fast Facts—Programme of Assistance to the Palestinian People (Gaza)," United Nations Development Program.

104 B'tselem, The Israeli Information Center for Human Rights in the Occupied Territories.

Imperialist Failure: the 'New Middle East'

105 "Rumsfeld Accuses Syria of Sheltering Baathists," *Guardian* UK, April 10, 2003.
106 "Israel-Hezbollah conflict: Victims of rocket attacks and IDF casualties," Israel Ministry of Foreign Affairs. Retrieved June 15, 2009.
107 "Lebanon Under Siege," Presidency of the Council of Ministers—Higher Relief Council (Lebanon), November 9, 2006.
108 *Ha'aretz,* February 14, 2006.
109 Palestine Committee for Human Rights, Press Release, March 12, 2009.
110 "Dense Inert Metal Explosive," GlobalSecurity.org. Retrieved June 15, 2009.

US-Israeli Relations after Bush

111 "Israel: Netanyahu Demands Recognition of Israel First," *New York Times,* April 16, 2009.
112 "Palestinians Ask US Envoy to Press Israel on 'Two State Solution,'" *New York Times,* April 17, 2009.
113 "Highlights from Netanyahu Speech," Reuters, June 14, 2009. Netanyahu said that any Palestinian "state" would have no army, and no control of its airspace or borders. As a precondition, Palestinians would have to recognize Israel as a "Jewish state." Settlements would not stop—in Zionist parlance this is "allowing for natural growth." And Jerusalem would be the "united" capital of Israel.
114 Chakib Mouzaoui, "Los Angeles Palestinians and supporters reject Trump and Netanyahu's 'Joke of the Century,'" *Liberation News,* February 10, 2020.
115 Hazem Balousha and Oliver Holmes, "The Gaza Strip mourns its dead after protest is met with bullets," The Guardian, March 31, 2018.
116 "The Israelis set for new Jewish temple on Al-Aqsa site," *France 24,* May 6, 2023.
117 Sameena Rahman, "Huge Israeli attack on Jenin cannot break Palestine's spirit," *Liberation News,* July 5, 2023.

Is Israel an Apartheid State?

118 Jimmy Carter, *Palestine: Peace Not Apartheid* (New York: Simon & Schuster, 2006).
119 Gideon Levy, "Twilight Zone / 'Worse than apartheid'," *Ha'aretz,* July 10, 2008.
120 Greg Myre, "Amid Political Upheaval, Israeli Economy Stays Healthy," *New York Times,* December 31, 2006. Patrick Cockburn, "'Gaza is a jail. Nobody is allowed to leave. We are all starving now'," *Independent UK,* September 8, 2006. The article cites the World Bank: "In the understated prose of a World Bank report published last month, the West Bank and Gaza face 'a year of unprecedented economic recession. Real incomes may contract by at least a third in 2006 and poverty to affect close to two thirds of the population.' Poverty in this case means a per capita income of under $2 a day."

121 Shulamit Aloni, "Indeed There Is Apartheid in Israel," *Yediot Aharonot,* January 5, 2006.

122 Ibid.

123 Shira Kamm, "The Arab Citizens of Israel: Status and Implications for the Middle East Conflict," Haifa, Mossawa Center, 2003, 15; Mada al-Carmel, "The Palestinians in Israel," undated. http://www.mada-research.org (accessed June 15, 2009).

124 Ibid., 53.

125 Hajo Meyer, interview by Adri Nieuwhof, "Auschwitz survivor: 'I can identify with Palestinian youth'," *Electronic Intifada,* June 2, 2009. See Appendix B for the complete interview.

126 Haim Hanegbi, Moshe Machover and Akiva Orr, "The Class Character of Israeli Society," *New Left Review 65* (1971), 3-26. Maztpen was a left split from the Israeli Communist Party. They were small in number and made up primarily of anti-Zionist Israeli Jews who worked closely with Palestinian activists. Maztpen was active from 1962 into the early 1980s. The cited document continues by demonstrating that Israel's policy toward Palestinians cannot be understood in its entirety without considering the role and interests of imperialism: "[I]t is clear that Israel's foreign and military policies cannot be deduced from the dynamics of the internal social conflicts alone. The entire Israeli economy is founded on the special political and military role which Zionism, and the settlers' society, fulfill in the Middle East as a whole."

127 *Electronic Intifada,* June 2, 2009.

128 "The State of Human Rights in Israel and the Occupied Territories," Association for Civil Rights in Israel, December 2007, 15-17; "Racism reaching new heights in Israel, civil rights group says," *Ha'aretz,* December 10, 2007.

129 Uri Blau, "Dead Palestinian babies and bombed mosques–IDF fashion 2009," *Ha'aretz,* April 7, 2009.

The Palestinian Right of Return

130 Salman Abu-Sitta, *The Palestinian Nakba 1948, The Register of Depopulated Localities in Palestine* (London: Palestine Return Centre, 1998).

131 Roane Carey, ed., *The New Intifada: Resisting Israel's Apartheid* (London: Verso, 2001).

132 Pappe, *The Ethnic Cleansing of Palestine,* 250.

Subsidizing Occupation: US Aid to Israel

133 Jeremy M. Sharp, "US Foreign Aid to Israel," *Congressional Research Service,* January 2, 2008.

134 The top four recipients in 2008 were, in descending order, Israel, Egypt, Pakistan and Jordan.

135 Washington Report on Middle East Affairs, http://www.wrmea.com (accessed June 15, 2009).

Palestine and the US Anti-war Movement

136 The ANSWER Coalition formed on September 14, 2001, as a coalition of hundreds of organizations and prominent individuals and scores of organizing centers in cities and towns across the country. It has organized most of the large-scale protests against the Iraq war since 2002 in Washington, DC, San Francisco, Los Angeles, New York, Florida, and elsewhere. ANSWER continues to organize anti-war and anti-racist demonstrations alongside many organizations across the US, notably with several Muslim, Arab and Palestinian organizations during the 2023 rise of the Palestinian solidarity movement.

137 Local BDS campaigns have taken place around the world for a number of years. The movement picked up steam in 2004 when the International Court of Justice in The Hague found Israel in violation of international law based on its construction of a wall in the West Bank.

One-year later, over 170 Palestinian political parties, trade unions, professional associations and other civil society organizations issued a "Call for boycott, divestment and sanctions against Israel until it fully complies with international law and the universal principles of human rights." The call has been gaining steam in the United States and across the world. South Africa's trade union federation, the Congress of South African Trade Unions, has been a major international force leading the divestment struggle. Read more about the BDS campaign in the September 2006 issue of *Socialism and Liberation*.

138 Hampshire College was the first college to divest from companies doing business with apartheid South Africa in 1977. Divestment campaigns also have been conducted at other US schools, including Columbia, Cornell, Duke, Harvard, MIT, New York University, University of North Carolina, Oberlin College, Ohio State, Rutgers, Tufts, University of Pennsylvania, University of Wisconsin at Madison, Virginia Commonwealth University, and the University of California.

139 For more, see https://www.hrw.org/news/2019/04/23/us-states-use-anti-boycott-laws-punish-responsible-businesses

140 Elias Rashmawi, interviewed by Richard Becker, "The US, Israel and the 'Project to End Palestine'," *Socialism and Liberation*, October 2004. See Appendix C for the full interview.

The 'Irreconcilable Conflict' and the Future

141 Yediot Aharonot, October 17, 1969; quoted in Arie Bober, ed., *The Other Israel* (New York, Doubleday, 1972), 27.

142 Former President Jimmy Carter has characterized the one-state solution as a "catastrophe" for Israel.

143 "Saadat: Our quest is a democratic and free society," *Green Left Weekly*, July 9, 2003 (reprinted from *Fightback!*).

Israel: Base of Western Imperialism

144 Theodore Herzl, vol. 3 of *Complete Diaries of Theodor Herzl,* ed. Raphael Patai, trans. Harry Zohn (New York/London: Herzl Press and Thomas Yoseloff, 1960), 1179.

145 Ibid., vol. 3, 1194.

146 Ibid., vol. 1, 343.

147 Ibid., vol. 1, 338.

148 Uri Avnery, "A War Between Two Semitic Brothers," *Contemporary Zionist Thought* (in Arabic) (Beirut: Pal-estine Liberation Organization, 1963), 341.

149 Quoted by Fayez Sayegh "The 'Non-Colonial' Zionism of Mr. Abba Eban," *Middle East Forum,* (XLII, 1966), 50.

ß150   Ibid.

151 Harry S. Truman, vol. 2 of *Memoirs* (Garden City, New York: Doubleday, 1955), 159.

152 Joseph Schechtrnan, *Fighter and Prophet: The Vladimir Jabotinsky Story. The Last Years,* (New York: Thomas Yoseloff, 1961), 324.

153 Quoted by Ben Herrnan, "Zionism and the Lion," Zionism, *Israel and the Arabs,* ed. Hal Draper (Berkeley, California: Independent Socialist Clippingbooks, 1967), 31.

154 Arthur Hertzberg, ed., *The Zionist Idea: A Historical Analysis and Reader.*

155 Conference of Zionists, 1961. Quoted by Erskine Childers in his speech to the Palestine Day Conference held in London, May 15, 1966.

156 Abba Eban, *Voice of Israel* (New York: Horizon Press, 1957), 76.

157 Ibid.

158 William R. Polk et. al., *Backdrop to Tragedy* (Boston: Beacon Press, 1957), 136.

159 Ibid. 137.

160 Ibid. 160.

161 From a speech by Erskine Childers at the Palestine Day Conference in London, May 15th, 1966.

162 Quoted by *Labour Monthly,* August 1967, 342.

163 *Diaries,* vol. 2, 500.

164 Ibid. vol. 2, 526.

165 Ibid. vol. 4, 1309.

166 Ibid.

167 Alfred M. Lilienthal, *What Price Israel?* (Chicago: Henry Regnery Company, 1953), 22.

168 Ibid., 26.

169 J. Arrusky, "The Tragedy of Israeli Chauvinism," Ibid., 191.

170 Rita Freed, *The War in the Mideast: June 1967* (New York: The Ad Hoc Committee on the Middle East, n.d.), 15

171 Ibid., 15–16.

172 Quoted by Hyman Lumer, *The Middle East Crisis* (New York: New Outlook Publishers, 1967), 8.

173 Fayez Sayegh, "Twenty Basic Facts About Israel" (New York: Arab Information Center, 1960), 4

174 In this section I relied heavily on Dr. Sayegh's book *Zionist Colonialism in Palestine* (Beirut: Palestine Liberation Organization, 1965) and Larla al-Kadi, *The Palestine Question in Thirty Three International Conferences* (Beirut: Palestine Liberation Organization, 1966).

175 N. Kirschner, "Zionism and the Union of South Africa," *Jewish Affairs,* May 1960, 42.

176 Ibid., 45.

177 Ibid.

178 Ibid., 42.

179 *Hayuon,* January 4, 1968.

180 Don Barnett, "In the Liberated Areas of Angola," *Guardian,* May 11, 1968, 12.

181 *Al-Itihad* (an Israeli newspaper in Arabic), April 14, l967.

The US, Israel, and the 'Project to End Palestine'

182 Bantustans were puppet "homelands" for Black Africans created by the white ruling class in apartheid South Africa.

183 The "1948 Palestinians" are the Palestinians living inside the borders of the Israeli state that was established in 1948. Those borders include 78 percent of historic Palestine.

184 The "1967 Palestinians" refer to the Palestinians living in the West Bank and Gaza, which formed the other 22 percent of historic Palestine conquered by Israel in the Six-Day War in June 1967.

185 The right of return refers to the right of Palestinians expelled in 1948, 1967 and at other times to return to their homes in Palestine and have their lands and other property restored. The Palestinian right of return has been upheld in many UN resolutions, but is adamantly opposed by Israel and the US government. A Jewish person from anywhere in the world is accorded the right "to return" to Israel and be granted citizenship. No expelled Palestinians have ever been allowed to return by Israeli authorities.

186 During apartheid in South Africa, Mangosuthu Gatsha Buthelezi was a puppet ruler of KwaZulu, the largest of the bantustans.

187 The population of Israel is today around 6 million, of whom about 1.2 million are Palestinians. There are 3.4 million Palestinians living in the West Bank and Gaza. Another 4.5 million living outside historic Palestine in Jordan, Lebanon, Syria, Iraq, Egypt, the Gulf states and elsewhere.

INDEX

207